Flutter Recipes

Mobile Development Solutions for iOS and Android

Fu Cheng

Apress®

Flutter Recipes: Mobile Development Solutions for iOS and Android

Fu Cheng
Sandringham, Auckland, New Zealand

ISBN-13 (pbk): 978-1-4842-4981-9   ISBN-13 (electronic): 978-1-4842-4982-6
https://doi.org/10.1007/978-1-4842-4982-6

Managing Director, Apress Media LLC: Welmoed Spahr
Acquisitions Editor: Aaron Black
Development Editor: James Markham
Coordinating Editor: Jessica Vakili

Cover image designed by Freepik (www.freepik.com)

Distributed to the book trade worldwide by Springer Science+Business Media New York, 233 Spring Street, 6th Floor, New York, NY 10013. Phone 1-800-SPRINGER, fax (201) 348-4505, e-mail orders-ny@springer-sbm.com, or visit www.springeronline.com. Apress Media, LLC is a California LLC and the sole member (owner) is Springer Science + Business Media Finance Inc (SSBM Finance Inc). SSBM Finance Inc is a **Delaware** corporation.

For information on translations, please e-mail rights@apress.com, or visit http://www.apress.com/rights-permissions.

Apress titles may be purchased in bulk for academic, corporate, or promotional use. eBook versions and licenses are also available for most titles. For more information, reference our Print and eBook Bulk Sales web page at http://www.apress.com/bulk-sales.

Any source code or other supplementary material referenced by the author in this book is available to readers on GitHub via the book's product page, located at www.apress.com/978-1-4842-4981-9. For more detailed information, please visit http://www.apress.com/source-code.

Printed on acid-free paper

Table of Contents

About the Author

Fu Cheng is a full-stack software developer living in Auckland, New Zealand, with rich experience in applying best practices in real product development and strong problem-solving skills. He is the author of the book *Exploring Java 9: Build Modularized Applications in Java*, which covers the new features of Java SE 9 and provides a deep dive of Java platform core features. He is also a regular contributor to IBM developerWorks China and InfoQ China, with more than 50 published technical articles covering various technical topics.

About the Technical Reviewer

Jason Whitehorn is an experienced entrepreneur and software developer and has helped many oil and gas companies automate and enhance their oil field solutions through field data capture, SCADA, and machine learning. Jason obtained his Bachelor of Science in Computer Science from Arkansas State University, but he traces his passion for development back many years before then, having first taught himself to program BASIC on his family's computer while still in middle school.

When he's not mentoring and helping his team at work, writing, or pursuing one of his many side projects, Jason enjoys spending time with his wife and four children and living in the Tulsa, Oklahoma, region. More information about Jason can be found on his web site `https://jason.whitehorn.us`.

CHAPTER 1

Get Started

Recipes in this chapter help you set up your local development environment to get ready for building Flutter apps. Depending on the operating system of your machine, the steps to set up may be different. You only need to use the recipes for your own requirement. After using recipes in this chapter, you should be able to get the first Flutter app running on emulators or physical devices.

1-1. Installing Flutter SDK on Windows

Problem

You have a Windows machine, and you want to start Flutter development on this machine.

Solution

Install Flutter SDK and set up Android platform on the Windows machine.

Discussion

Flutter SDK supports Windows platform. Installing Flutter on Windows is not a hard task as you may think. First of all, you need to make sure that your local development environment meets the minimum requirements. You'll need to have 64-bit Windows 7 SP1 or later and at least 400MB free disk

© Fu Cheng 2019
F. Cheng, *Flutter Recipes*, https://doi.org/10.1007/978-1-4842-4982-6_1

space for Flutter SDK to use. Flutter SDK also requires Windows PowerShell 5.0 or newer and Git for Windows to be available on the machine.

Windows PowerShell 5.0 is pre-installed with Windows 10. For Windows versions older than Windows 10, you need to install PowerShell 5.0 manually by following instructions from Microsoft (`https://docs.microsoft.com/en-us/powershell/scripting/setup/installing-windows-powershell`). You may already have Git for Windows installed since Git is a very popular tool for development. If you can run Git commands in PowerShell, then you are good to go. Otherwise, you need to download Git for Windows (`https://git-scm.com/download/win`) and install it. When installing Git for Windows, make sure the option "Git from the command line and also from 3rd-party software" is selected in the page "Adjusting your PATH environment"; see Figure 1-1.

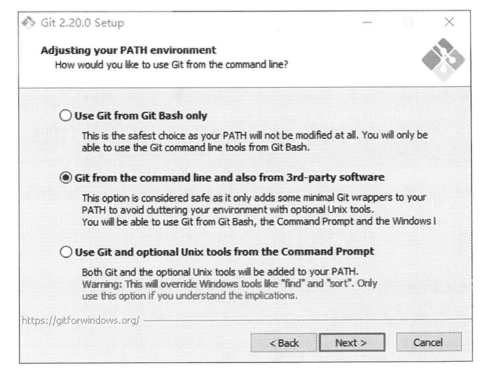

Figure 1-1. *Git for Windows setup*

After these minimum requirements have been satisfied, you can download the Flutter SDK zip bundles from the official web site (`https://flutter.dev/docs/get-started/install/windows`). Extract the downloaded zip file to the desired location on the local machine. It's recommended to avoid using the system driver where Windows is installed. In the extracted directory, double-click the file `flutter_console.bat` to start Flutter Console and run Flutter SDK commands.

To be able to run Flutter SDK commands in any Windows console, we need to add Flutter SDK to the `PATH` environment variable. The full path to `bin` of the installation directory should be added to the `PATH`. To modify the PATH on Windows 10

1. Open the Start Search and type "env" and select "Edit the system environment variables".

2. Click the "Environment Variables..." button and find the row with "Path" in the first column under the "System Variables" section.

3. In the "Edit environment variable" dialog, click "New" and input the path of the bin directory of installed Flutter SDK.

4. Close all dialogs by clicking "OK".

Now you can open a new PowerShell windows and type the command `flutter --version` to verify the installation; see Figure 1-2.

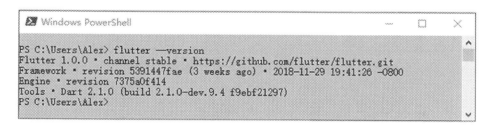

Figure 1-2. *Success installation of Flutter SDK on Windows*

Only Android platform is supported on Windows. Continue the setup following Recipe 1-7.

1-2. Installing Flutter SDK on Linux

Problem

You have a Linux machine, and you want to start Flutter development on this machine.

Solution

Install Flutter SDK and set up Android platform on the Linux machine.

Discussion

Flutter SDK supports Linux platform. However, given that there are many different Linux distributions available, the actual steps to get Flutter SDK installed may be slightly different. This recipe is based on installing Flutter SDK on Ubuntu 18.04 LTS.

Flutter SDK requires several command-line tools to be available in the local environment, including bash, mkdir, rm, git, curl, unzip, and which. For most Linux distributions, the commands bash, mkdir, rm, unzip, and which should already be included by default. The easiest way to verify that is to open a terminal window and type these commands to see the output. You'll see "command not found" error if a command is not installed. git and curl are unlikely to be included by default. Most Linux distributions provide built-in package managers to install these tools. For Ubuntu, you can use apt-get; see the following command.

```
$ sudo apt-get update
$ sudo apt-get install -y curl git
```

4

After the installation finishes successfully, you can type commands curl and git to verify.

Now you can download the Flutter SDK zip bundles from the official web site (https://flutter.dev/docs/get-started/install/linux). Extract the downloaded zip file to the desired location on the local machine. Open a terminal window, navigate to the directory of extracted Flutter SDK, and run the following command to verify the installation.

```
$ bin/flutter --version
```

It's recommended to add the bin directory of Flutter SDK to the PATH environment variable, so the flutter command can be run in any terminal session. For Ubuntu, you can edit the file ~/.profile.

```
$ nano ~/.profile
```

Add the following line to this file and save.

```
export PATH="<flutter_dir>/bin:$PATH"
```

In the current terminal window, you need to run source ~/.profile for the change to take effect. Or you can simply create a new terminal window. Type flutter --version in any terminal window to verify. You'll see the same output as Figure 1-2.

Only Android platform is supported on Linux. Continue the setup following Recipe 1-7.

1-3. Installing Flutter SDK on macOS

Problem

You have a macOS machine, and you want to start Flutter development on this machine.

Solution

Install Flutter SDK and set up Android and iOS platforms on the macOS machine.

Discussion

For macOS, Flutter SDK requires several command-line tools to be available in the local environment. These tools are `bash`, `mkdir`, `rm`, `git`, `curl`, `unzip`, and `which`. macOS should already have these tools as part of the system. You can simply type these commands in the terminal to verify. The easiest way to install missing tools is to use Homebrew (`https://brew.sh/`). Homebrew is also important when setting up the iOS development environment. Use `brew install` to install tools, for example, `brew install git` to install Git.

After installing required tools, we can download the Flutter SDK zip bundle from the official web site (`https://flutter.dev/docs/get-started/install/macos`). Extract the downloaded zip file to the desired location on the local machine. The `flutter` command is located under the `bin` directory of the extracted location.

To run `flutter` command in any terminal session, the PATH environment variable should be updated to include the `bin` directory of the Flutter SDK. This is typically done by updating the profile of the shell. For the default bash, this file is `~/.bash_profile`. For zsh, this file is `~/.zshrc`. Modify this file to include the following line.

```
export PATH=<flutter_install_dir>/bin:$PATH
```

To make the current terminal window use the updated PATH, you need to run `source ~/.bash_profile`. You can also start a new terminal window which will automatically use the updated value of PATH.

Run `flutter --version` in any terminal window to verify the installation. You'll see the same output as Figure 1-2.

Both Android and iOS platforms are supported on macOS. Continue the setup following Recipes 1-4 and 1-7.

1-4. Setting Up iOS Platform

Problem

You want to develop Flutter apps for iOS platform.

Solution

Set up iOS platform for Flutter SDK on your Mac.

Discussion

To develop Flutter apps for iOS, you need to have a Mac with at least Xcode 9.0. To set up the iOS platform, you need to go through the following steps:

1. Install Xcode (`https://developer.apple.com/xcode/`) from App Store.

2. Verify the path of the Xcode command-line tools. Run the following command to show the current path to the command-line tools. Usually you should see output like `/Applications/Xcode.app/Contents/Developer`.

   ```
   $ xcode-select -p
   ```

If the path shown in the output is not the one you want, for example, you have different versions of Xcode command-line tools installed, use xcode-select -s to switch to a different path. If you don't have the command-line tools installed, use xcode-select --install to open the installation dialog.

3. You need to open Xcode once to accept its license agreement. Or you can choose to run the command sudo xcodebuild -license to view and accept it.

4. Flutter SDK requires other tools for iOS platform, including libimobiledevice, usbmuxd, ideviceinstaller, ios-deploy, and CocoaPods (https://cocoapods.org/). All these tools can be installed using Homebrew. If you run the command flutter doctor, it shows the commands to install these tools using Homebrew. Simply run these commands and use flutter doctor to check again. When you see the green tick of "iOS toolchain," the iOS platform is set up successfully for Flutter SDK to use; see Figure 1-3 for a sample output.

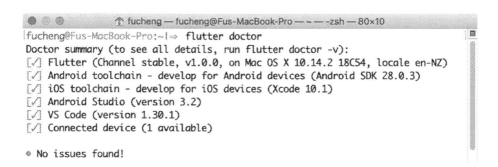

Figure 1-3. *Output of flutter doctor*

1-5. Setting Up iOS Simulators

Problem

You need a quick way to test Flutter apps on iOS platform.

Solution

Set up the iOS simulator.

Discussion

Xcode provides simulators for different iOS versions. You can download additional simulators using the tab Components in Xcode ➤ Preferences. To open the simulator, run the following command.

```
$ open -a Simulator
```

When the simulator is opened, you can switch the combination of different devices and iOS versions using the menu **Hardware ➤ Device**.

After the simulator is started, running `flutter devices` should show the simulator.

1-6. Setting Up iOS Devices

Problem

You have finished the testing of your Flutter apps on iOS simulator, and you want to test them on real iOS devices.

Solution

Deploy Flutter apps to iOS devices.

Discussion

Before deploying Flutter apps to iOS devices, you need to run `flutter doctor` to verify that iOS toolchain is set up correctly. To develop and test Flutter apps on devices, you need to have an Apple ID. If you want to distribute apps to App Store, you also need to enroll Apple Developer Program.

The first time you connect a physical device for iOS development, you need to trust the Mac to connect your device. Flutter apps need to be signed before deploying to devices. Open the `ios/Runner.xcworkspace` file of the Flutter app in Xcode. In the **General** tab, select the correct team in the **Signing** section. If you select the connected device as the running target, Xcode will finish the necessary configurations for code signing. The Bundle Identifier must be unique.

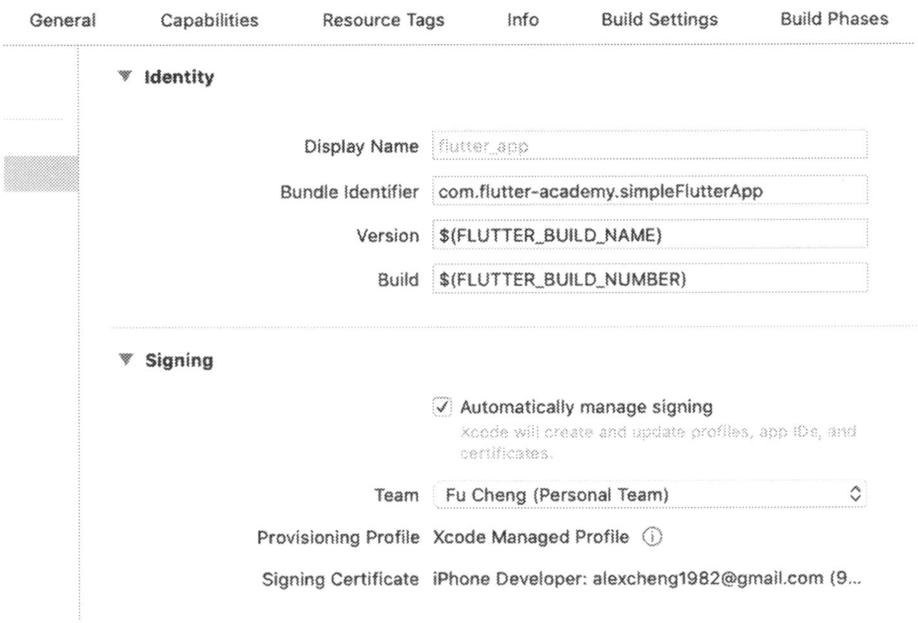

Figure 1-4. *App signing in Xcode*

The Flutter app can be deployed to the device using Xcode or the command `flutter run`. The first time you deploy the app, you may need to trust the development certificate in **General ➤ Device Management** of the Settings app on the iOS device.

1-7. Setting Up Android Platform
Problem

You want to develop Flutter apps for Android platform.

Solution

Install Android Studio to set up Android platform on your local machine.

Discussion

To develop Flutter apps for Android platform, we need to set up Android platform first. Flutter SDK requires a full installation of Android Studio for its Android platform dependencies, so we have to install Android Studio.

Go to Android Studio download page (`https://developer.android.com/studio/`) and click the "DOWNLOAD ANDROID STUDIO" button. You need to accept the terms and conditions to download it. The download page checks your platform and provides the most suitable version to download. If the provided option is not what you want, click the "DOWNLOAD OPTIONS" and select from the list of all download options; see Figure 1-5.

Android Studio downloads

Platform	Android Studio package	Size	SHA-256 checksum
Windows (64-bit)	android-studio-ide-181.5056338-windows.exe Recommended	927 MB	6ee509f3391757fe87cc5c1e4970a0228fc1ad6ca34a8b31c0a28926179353a9
	android-studio-ide-181.5056338-windows.zip No .exe installer	1001 MB	21aebb3a7fab4931b830ec40d836d6945eabb4f32acf1b52fae148d33599fd7c
Windows (32-bit)	android-studio-ide-181.5056338-windows32.zip No .exe installer	1000 MB	3a61a587c90e358ab15d076d0306550564ad4cc5a8aa1dd0c22c6afd092e976a
Mac	android-studio-ide-181.5056338-mac.dmg	989 MB	b8d2b7add6a7c776d16a8e48bd35c3e2bba18b4717131d7b9a00fa416ebe4480
Linux	android-studio-ide-181.5056338-linux.zip	1007 MB	b9ec0d44f2feaafe1e3fbd1ed696bf325f9e05cfb6c1ace84dbf87ae249efa84

See the Android Studio release notes

Figure 1-5. *Download options of Android Studio*

Android Studio provides a GUI-based installer, so it's very easy to get it installed and running on the local machine. Installing Android Studio also installs Android SDK, Android SDK platform tools, and Android SDK build tools. Even you choose not to use Android Studio as the IDE, Android SDK and related tools are still required for Android development.

In the Android SDK page of preferences in Android Studio, you can also install additional Android SDK platforms and tools; see Figure 1-6. Android Studio also prompts available updates to installed Android SDK platforms and tools.

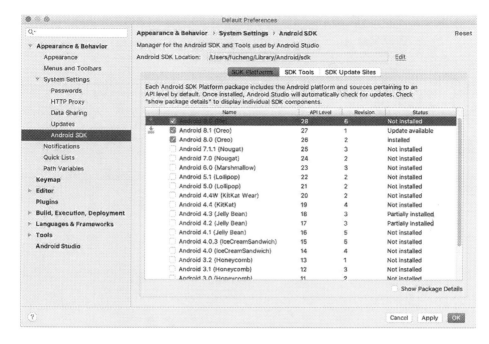

Figure 1-6. *Manage Android SDK in Android Studio*

1-8. Setting Up Android Emulators

Problem

You need a quick way to test Flutter apps for Android platform.

Solution

Set up the Android emulators.

Discussion

When developing Flutter apps, you can run them on Android emulators to see the results of running apps. To set up Android emulators, you can go through the following steps.

Open an Android project in Android Studio and select **Tools ➤** Android ➤ **AVD Manager** to open AVD Manager and click "Create Virtual Device..."; see Figure 1-7.

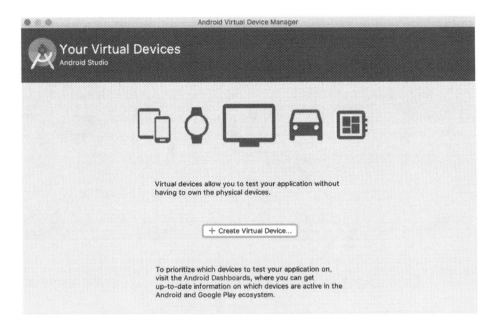

Figure 1-7. *Android Virtual Device Manager*

Choose a device definition, for example, Nexus 6P, and click Next; see Figure 1-8.

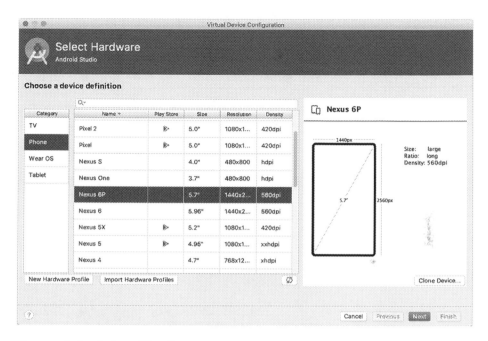

Figure 1-8. *Select Hardware*

Select a system image for the Android version you want to emulate and click Next; see Figure 1-9.

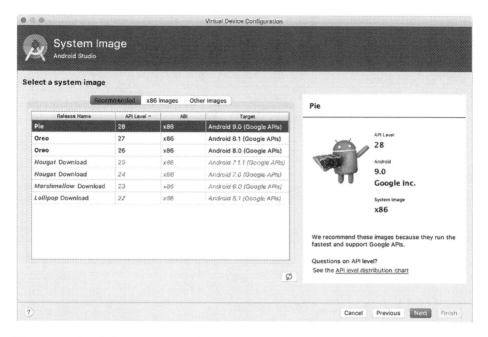

Figure 1-9. *Select a system image*

Select Hardware - GLE 2.0 for Emulated Performance to enable hardware acceleration and click Finish; see Figure 1-10.

Figure 1-10. *Select emulated performance*

A new AVD is created and listed in AVD Manager. Android Studio
official web site provides a comprehensive guide (`https://developer.`
`android.com/studio/run/managing-avds`) on how to manage AVDs, if you
want to know more details about AVD configurations.

In the AVD Manager, click the green triangle button to start the
emulator. It may take some time for the emulator to start up and show the
default Android home screen.

1-9. Setting Up Android Devices

Problem

You have finished the testing of your Flutter apps on emulators, and you want to test them on real Android devices.

Solution

Set up your Android device to run Flutter apps.

Discussion

To set up your Android device, you can go through the following steps:

1. You need to enable Developer options and USB debugging on your device. Check the instructions on the official Android web site (`https://developer.android.com/studio/debug/dev-options#enable`). You may also need to install Google USB driver (`https://developer.android.com/studio/run/win-usb`) on Windows machines.

2. Plug your device into your computer with a USB cable. The device prompts a dialog to ask for permissions, authorizing your computer to access your device.

3. Run the command `flutter devices` to verify Flutter SDK can recognize your device.

The Flutter app can be deployed to the device using Android Studio or the command `flutter run`.

1-10. Creating Flutter Apps Using Command Line

Problem

You have already set up your local environment to develop Flutter apps. Even though using Android Studio or VS Code is a good choice for development, you may still want to know how to do this from command line.

Solution

Use the commands from Flutter SDK to create and build Flutter apps.

Discussion

Using tools like Android Studio and VS Code can make Flutter development much easier. However, it's still valuable to know how to build Flutter apps using the command-line tools. This is important for continuous integration. It also allows you to use any other editors to develop Flutter apps.

The command `flutter create` can be used to create a new Flutter app. Actually, Android Studio and VS Code both use this command to create new Flutter apps. The following command creates a new Flutter app in the directory `flutter_app`.

```
$ flutter create flutter_app
```

This command creates various files in the specified directory as the skeleton code of the new app. Navigate to the directory `flutter_app` and use `flutter run` to run this app.

1-11. Creating Flutter Apps Using Android Studio

Problem

You want to have a powerful IDE that meets most of the requirements when developing Flutter apps.

Solution

Use Android Studio to create Flutter apps.

Discussion

Since we already have Android Studio installed to set up Android platform for Flutter SDK, it's a natural choice to use Android Studio as the IDE to develop Flutter apps. Android Studio itself is a powerful IDE based on IntelliJ platform. If you have used other products from JetBrains, like IntelliJ IDEA or WebStorm, you may find it's quite easy to get started with Android Studio.

To use Android Studio for Flutter development, Flutter and Dart plugins are required. To install these two plugins, open the **Plugins** page in **Preferences** dialog of Android Studio and click the "Browse repositories…" button. In the opened dialog, type in "Flutter" to search for the Flutter plugin to install; see Figure 1-11. Click the green Install button to install it. This will also prompt you to install the Dart plugin. Click Yes to install that as well. Restart Android Studio.

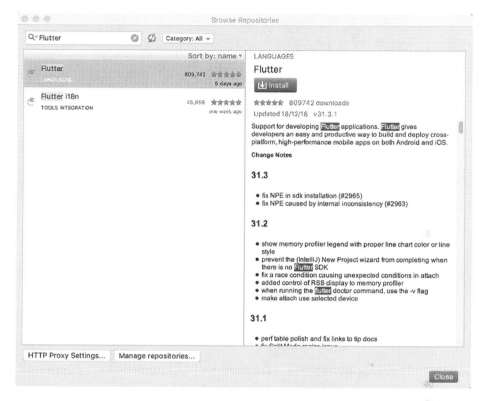

Figure 1-11. *Install Flutter plugin in Android Studio*

After restarting Android Studio, you should see a new option to start a new Flutter project. The wizard for Flutter projects has different pages to configure the new project.

The first page allows you to select type of the new Flutter project. The description in the page shows the difference of these four different project types. Most of the time, we are going to create a Flutter Application.

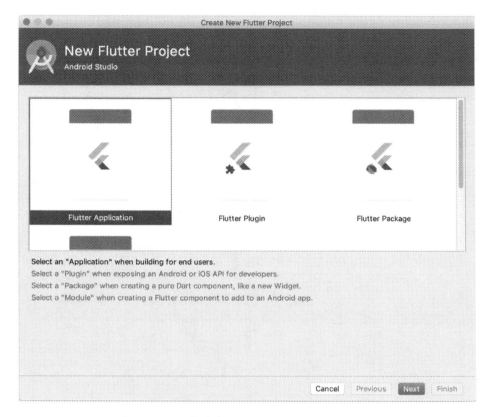

Figure 1-12. *Select type of Flutter project*

The second page allows you to customize basic configurations of the new Flutter project, including project name, location, and description.

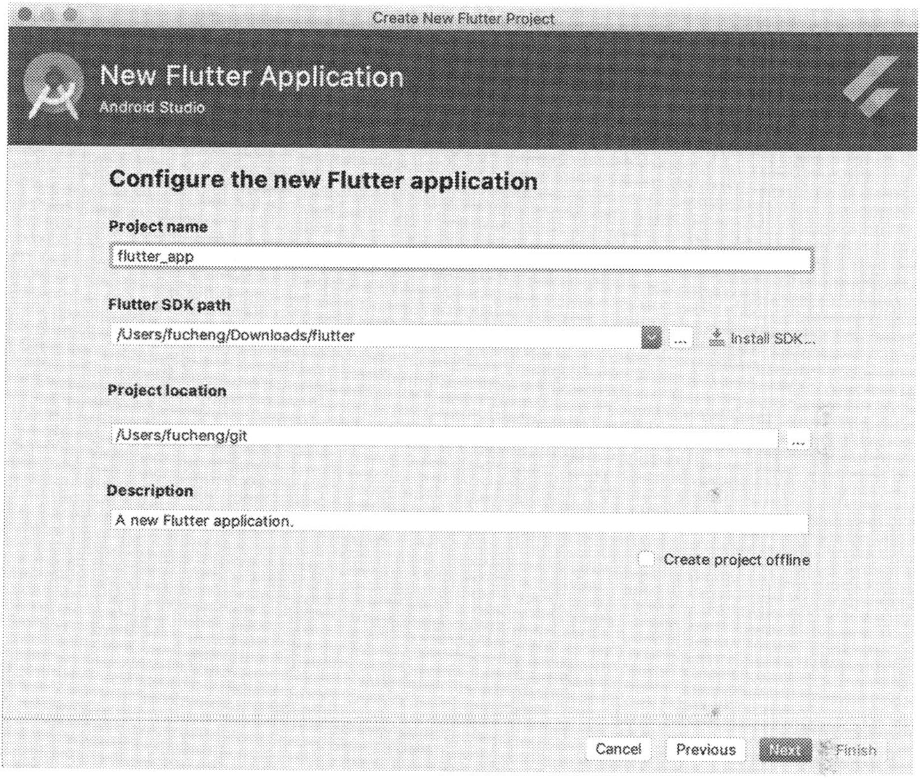

Figure 1-13. *Basic project configurations*

The last page allows you to customize some advanced project configurations. The company domain is used to create unique identifier for the project.

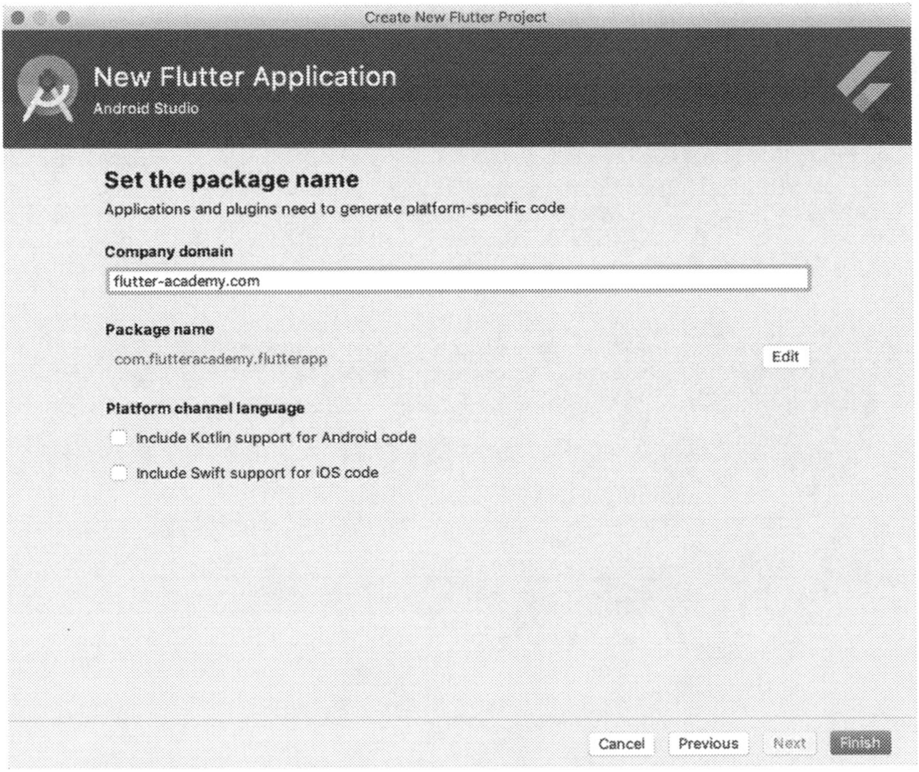

Figure 1-14. *Advanced project configurations*

After finishing the wizard, a new project is created and opened in Android Studio.

1-12. Creating Flutter Apps Using VS Code

Problem

You want to use a light-weight editor to develop Flutter apps.

Solution

Use VS Code to create Flutter apps.

Discussion

VS Code (https://code.visualstudio.com/) is a popular light-weight editor in the community of front-end developers. With the extensions for Flutter and Dart, we can also use VS Code for Flutter development. Open the Extensions tab in VS Code and search for "flutter" to install the Flutter extension; see Figure 1-15. Flutter extension depends on the Dart extension, which will also be installed. After installing these two extensions, we can open the command palette and search "flutter" for available Flutter commands.

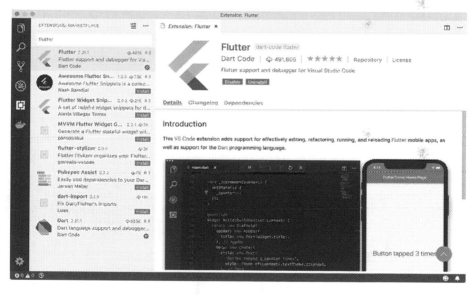

Figure 1-15. *Install Flutter extension in VS Code*

To create a new Flutter in VS Code, open the command palette and run the **Flutter: New Project** command. Input the name of the new project in the opened dialog. Select the directory of the project. VS Code opens a new window for the newly created project.

1-13. Running Flutter Apps

Problem

You want to run Flutter apps on emulators or devices.

Solution

Use flutter run command or IDEs to run Flutter apps.

Discussion

Depending on your preferred approach to develop Flutter apps, there are different ways to run Flutter apps. Before running Flutter apps, you must have at least one running emulator or connected device:

- The command flutter run starts the current Flutter app.

- In Android Studio, select the emulator or device from the dropdown menu shown in Figure 1-16, then click the **Run** button to start the app.

- In VS Code, select **Debug ➤ Start Without Debugging** to start the app.

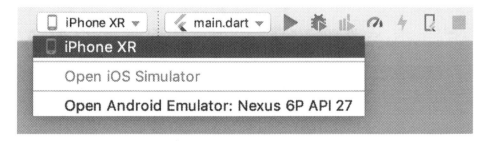

Figure 1-16. *Select device in Android Studio*

1-14. Understanding Code Structure of Flutter Apps

Problem

You want to know the typical structure of Flutter apps.

Solution

Go through the sample app generated by Flutter SDK and understand the files.

Discussion

Before going into details of developing Flutter apps, you should know about the code structure of Flutter apps, so you know where to add new files. Flutter apps have a predefined directory structure for various files in the app. When a new app is created, you can take a look of the generated files and have a basic understanding of them. Table 1-1 shows directories and files of the created app.

Table 1-1. *Directories and files of a Flutter app*

Name	Description
lib	Main directory of app source code. The file `main.dart` is usually the entry point of the app.
test	Directory that contains test files.
android	Files for Android platform.
ios	Files for iOS platform.
pubspec.yaml	Package description for Dart pub tool.
pubspec.lock	Lock file for Dart pub tool.
.metadata	Flutter project description used by Flutter SDK.

1-15. Fixing Configuration Issues of Flutter SDK

Problem

You want to make sure the configuration of your local development environment is correct for Flutter development.

Solution

Use the command `flutter doctor`.

Discussion

After Flutter SDK is installed, it needs to be configured with other supporting tools. The command `flutter doctor` is the primary tool to provide necessary help. This command checks the local environment and reports status of the Flutter SDK installation. For each problem it finds, it also gives instructions on how to fix them. All you need to do is to apply the suggested fixes and run `flutter doctor` again to verify the result. It's not necessary to fix all issues reported by `flutter doctor`. You can safely ignore some issues if they are not relevant. For example, if you are not going to use VS Code as the primary IDE, then it doesn't matter if VS Code is installed or not.

1-16. Summary

Recipes in this chapter provide instructions on how to get your local machine prepared for Flutter apps development. `flutter doctor` is a useful tool for setup. You should be able to fix most of the configuration issues by following instructions provided by this command. In the next chapter, we'll see recipes about using tools provided by Dart SDK, Flutter SDK, and IDEs.

CHAPTER 2

Know the Tools

Building Flutter apps cannot succeed without the help of various tools. During the development, we may need to use tools from Dart SDK, Flutter SDK, and IDEs. Making good use of these tools can increase your productivity. This chapter covers usage of tools from Dart SDK, Flutter SDK, Android Studio, and VS Code.

2-1. Using Dart Observatory

Problem

You want to know the internals of a running Flutter app.

Solution

Use Dart Observatory provided by Dart SDK.

Discussion

Dart Observatory is a tool provided by Dart SDK to profile and debug Dart applications. Since Flutter apps are also Dart applications, Observatory is also available for Flutter apps. Observatory is an important tool for debugging, tracing, and profiling Flutter apps. Observatory allows you to

- View an app's CPU profile.
- View an app's memory allocation profile.

© Fu Cheng 2019

F. Cheng, *Flutter Recipes*, https://doi.org/10.1007/978-1-4842-4982-6_2

- Debug an app interactively.

- View snapshots of an app's heap.

- View logs generated by an app.

When a Flutter app is started using `flutter run`, Observatory is also started and waiting for connections. You can specify the port for Observatory to listen on, or let it listen on a random port by default. You can see the URL to access the Observatory in the command output. Navigate to the URL in the browser and you can see the UI of Observatory.

Note   For best results, Google Chrome is recommended when using the Observatory. Other browsers may not function properly.

The top section of the Observatory UI shows the Dart VM information; see Figure 2-1. Click the **Refresh** button to update the information.

Figure 2-1.   *VM information in Dart Observatory*

The bottom section shows a list of isolates; see Figure 2-2. Every Flutter app has an initial isolate for its entry point file. For each isolate, a pie chart shows the breakdown of activities of the VM. On the right side of the pie chart, a list of links points to different screens of other Observatory functionalities.

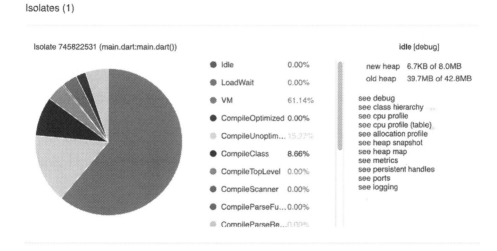

Figure 2-2. *Isolate information in Dart Observatory*

The details of these Observatory screens are out of the scope of this recipe; refer to the official documentation (`https://dart-lang.github.io/observatory/`) for instructions.

2-2. Using Hot Reload and Hot Restart
Problem

When developing Flutter apps, after you made some code changes, you want to see the result quickly.

Solution

Use hot reload and hot restart provided by Flutter SDK.

Discussion

When building mobile apps, it's crucial to be able to view effects of code changes efficiently, especially when building the UI. This enables us to quickly see the actual UI and update code iteratively. It's also very important to keep the app's current state when updating the app. Otherwise, it'll be very painful to manually reset the app to the previous state and continue testing. Suppose that the component you are developing is only accessible to registered users, to actually test the component, you may need to log in every time you made a code change, if the state is not preserved between app updates.

Hot reload provided by Flutter SDK is a killer feature that can significantly increase developers' productivity. With hot reload, the state is perverse between app updates, so you can see the UI updates instantly and continue the development and testing from the last execution point where you made the changes.

Depending on how a Flutter app is started, there are different ways to trigger hot reload. Only Flutter apps in debug mode can be hot reloaded:

- When the app is started by the command flutter run, enter r in the terminal window to trigger hot reload.

- When the app is started by Android Studio, saving the files automatically triggers hot reload. You can also click the **Flutter Hot Reload** button to manually trigger it.

- When the app is started by VS Code, saving the files automatically triggers hot reload. You can also run the command **Flutter: Hot Reload** with the keyboard shortcut Control-F5 to manually trigger it.

If the app is hot reloaded successfully, you can see output in the console with details of the hot reload. Figure 2-3 shows the console output when a hot reload is triggered by saving files in Android Studio.

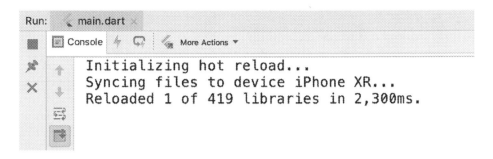

Figure 2-3. *Hot reload output*

Hot reload is so useful that you may want it to be available for all code changes you made. Unfortunately, there are still some cases that hot reload may not work:

- Your code change introduces compilation errors. You need to fix these compilation errors before hot reload can continue.

- Hot reload preserves the app state, and it tries to rebuild the widgets tree using the preserved state to reflect new changes. If your code change modifies the state, then the change to widgets may not be able to work with the old preserved state. Suppose that we have a widget that is designed to display a user's profile information. In the previous version, the state for a user only contains the username and name. In the new version, the state is updated to include a new property email, and the widget is updated to display the new property. After hot reload, the widget still uses the old state and doesn't see the new property. A hot restart is required in this case to pick up the state change.

- Changes to initializers of global variables and static fields can only be reflected after a hot restart.

- Changes to the app's `main()` method may only be reflected after a hot restart.

- Hot reload is not supported when an enumerated type is changed to a regular class or a regular class is changed to an enumerated type.

- Hot reload is not supported when changing the generic declarations of types.

If hot reload doesn't work, you can still use hot restart, which restarts the app from scratch. You can be sure that hot restart will reflect all changes you made. Depending on how a Flutter app is started, there are different ways to trigger hot restart:

- When the app is started by `flutter run`, enter R in the terminal window to trigger hot restart.

- When the app is started by Android Studio, click the **Flutter Hot Restart** button to trigger hot restart.

- When the app is started by VS Code, click the Restart button, or run the command **Flutter: Hot Restart** from command palette to trigger hot restart.

2-3. Upgrading Flutter SDK

Problem

You want to keep the Flutter SDK up to date to get latest features, bug fixes, and performance improvements.

Solution

Track different Flutter SDK channels and upgrade the SDK.

Discussion

From time to time, we may need to upgrade Flutter SDK to get new features, bug fixes, and performance improvements. Flutter SDK has different channels to get updates. Each channel is actually a Git branch in Flutter SDK's repository. Executing the command flutter channel shows all available channels; see Figure 2-4. The channel marked with a star symbol is the current channel. In Figure 2-4, the current channel is stable.

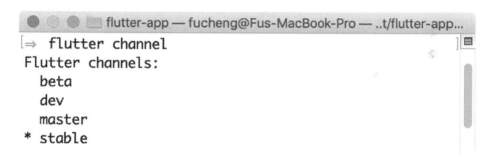

Figure 2-4. *Output of the command* flutter channel

Table 2-1 shows four channels of Flutter SDK.

Table 2-1. *Flutter SDK channels*

Channel	Description
stable	Channel for stable builds. It's the recommended channel for product development.
beta	Channel for best build of the previous month.
dev	Channel for latest fully tested build. More tests are run in this channel than master.
master	Channel for active development with latest changes. If you want to try the latest features, this is the channel to track. Code in this channel usually works, but sometimes it may break accidentally. Use this channel at your own risk.

We can use the command `flutter channel [<channel-name>]` to switch to a different channel. For example, `flutter channel master` changes to the `master` channel. To get updates of the current channel, run the command `flutter upgrade`. The following command shows a typical way to switch channels.

```
$ flutter channel master
$ flutter upgrade
```

2-4. Debugging Flutter Apps in Android Studio

Problem

You are using Android Studio to develop Flutter apps and want to find out why the code doesn't work the way you expected.

Solution

Use the built-in Flutter debugging support in Android Studio.

Discussion

Debugging is an important part of developers' daily routines. When debugging, we can see the actual code execution path in the runtime and inspect values of variables. If you have experiences with other programming languages, you should already have the basic debugging skills.

In Android Studio, you can click on the left gutter of a line in the editor to add breakpoints to that line. Click the **Debug** icon or use the menu **Run ➤ Debug** to start the app in debug mode; see Figure 2-5.

Figure 2-5. *Click Debug icon to start debugging*

Once the code execution hits a breakpoint, the execution is paused. You can inspect values of variables and interactively continue the execution using the buttons in the debug toolbar. There are different panels to see related information in debug mode.

Frames view in Figure 2-6 shows the current execution frames.

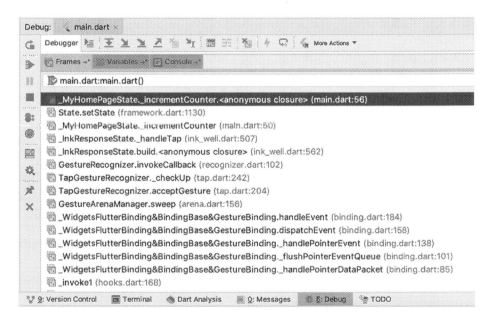

Figure 2-6. *Frames view in Android Studio*

Variables view in Figure 2-7 shows values of variables and objects. In this view, we can also add expressions to watch for values.

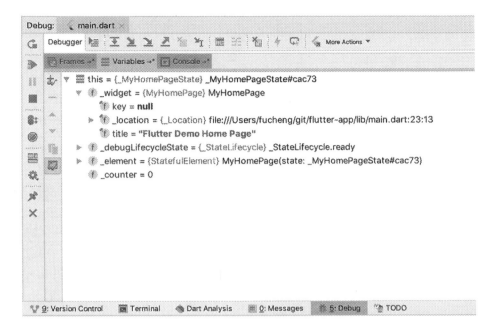

Figure 2-7.   *Variables view in Android Studio*

Console view in Figure 2-8 shows messages displayed to the console.

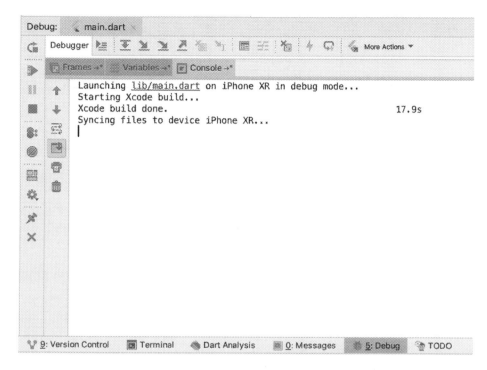

Figure 2-8. *Console view in Android Studio*

2-5. Viewing Outline of Flutter Apps in Android Studio

Problem

You want to see outline of Flutter apps to have a clear view of how widgets are organized.

Solution

Use Flutter Outline view in Android Studio.

Discussion

In Android Studio, Flutter Outline view can be opened from menu **View ➤ Tool Windows ➤ Flutter Outline**. This view displays a tree-like hierarchy of current open file; see Figure 2-9. Flutter Outline view is linked with the file editor. Selecting an element in the Flutter Outline view makes the editor to scroll and highlight the source code of this element. This link is bidirectional; selection in the editor also causes corresponding element to be selected in the Flutter Outline view.

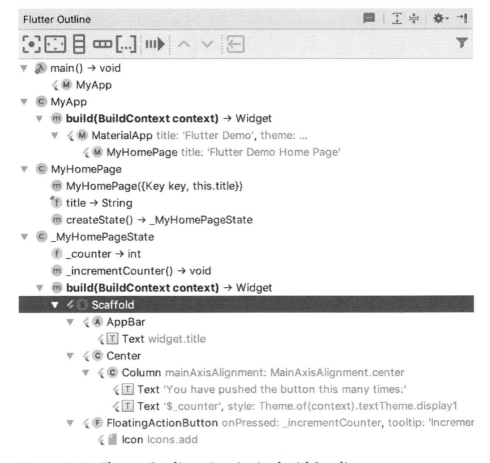

Figure 2-9. *Flutter Outline view in Android Studio*

The toolbar in Flutter Outline view has different actions to manage widgets. For example, Center widget button wraps the current widget with a Center widget.

2-6. Debugging Flutter Apps in VS Code

Problem

You are using VS Code to develop Flutter apps and want to find out why the code doesn't work the way you expected.

Solution

Use the built-in Flutter debugging support in VS Code.

Discussion

In VS Code, you can click on the left gutter of a line in the editor to add breakpoints to that line. Use the menu **Debug ➤ Start Debugging** to start the app in debug mode.

Figure 2-10 shows the VS Code view in debug mode. There are different panels in this view:

- Variables – Shows values of variables.

- Watch – Manages watch expressions and views their values.

- Call stack – Views current call stack.

- Breakpoints – Views added breakpoints.

- Debug console – Views messages output to the console.

The actions bar in the top contains actions including Continue, Step Over, Step Into, Step Out, Restart, and Stop.

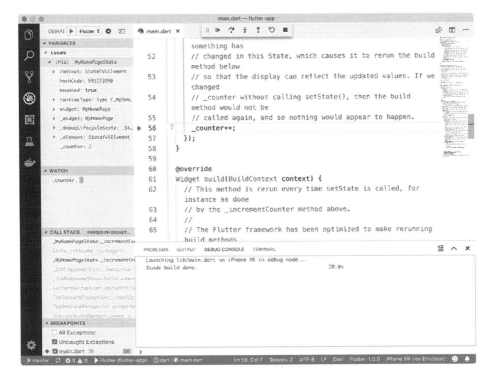

Figure 2-10. *Debug in VS Code*

2-7. Creating Flutter Projects

Problem

You want to create different types of Flutter projects.

Solution

Use the command `flutter create` with different arguments.

Discussion

`flutter create` is the command provided by Flutter SDK to create Flutter projects. In Recipe 1-10, we use this command to create a simple Flutter app. In Recipe 1-11, we also see the wizard provided by Android to create new Flutter projects, which allows customizations of the created projects. Under the hood, Android Studio also uses `flutter create` command. This command supports different arguments for various scenarios. The following code is the basic usage of `flutter create`. The output directory will contain files of the new project.

```
$ flutter create <output directory>
```

Type of Project

Use the argument `-t` or `--template` to specify the type of project to create. There are four types of projects; see Table 2-2.

Table 2-2. *Flutter project types*

Project type	Description
app	A Flutter application. This is the default type.
package	A sharable Flutter project that contains modular Dart code.
plugin	A sharable Flutter project that contains platform-specific code for Android and iOS.

The following command shows how to create a Flutter package and plugin.

```
$ flutter create -t package my_package
$ flutter create -t plugin my_plugin
```

When creating plugins, we can also use the argument `-i` or `--ios-language` to specify the programming language of iOS code. Possible values are `objc` for Objective-C and `swift` for Swift. The default value is `objc`. For Android code, we can use the argument `-a` or `--android-language` to specify the programming language of Android code. Possible values are `java` for Java and `kotlin` for Kotlin. The default value is `java`. The following command shows how to create a Flutter plugin with Swift for iOS and Kotlin for Android.

```
$ flutter create -t plugin -i swift -a kotlin my_plugin
```

Code Sample

When creating a Flutter application, we can use the argument `-s` or `--sample` to specify the sample code to use as the file `lib/main.dart` of the new app. Given a sample id, the command tries to load the dart file with the URL `https://docs.flutter.dev/snippets/<sample_id>.dart`.

Project Configurations

There are some general configurations available when creating projects; see Table 2-3.

Table 2-3. *Flutter project configurations*

Argument	Description	Default value
`--project-name`	Name of this new Flutter project. The name must be a valid dart package name.	Derived from the output directory name
`--org`	Organization name of this new Flutter project. The value should be in reverse domain notation, for example, `com.example`. The value is used as the Java package name for Android code and the prefix in the iOS bundle identifier.	`com.example`
`--description`	The description of this new Flutter project.	A new Flutter project

The following command uses the project configurations in Table 2-3.

```
$ flutter create --org=com.mycompany --description="E-commerce
app" my_ecommerce_app
```

Enable or Disable Features

There are additional flags to enable or disable some features; see Table 2-4. Only one argument of each pair can be specified at a time. The argument name with the prefix `--no` means disabling a feature, while the other one means enabling a feature. For example, `--overwrite` means enabling overwriting, while `--no-overwrite` means disabling overwriting. The default value On or Off means whether the feature is enabled or disabled by default, respectively. For example, the default value Off for the pair `--overwrite` and `--no-overwrite` means the `--no-overwrite` is used by default.

Table 2-4. *Features of* `flutter create`

Arguments	Description	Default value
`--overwrite` / `--no-overwrite`	Whether to overwrite existing files.	Off
`--pub` / `--no-pub`	Whether to run `flutter packages get` after the project has been created.	On
`--offline` / `--no-offline`	Whether to run `flutter packages get` in offline mode or not. Only applicable when `--pub` is on.	Off
`--with-driver-test` / `--no-with-driver-test`	Whether to add a `flutter_driver` dependency and generate a sample Flutter Drive test.	Off

2-8. Running Flutter Apps

Problem

You want to run Flutter apps.

Solution

Use the command `flutter run` with different arguments.

Discussion

`flutter run` is the command provided by Flutter SDK to start Flutter apps.
`flutter run` has a lot of arguments for different usage scenarios.

Different Build Flavors

By default, flutter run builds a debug version of the app. Debug version is good for development and testing with hot reload support. There are other build flavors you can use for different scenarios; see Table 2-5.

Table 2-5. *Build flavors of flutter run*

Argument	Description
--debug	A debug version. This is the default build flavor.
--profile	A version specialized for performance profiling. This option does not currently support emulator targets.
--release	A release version ready for publishing to app store.
--flavor	A custom app flavor defined by platform-specific build setup. This requires using product flavors in Android Gradle scripts and custom Xcode schemes.

Other Options

The argument -t or --target specifies the main entry point file of the app. It must be a Dart file that contains the main() method. The default value is lib/main.dart. The following command uses lib/app.dart as the entry point file.

```
$ flutter run -t lib/app.dart
```

If your app has different routes, use the argument --route to specify the route to load when running the app.

If you want to record the process id of the running Flutter app, use the argument --pid-file to specify the file to write the process id. With the process id, you can send the signal SIGUSR1 to trigger a hot reload and

SIGUSR2 to trigger a hot restart. In the following command, the process id is written to the file ~/app.pid.

```
$ flutter run --pid-file ~/app.pid
```

Now we can send signals to the running Flutter app using kill.

```
$ kill -SIGUSR1 $(<~/app.pid)
$ kill -SIGUSR2 $(<~/app.pid)
```

Table 2-6 shows other arguments supported by flutter run.

Table 2-6. *Extra arguments of flutter run*

Arguments	Description	Default value
--hot / --not-hot	Whether hot reload should be enabled.	On
--build / --no-build	Whether the app should be built if necessary before running it.	On
--pub / --no-pub	Whether to run flutter packages get before running it.	On
--target-platform	Specify the target platform when building the app for Android devices. Possible values are default, android-arm, and android-arm64.	default
--observatory-port	Specify the port for Observatory debugger connections.	0 (a random free port)
--start-paused	Make the app to start in a paused mode and wait for a debugger to connect.	
--trace-startup	Start tracing.	

(*continued*)

Table 2-6. (*continued*)

Arguments	Description	Default value
`--enable-software-rendering`	Enable rendering using Skia.	
`--skia-deterministic-rendering`	Provide 100% deterministic Skia rendering when used with `--enable-software-rendering`.	
`--trace-skia`	Enable tracing of Skia code.	

Figure 2-11 shows the output of running the command `flutter run`. From the output, we can see the Observatory port of the running app, which is very important for other Flutter SDK commands to work with the running app. We can interact with the console by pressing different keys. For example, pressing "r" triggers hot reload. After pressing "h", `flutter run` shows a help message about all commands it can accept.

```
● ● ●          flutter-app — flutter run — flutter — dart ‹ flutter run — 80×37
⇒  flutter run
Launching lib/main.dart on iPhone XR in debug mode...
Starting Xcode build...
 ├─Assembling Flutter resources...                2.1s


 └─Compiling, linking and signing...              4.3s


Xcode build done.                                            8.8s
 6.3s
Syncing files to device iPhone XR...                         2.5s


🔥  To hot reload changes while running, press "r". To hot restart (and rebuild
state), press "R".
An Observatory debugger and profiler on iPhone XR is available at:
http://127.0.0.1:51384/
For a more detailed help message, press "h". To detach, press "d"; to quit,
press "q".


🔥  To hot reload changes while running, press "r". To hot restart (and rebuild
state), press "R".
An Observatory debugger and profiler on iPhone XR is available at:
http://127.0.0.1:51384/
You can dump the widget hierarchy of the app (debugDumpApp) by pressing "w".
To dump the rendering tree of the app (debugDumpRenderTree), press "t".
For layers (debugDumpLayerTree), use "L"; for accessibility
(debugDumpSemantics), use "S" (for traversal order) or "U" (for inverse hit test
order).
To toggle the widget inspector (WidgetsApp.showWidgetInspectorOverride), press
"i".
To toggle the display of construction lines (debugPaintSizeEnabled), press "p".
To simulate different operating systems, (defaultTargetPlatform), press "o".
To display the performance overlay (WidgetsApp.showPerformanceOverlay), press
"P".
To save a screenshot to flutter.png, press "s".
To repeat this help message, press "h". To detach, press "d"; to quit, press
"q".
▌
```

Figure 2-11. *Output of the command flutter run*

2-9. Building Flutter App Binaries

Problem

You want to build app binaries for Android and iOS platforms.

Solution

Use the command `flutter build`.

Discussion

To deploy Flutter apps to devices and publish to app stores, we need to build the binaries for Android and iOS platforms. The command `flutter build` supports building these binaries.

Build APK Files for Android

The command `flutter build apk` builds the APK file for your app. Table 2-7 shows the arguments supported by this command.

Table 2-7. *Arguments of flutter build apk*

Argument	Description
--debug	Build a debug version.
--profile	Build a version specialized for performance profiling.
--release	Build a release version ready for publishing to app store.
--flavor	Build a custom app flavor defined by platform-specific build setup. This requires using product flavors in Android Gradle scripts and custom Xcode schemes.

(continued)

Table 2-7. (*continued*)

Argument	Description
--pub / --no-pub	Whether to run flutter packages get before building the app.
--build-number=<int>	An integer to specify an increasing internal version number. This value must be unique for each build. The value is used as "versionCode".
--build-name=<x.y.z>	A string version number in the format of x.y.z. The value is used as "versionName".
--build-shared-library	Compile to a *.so file.
--target-platform	The target platform. Possible values are android-arm and android-arm64.

When building APK file, --release is the default mode. The following command builds a release version with build number 5 and version name 0.1.0.

```
$ flutter build apk --build-number=5 --build-name=0.1.0
```

Build for iOS

The command flutter build ios builds iOS application bundles. This command has the same arguments --debug, --profile, --release, --flavor, --pub, --no-pub, --build-number, and --build-version as flutter build apk. The value of --build-number is used as "CFBundleVersion", while the value of --build-name is used as "CFBundleShortVersionString".

It also has other arguments; see Table 2-8.

Table 2-8. *Extra arguments of flutter build ios*

Argument	Description
--simulator	Build a version for the iOS simulator.
--no-simulator	Build a version for the iOS device.
--codesign / --no-codesign	Whether to sign the application bundle. Default value is --codesign.

By default, `flutter build ios` builds the app for device, that is, `--no-simulator` is used. The following command builds a debug version for the simulator without signing the application bundle.

```
$ flutter build ios --debug --no-codesign --simulator
```

2-10. Installing Flutter Apps
Problem

You want to install Flutter apps to emulators or devices.

Solution

Use the command `flutter install`.

Discussion

The command `flutter install` installs the current Flutter app to emulators or devices. To install the app, you need to have at least one emulator started or one device connected. Before installing the app, a binary file should be available for the target emulator or device. Use `flutter build` to build the binary file first.

The following command installs the built binary.

```
$ flutter install
```

2-11. Managing Packages

Problem

You want to manage dependencies of Flutter apps.

Solution

Use the command `flutter packages`.

Discussion

Using packages is the Dart way to manage project dependencies. Flutter inherits the same way for dependency management. You may have seen similar concepts in other programming platforms. For the dependency management to work, we need to have a way to describe sharable components and their dependencies. We also need a tool to fetch dependencies. Table 2-9 shows package management tools for different platforms. Flutter SDK uses command `flutter packages` to manage dependencies, which uses Dart `pub` tool under the hood.

Table 2-9. *Package management tools*

Platform	Description file	Tool
Node.js	`package.json`	npm
		Yarn
Dart	`pubspec.yaml`	pub
Flutter		`flutter packages`
Java	`pom.xml`	Maven
	`build.gradle`	Gradle
Ruby	`Gemfile`	Bundler

The command `flutter packages` get downloads dependent packages in a Flutter project. The command `flutter packages upgrade` upgrades packages in a Flutter project. These two commands simply wrap around the underlying pub tool from Dart. We can also use `flutter packages pub` to directly invoke Dart pub tool. The command `flutter packages` cannot do much as functionalities it provides are limited. You can always use `flutter packages pub` to delegate tasks to Dart pub tool.

Note   You should use `flutter packages get` and `flutter packages upgrade` to manage dependencies of Flutter apps. Commands `pub get` and `pub upgrade` from Dart pub tool shouldn't be used. If you need more functionalities from Dart pub tool, use `flutter packages pub`.

The command `flutter packages test` is the same as `pub run test`, but different from `flutter test`. The tests run by `flutter packages test` are hosted in a pure Dart environment, so libraries like `dart:ui` are not available. This makes the tests run faster. If you are building libraries that don't depend on any packages from Flutter SDK, you should use this command to run tests.

2-12. Running Flutter Tests

Problem

You have written tests for Flutter apps, and you want to make sure these tests passed.

Solution

Use the command `flutter test`.

Discussion

Tests are essential part of maintainable software projects. You should have tests for Flutter apps. The command `flutter test` runs tests for a Flutter app. When running the command, you can provide a list of space-separated relative file paths to specify the test files to run. If no files provided, all files in the `test` directory that have file name ending with `_test.dart` are included. The following command runs the test file `test/mytest.dart`.

```
$ flutter test test/mytest.dart
```

Filter the Tests to Run

The argument --name specifies the regular expression to match the names of tests to run. A test file may contain multiple tests. If you only need to do simple substring matching, use --plain-name instead. The following commands show the usage of --name and --plain-name.

```
$ flutter test --name="smoke\d+"
$ flutter test --plain-name=smoke
```

You can specify multiple matching conditions using --name and --plain-name. The tests to run need to match all given conditions. The following command uses both --name and --plain-name.

```
$ flutter test --name="smoke.*" --plain-name=test
```

Test Coverage

If you want to know the coverage of your tests, use the argument --coverage. After the testing, flutter test generates test coverage information and saves to the file coverage/lcov.info. The output path of the coverage information can be specified using the argument --coverage-path. If you have base coverage data, you can put it into the path coverage/lcov.base.info and pass the argument --merge-coverage to flutter test, then Flutter SDK will use lcov to merge these two coverage files.

To view the coverage report, you need to have lcov installed. On macOS, lcov can be installed using Homebrew.

```
$ brew install lcov
```

The command genhtml generates HTML files from the lcov coverage information file. The following command generates the HTML coverage report. Open the generated file index.html to view the report.

```
$ genhtml coverage/lcov.info --output-directory coverage_report
```

Debug a Test

If you want to debug a test file, you can use the argument --start-paused. Only a single test file is allowed in this mode. The execution is paused until a debugger is connected. The following command debugs the file test/simple.dart.

```
$ flutter test --start-paused test/simple.dart
```

Other Options

There are other useful arguments; see Table 2-10.

Table 2-10. *Extra arguments of* flutter test

Arguments	Description	Default value
--j, --concurrency	The number of concurrent tests to run.	6
--pub / --no-pub	Whether to run flutter packages get before running the tests.	On

2-13. Analyzing the Code
Problem

Your Flutter code compiles successfully and looks good in tests. However, you want to know if there are any potential errors or bad code practices in your code.

Solution

Use the command `flutter analyze`.

Discussion

Even though your code compiles successfully and passes all tests, it's still possible for the code to have potential errors or bad smells. For example, a local variable is declared but never used. It's a good practice to keep the code as clean as possible. Dart provides the analyzer to analyze source code to find potential errors.

The command `flutter analyze` accepts a list of directories to scan Dart files. If no path is provided, flutter analyze simply analyzes current working directory. The following command analyzes the directory `~/my_app/lib`.

```
$ flutter analyze ~/my_app/lib
```

The analysis result can be written to a file with the argument `--write`. By default, the result is written to the console. You can also pass the argument `--watch` to let the analyzer watch for file system changes and run analysis continuously.

Table 2-11 shows extra arguments of `flutter analyze`.

Table 2-11. *Extra arguments of* flutter analyze

Arguments	Description	Default value
--current-package / --no-current-package	Whether to analyze current project. If --no-current-package is enabled and no directory is specified, then nothing will be analyzed.	On
--pub / --no-pub	Whether to run flutter packages get before running the analysis.	On
--preamble / --no-preamble	Whether to show the current file being analyzed.	On
--congratulate / --no-congratulate	Whether to show output even there are no errors, warnings, hints, or lints.	On
--watch	Continuously monitors for file system changes, and runs analysis in response.	

The command flutter analyze delegates the code analysis to Dart dartanalyzer tool. We can use the file analysis_options.yaml in the project's root directory to customize the analysis behavior.

Figure 2-12 shows the output of flutter analyze with one issue found in the code.

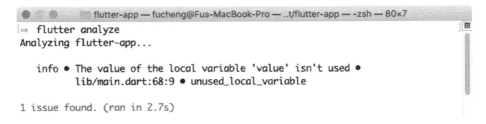

Figure 2-12. *Output of the command flutter analyze*

2-14. Managing Emulators

Problem

You want to manage different emulators used by Flutter SDK.

Solution

Use the command `flutter emulators`.

Discussion

When setting up the Android and iOS platforms for Flutter SDK, we also created emulators for Android and iOS. For Android, we can use AVD Manager to manage emulators. For iOS, we can use Xcode to manage simulators. It will be convenient if we can manage both Android emulators and iOS simulators in the same way. The command `flutter emulators` is the tool for managing emulators.

Running `flutter emulators` shows all available emulators for Flutter SDK to use; see Figure 2-13.

```
flutter-app — fucheng@Fus-MacBook-Pro — ..t/flutter-app — -zsh — 80×12
⇒ flutter emulators
2 available emulators:

Nexus_6P_API_28     • Nexus 6P      • Google • Nexus 6P API 28
apple_ios_simulator • iOS Simulator • Apple

To run an emulator, run 'flutter emulators --launch <emulator id>'.
To create a new emulator, run 'flutter emulators --create [--name xyz]'.

You can find more information on managing emulators at the links below:
   https://developer.android.com/studio/run/managing-avds
   https://developer.android.com/studio/command-line/avdmanager
```

Figure 2-13. *Output of the command flutter emulators*

To start a simulator, use `flutter emulators --launch <emulator_id>`. The following command launches the `Nexus_6P_API_28` emulator. You only need to provide a partial ID to find the exact emulator to launch. The partial ID must only match one emulator.

```
$ flutter emulators --launch Nexus
```

We can also create a new Android emulator using `flutter emulators --create`. The following command creates a new emulator with the name `Pixel`. This command can only create emulators based on Pixel devices.

```
$ flutter emulators --create --name Pixel
```

2-15. Taking Screenshots

Problem

You want to take screenshots of your running apps.

Solution

Use the command `flutter screenshot`.

Discussion

Android emulators and iOS simulators both provide the native functionalities to take screenshots. For iOS simulators, this can be done using the menu **File ➤ New Screen Shot**. For Android emulators, this can be done by clicking the Screenshot icon in the floating control bar. But using the UI controls is not quite convenient. The screenshots taken by emulators are saved to the desktop by default. You have to configure the emulators to save to the desired location.

The command flutter screenshot is much easier to use than the built-in features in emulators. You can use the argument -o or --output to specify the location to save the screenshot; see the following command.

```
$ flutter screenshot -o ~/myapp/screenshots/home.png
```

flutter screenshot can take different types of screenshots. The argument --type accepts values in Table 2-12.

Table 2-12. *Types of screenshots*

Type	Description
Device	Use the device's native screenshot capabilities. The screenshot includes the entire screen currently being displayed. This is the default type.
Rasterizer	Screenshot of the Flutter app rendered using the rasterizer.
skia	Screenshot of the Flutter app rendered as a Skia picture.

For the types of rasterizer and skia, the argument --observatory-port is required to provide the Dart Observatory port number of the running app. This port is displayed in the output of the command flutter run.

2-16. Attaching to Running Apps
Problem

Your Flutter app is not launched using flutter run, but you need want to interact with it.

Solution

Use the command flutter attach.

Discussion

When a Flutter app is launched using `flutter run`, we can interact with
using the console. However, the app can also be launched in other ways.
For example, we can close the app on the device and open it again. In this
case, we lose the control of the running app. `flutter attach` provides a
way to attach to running apps.

If the app is already running and you know the port of its observatory,
use `flutter attach --debug-port` to attach to it. The following
command attaches to a running app.

```
$ flutter attach --debug-port 10010
```

If no observatory port is provided, `flutter attach` starts listening
and scanning for new apps that become active. When a new observatory is
detected, this command attaches to the app automatically.

```
$ flutter attach
```

In Figure 2-14, `flutter attach` is initially waiting for a new Flutter app
to start. Once a Flutter app is started, `flutter attach` connects to it and
shows the same console as `flutter run`.

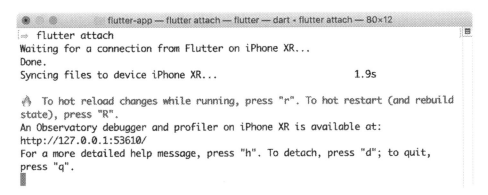

Figure 2-14. *Output of the command flutter attach*

2-17. Tracing Running Flutter Apps

Problem

You want to trace the execution of a running app.

Solution

Use the command `flutter trace`.

Discussion

To start tracing, we need to know the observatory port of the running app and provide this port to `flutter trace` with the argument `--debug-port`. By default the tracing runs for 10 seconds and writes the result JSON file to the current directory with names like `trace_01.json`, `trace_02.json`, and so on. In the following command, the observatory port is `51240`.

```
$ flutter trace --debug-port=51240
```

Use the argument `-d` or `--duration` to specify the duration in seconds for the tracing to run. The following command runs the tracing for 5 seconds.

```
$ flutter trace --debug-port=51240 -d 5
```

If you prefer to manually control the tracing progress, you can use `flutter trace --start` to start the tracing first, then use `flutter trace --stop` to stop the tracing at a later time. It's worth noting that when calling `flutter trace --stop`, the tracing needs to wait for the time specified in `--duration` before it's stopped. In the following command, after the second `flutter trace --stop`, the tracing waits for another 10 seconds before stopping, which is the default value of `--duration`.

```
$ flutter trace --start
$ flutter trace --stop
```

To stop the tracing immediately, use the following command.

```
$ flutter trace --stop -d 0
```

2-18. Configuring Flutter SDK
Problem

You want to configure different settings of Flutter SDK.

Solution

Use the command `flutter config`.

Discussion

The command `flutter config` allows configuring some Flutter SDK settings. Table 2-13 shows arguments of `flutter config`.

Table 2-13. *Arguments of* `flutter config`

Arguments	Description	Default value
`--analytics /` `--no-analytics`	Whether to report anonymous tool usage statistics and crash reports.	On
`--clear-ios-` `signing-cert`	Clear the saved development certificate used to sign apps for iOS device deployment.	
`--gradle-dir`	Set the Gradle install directory.	
`--android-sdk`	Set the Android SDK directory.	
`--android-` `studio-dir`	Set the Android Studio install directory.	

To remove a setting, simply configure it to an empty string. The following command disables analytics reporting.

```
$ flutter config --no-analytics
```

2-19. Showing App Logs
Problem

You want to see logs generated by Flutter apps running on emulators or devices.

Solution

Use the command `flutter logs`.

Discussion

Even though we can debug a Flutter app's code to find out causes of certain problems, logs are still very valuable for error diagnosis. The easiest way to generate logs in Flutter apps is calling the `print()` method. The command `flutter logs` watches for logs generated on the device and prints out to the console.

```
$ flutter logs
```

Use the argument `-c` or `--clear` if you want to clear the log history before reading the logs.

```
$ flutter logs -c
```

Figure 2-15 shows the output of `flutter logs`.

```
flutter-app — flutter logs — flutter — script • flutter logs — 80×8
:⇒  flutter logs
Showing iPhone XR logs:
Runner: flutter: Counter is 0
Runner: flutter: Counter is 1
Runner: flutter: Counter is 2
Runner: flutter: Counter is 3
Runner: flutter: Counter is 4
```

Figure 2-15. *Output of the command flutter logs*

2-20. Formatting Source Code

Problem

You want to make sure that the source code of your app follows the same code style.

Solution

Use the command `flutter format`.

Discussion

It's a good practice to have the same code style for your app, especially for a development team. The consistent code style is also good for code reviews. The command `flutter format` can format the source code files to match the default code style of Dart.

To run `flutter format`, you need to provide a space-separated list of paths. The following command formats the current directory.

```
$ flutter format .
```

`flutter format` simply delegates the formatting task to Dart `dartfmt` tool. The code style is described in the official guide (`https://dart.dev/guides/language/effective-dart/style`) of Dart language. Table 2-14 shows extra arguments of `flutter format`.

Table 2-14. *Extra arguments of flutter format*

Argument	Description
-n, --dry-run	Just show which files would be modified without actually modifying them.
--set-exit-if-changed	Return exit code 1 if there are any formatting changes made by this command.
-m, --machine	Set the output format to JSON.

2-21. Listing Connected Devices

Problem

You want to see all connected devices that can be used by Flutter SDK.

Solution

Use the command `flutter devices`.

Discussion

Flutter SDK requires at least one emulator or device to be ready before running certain commands. Flutter SDK uses the term "device" to reference Android emulators, iOS simulators, and real devices. The command `flutter devices` lists all devices that can be used by Flutter SDK. Figure 2-16 shows the output of `flutter devices`.

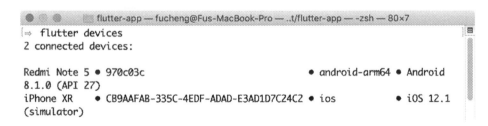

Figure 2-16. *Output of flutter devices*

2-22. Running Integration Tests

Problem

You have written integration tests using Flutter Driver, and you want to run these tests.

Solution

Use the command `flutter drive`.

Discussion

Flutter Driver is the tool provided by Flutter SDK to run integration tests. When running integration tests, the app itself is running in an emulator or a device, but the test scripts run on your local machine. During the tests, the test script connects to the running app and sends commands to the app to simulate different user actions. The test script can perform actions like tapping and scrolling. It can also read widget properties and verify their correctness.

`flutter drive` is the command to run integration tests. It can launch the app itself or connect to an existing running app. When `flutter drive` launches the app, it can take the same arguments as `flutter run`, including `--debug`, `--profile`, `--flavor`, `--route`, `--target`, `--observatory-port`, `--pub`, `--no-pub`, and `--trace-startup`. These arguments have the same meaning as in `flutter run`. When connecting to an existing app, the argument `--use-existing-app` needs to be specified with the observatory URL of the existing app; see the following command.

```
$ flutter drive --use-existing-app=http://localhost:50124
```

When launching the test script, `flutter drive` uses a convention to locate the test script file based on the entry point file of the app. The entry point file is specified using the argument `--target` with a default value of `lib/main.dart`. `flutter drive` tries to find the test script file in the `test_driver` directory with the same name but with a suffix `_test.dart`. For example, if the entry point file is `lib/main.dart`, it tries to find the test script file `test_driver/main_test.dart`. You can explicitly specify the test script file using the argument `--driver`; see the following command.

```
$ flutter drive --driver=test_driver/simple.dart
```

71

If the app is started by `flutter drive`, then the app will be stopped after test script finishes, unless the argument `--keep-app-running` is specified to keep it running. When connecting to an existing app, the app keeps running after test script finishes, unless the argument `--no-keep-app-running` is specified to stop it. The following command keeps the app running after the test.

```
$ flutter drive --keep-app-running
```

2-23. Enabling Bash Completion of Flutter SDK Commands

Problem

When typing Flutter SDK commands, you want to have the completion support for your shell.

Solution

Use the command `flutter bash-completion` to set up completion.

Discussion

With shell completion support, when you type some commands, the shell tries to complete it. `flutter bash-completion` prints the setup script to enable completion for bash and zsh. If no argument is provided, the setup script is printed out to the console. If a file path is provided, the setup script is then written to this file.

On macOS, we can use Homebrew to install `bash-completion` first.

```
$ brew install bash-completion
```

If you are using bash, you need to modify the file `~/.bash_profile` to add the following line.

```
[ -f /usr/local/etc/bash_completion ] && . /usr/local/etc/bash_completion
```

Then you can run `flutter bash-completion` to save the setup script to the directory `/usr/local/etc/bash_completion.d`; see the following command.

```
$ flutter bash-completion /usr/local/etc/bash_completion.d/flutter
```

Finally, you should run `source ~/.bash_profile` or restart the shell to enable the completion.

If you are using zsh, you can add the setup script to the file `~/.zshrc`. First you need to add the following line to the top of `~/.zshrc`.

```
autoload bashcompinit
bashcompinit
```

Then you need to run the following command to add the setup script to `~/.zshrc`.

```
$ flutter bash-completion >> ~/.zshrc
```

Finally, you should run `source ~/.zshrc` or restart the shell to enable the completion.

2-24. Cleaning Build Files of Flutter Apps

Problem

You want to clean build files of Flutter apps.

Solution

Use the command `flutter clean`.

Discussion

The command `flutter clean` deletes files in the `build` directory. The disk size of the `build` directory can be large even for small apps. For example, after building the Flutter sample app, the size of the `build` directory is about 200M. When learning Flutter, you may create many small apps for testing. It's a good idea to run `flutter clean` for those apps when you think you have done with them. You'll find out that you can reclaim a large amount of disk space.

2-25. Managing Flutter SDK Cache

Problem

You want to explicitly manage the cache of Flutter SDK.

Solution

Use the command `flutter precache`.

Discussion

Flutter SDK keeps a cache of required artifacts in the `bin/cache` directory. This directory contains binary files of Dart SDK, Flutter Engine, Material fonts, and Gradle wrapper. This cache is populated automatically if it doesn't exist. The command `flutter precache` explicitly updates the cache. Most of Flutter commands update the cache automatically before execution, except for commands `config`, `precache`, `bash-completion`, and `upgrade`, so most of the time you don't need to explicitly run this command.

`flutter precache` has the argument `-a` or `--all-platforms` to specify whether artifacts for all platforms should be downloaded. By default, only artifacts of the current platform are downloaded.

```
$ flutter precache -a
```

2-26. Summary

This chapter is about the tools you may need to use when developing Flutter apps. You may not need to use all of these tools. With the help of IDEs, you can perform most of the actions inside of IDEs. Knowledge of these tools is still valuable because you can do more with these tools. In the next chapter, we'll see recipes about essential parts of Dart language.

CHAPTER 3

Essential Dart

Flutter projects can have cross-platform code and platform-specific code. Cross-platform code is written in Dart. Sufficient knowledge of Dart is a prerequisite for building Flutter apps. Details of Dart language is out of the scope of this book. You can find plenty of online resources related to Dart. However, it's still very helpful to cover essential part of Dart for building Flutter apps. Recipes in this chapter cover different aspects of Dart. You can skip this chapter if you are confident about your knowledge of Dart.

3-1. Understanding Built-In Types

Problem

You want to know the built-in types of Dart.

Solution

Dart has built-in types of numbers, strings, booleans, lists, maps, runes, and symbols.

Discussion

Dart has several built-in types, including numbers, strings, booleans, lists, maps, runes, and symbols.

© Fu Cheng 2019
F. Cheng, *Flutter Recipes*, https://doi.org/10.1007/978-1-4842-4982-6_3

Numbers

Numbers in Dart can be integer values no larger than 64 bits or 64-bit double-precision floating-point number specified by the IEEE 754 standard. Types int and double represent these two types of numbers, respectively. Type num is the supertype of int and double. Unlike primitive types in Java, numbers in Dart are also objects. They have methods to work with them.

In Listing 3-1, the type of x is int, while the type of y is double. The method toRadixString() returns a string value by converting the value to the specified radix. The method toStringAsFixed() makes sure that the given number of fraction digits is kept in the string representation. The static method tryParse() of double tries to parse a string as a double literal.

Listing 3-1. Numbers

```
var x = 10;
var y = 1.5;
assert(x.toRadixString(8) == '12');
assert(y.toStringAsFixed(2) == '1.50');
var z = double.tryParse('3.14');
assert(z == 3.14);
```

Strings

Dart strings are sequences of UTF-16 code units. Either single or double quotes can be used to create strings. It doesn't matter which quote is used. The key point is to be consistent across the whole code base. Dart has built-in support for string interpolation. Expressions can be embedded into strings using the form ${expression}. Values of embedded expressions are evaluated when strings are used. If the expression is an identifier, then {} can be omitted. In Listing 3-2, name is an identifier, so we can use $name in the string.

Listing 3-2. String interpolation

```
var name = 'Alex';
assert('The length of $name is ${name.length}' == 'The length
of Alex is 4');
```

If you want to concatenate strings, you can simply place these string literals next to each other without the + operator; see Listing 3-3.

Listing 3-3. String concatenation

```
var longString = 'This is a long'
  'long'
  'long'
  'string';
```

Another way to create a multi-line string is to use a triple quote with either single or double quotes; see Listing 3-4.

Listing 3-4. Multi-line string

```
var longString2 = "'
This is also a long
  long
  long
  string
"';
```

Booleans

Boolean values are represented using the type bool. bool type has only two objects: true and false. It's worth noting that only bool values can be used in if, while, and assert as conditions to check. JavaScript has a broader concept of truthy and falsy values, while Dart follows a stricter rule. For example, if ('abc') is valid in JavaScript, but not in Dart.

In Listing 3-5, name is an empty string. To use it in if, we need to invoke the getter isEmpty. We also need explicit check for null and 0.

Listing 3-5. Booleans

```
var name = '';
if (name.isEmpty) {
  print('name is emtpy');
}
var value;
assert(value == null);

var count = 5;
while(count-- != 0) {
  print(count);
}
```

Lists and Maps

Lists and maps are commonly used collection types. In Dart, arrays are List objects. Lists and maps can be created using literals or constructors. It's recommended to use collection literals when possible. Listing 3-6 shows how to create lists and maps using literals and constructors.

Listing 3-6. Lists and maps

```
var list1 = [1, 2, 3];
var list2 = List<int>(3);
var map1 = {'a': 'A', 'b': 'B'};
var map2 = Map<String, String>();
```

Runes

Runes are UTF-32 code points of a string. To express 32-bit Unicode values in a string, we can use the form \uXXXX, where XXXX is the four-digit hexadecimal value of the code point. If the code point cannot be expressed as four-digit hexadecimal value, then {} is required to wrap those digits, for example, \u{XXXXX}. In Listing 3-7, the string value contains two emojis.

Listing 3-7. Runes

```
var value = '\u{1F686} \u{1F6B4}';
print(value);
```

Symbols

A Symbol object represents an operator or identifier. Symbols can be created using constructor Symbol(<name>) or symbol literal #<name>. Symbols created with the same name are equal; see Listing 3-8. Symbols should be used when you want to reference identifiers by name.

Listing 3-8. Symbols

```
assert(Symbol('a') == #a);
```

3-2. Using Enumerated Types
Problem

You want to have a type-safe way to declare a set of constant values.

Solution

Use enumerated type.

Discussion

Like other programming languages, Dart has enumerated types. To declare an enumerated type, use the enum keyword. Each value in an enum has an index getter to get the zero-based position of the value. Use values to get a list of all values in an enum. Enums are usually used in switch statements. In Listing 3-9, the enum type TrafficColor has three values. The index of first value red is 0.

Listing 3-9. Enumerated type

```dart
enum TrafficColor { red, green, yellow }

void main() {
  assert(TrafficColor.red.index == 0);
  assert(TrafficColor.values.length == 3);

  var color = TrafficColor.red;
  switch (color) {
    case TrafficColor.red:
      print('stop');
      break;
    case TrafficColor.green:
      print('go');
      break;
    case TrafficColor.yellow:
      print('be careful');
  }
}
```

3-3. Using Dynamic Type
Problem

You don't know the type of an object or you don't care about the type.

Solution

Use the dynamic type.

Discussion

Dart is a strong-typed language. Most of the time, we want an object to have a defined type. However, sometimes we may not know or don't care about the actual type; we can use dynamic as the type. The dynamic type is often confused with the Object type. Both Object and dynamic permit all values. Object should be used if you want to state that all objects are accepted. If the type is dynamic, we can use is operator to check whether it's the desired type. The actual type can be retrieved using runtimeType. In Listing 3-10, the actual type of value is int, then the type is changed to String.

Listing 3-10. Use dynamic type

```
dynamic value = 1;
print(value.runtimeType);
value = 'test';
if (value is String) {
  print('string');
}
```

3-4. Understanding Functions

Problem

You want to understand functions in Dart.

Solution

Functions in Dart are very powerful and flexible.

Discussion

Functions in Dart are objects and have the type Function. Functions can be assigned to values, passed in function arguments, and used as function return values. It's very easy to create high-order functions in Dart. A function may have zero or many parameters. Some parameters are required, while some are optional. Required arguments come first in the parameters list, followed by optional parameters. Optional positional parameters are wrapped in [ ].

When a function has a long list of parameters, it's hard to remember the position and meaning of these parameters. It's better to use named parameters. Named parameters can be marked as required using the @required annotation. Parameters can have default values specified using =. If no default value is provided, the default value is null.

In Listing 3-11, the function sum() has an optional positional argument initial with the default value 0. The function joinToString() has a required named argument separator and two optional named arguments prefix and suffix. The arrow syntax used in joinToString() is a shorthand for function body with only one expression. The syntax => expr is the same as { return expr; }. Using arrow syntax makes code shorter and easier to read.

Listing 3-11. Function parameters

```dart
import 'package:meta/meta.dart';

int sum(List<int> list, [int initial = 0]) {
  var total = initial;
  list.forEach((v) => total += v);
  return total;
}

String joinToString(List<String> list,
        {@required String separator, String prefix = '', String
        suffix = ''}) =>
    '$prefix${list.join(separator)}$suffix';

void main() {
  assert(sum([1, 2, 3]) == 6);
  assert(sum([1, 2, 3], 10) == 16);

  assert(joinToString(['a', 'b', 'c'], separator: ',') ==
  'a,b,c');
  assert(
      joinToString(['a', 'b', 'c'], separator: '-', prefix:
      '*', suffix: '?') ==
          '*a-b-c?');
}
```

Sometimes you may not need a name for a function. These anonymous functions are useful when providing callbacks. In Listing 3-12, an anonymous function is passed to the method forEach().

Listing 3-12. Anonymous functions

```dart
var list = [1, 2, 3];
list.forEach((v) => print(v * 10));
```

3-5. Using Typedefs

Problem

You want to have an alias of a function type.

Solution

Use typedefs.

Discussion

In Dart, functions are objects. Functions are instances of the type
Function. But the actual type of a function is defined by the types of its
parameters and the type of its return value. What matters is the actual
function type when a function is used as a parameter or return value.
typedef in Dart allows us to create an alias of a function type. The type
alias can be used just like other types. In Listing 3-13, Processor<T> is an
alias of the function type which has a parameter of type T and a return type
of void. This type is used as the parameter type in the function process().

Listing 3-13. typedef

```
typedef Processor<T> = void Function(T value);

void process<T>(List<T> list, Processor<T> processor) {
  list.forEach((item) {
    print('processing $item');
    processor(item);
    print('processed $item');
  });
}
```

```
void main() {
  process([1, 2, 3], print);
}
```

3-6. Using Cascade Operator

Problem

You want to make a sequence of operations on the same object.

Solution

Use the cascade operator (..) in Dart.

Discussion

Dart has a special cascade operator (..) which allows us to make a sequence of operations on the same object. To chain operations on the same object in other programming languages, we usually need to create a fluent API in which each method returns the current object. The cascade operator in Dart makes this requirement unnecessary. Methods can still be chained even though they don't return the current object. The cascade operator also supports field access. In Listing 3-14, cascade operator is used to access the fields and method in classes User and Address.

Listing 3-14. Using cascade operator

```
class User {
  String name, email;
  Address address;

  void sayHi() => print('hi, $name');
}
```

```
class Address {
  String street, suburb, zipCode;
  void log() => print('Address: $street');
}

void main() {
  User()
    ..name = 'Alex'
    ..email = 'alex@example.org'
    ..address = (Address()
      ..street = 'my street'
      ..suburb = 'my suburb'
      ..zipCode = '1000'
      ..log())
    ..sayHi();
}
```

3-7. Overriding Operators

Problem

You want to override operators in Dart.

Solution

Define overriding methods in class for operators.

Discussion

Dart has many operators. Only a subset of these operators can be overridden. These overridable operators are <, +, |, [ ], >, /, ^, [ ]=, <=, ~/, &, ~, >=, *, <<, ==, -, %, and >>. For some classes, using operators is more concise than using methods. For example, the List class overrides the + operator for list concatenation. The code [1] + [2] is very easy to understand. In Listing 3-15, the class Rectangle overrides operators < and > to compare instances by area.

Listing 3-15. Overriding operators

```dart
class Rectangle {
  int width, height;
  Rectangle(this.width, this.height);

  get area => width * height;

  bool operator <(Rectangle rect) => area < rect.area;
  bool operator >(Rectangle rect) => area > rect.area;
}

void main() {
  var rect1 = Rectangle(100, 100);
  var rect2 = Rectangle(200, 150);
  assert(rect1 < rect2);
  assert(rect2 > rect1);
}
```

3-8. Using Constructors
Problem

You want to create new instances of Dart classes.

Solution

Use constructors.

Discussion

Like other programming languages, objects in Dart are created by constructors. Usually, constructors are created by declaring functions with the same name as their classes. Constructors can have arguments to provide necessary values to initialize new objects. If no constructor is declared for a class, a default constructor with no arguments is provided. This default constructor simply invokes the no-argument constructor in the superclass. However, if a constructor is declared, this default constructor doesn't exist.

A class may have multiple constructors. You can name these constructors in the form `ClassName.identifier` to better clarify the meanings.

In Listing 3-16, the class `Rectangle` has a regular constructor that takes four arguments. It also has a named constructor `Rectangle.fromPosition`.

Listing 3-16. Constructors

```
class Rectangle {
  final num top, left, width, height;

  Rectangle(this.top, this.left, this.width, this.height);

Rectangle.fromPosition(this.top, this.left, num bottom, num
right)
      : assert(right > left),
        assert(bottom > top),
        width = right - left,
        height = bottom - top;

  @override
  String toString() {
```

```
    return 'Rectangle{top: $top, left: $left, width: $width,
    height: $height}';
  }
}

void main(List<String> args) {
  var rect1 = Rectangle(100, 100, 300, 200);
  var rect2 = Rectangle.fromPosition(100, 100, 300, 200);
  print(rect1);
  print(rect2);
}
```

It's common to use factories to create objects. Dart has a special kind of factory constructors that implements this pattern. A factory constructor doesn't always return a new instance of a class. It may return a cached instance, or an instance of a subtype. In Listing 3-17, the class ExpensiveObject has a named constructor ExpensiveObject._create() to actually create a new instance. The factory constructor only invokes ExpensiveObject._create() when _instance is null. When running the code, you can see that the message "created" is only printed once.

Listing 3-17. Facto+ry constructor

```
class ExpensiveObject {
  static ExpensiveObject _instance;
  ExpensiveObject._create() {
    print('created');
  }

  factory ExpensiveObject() {
    if (_instance == null) {
      _instance = ExpensiveObject._create();
    }
```

```
    return _instance;
  }
}

void main() {
  ExpensiveObject();
  ExpensiveObject();
}
```

3-9. Extending a Class

Problem

You want to inherit behavior from an existing class.

Solution

Extend from the existing class to create a subclass.

Discussion

Dart is an object-oriented programming language. It provides support for inheritance. A class can extend from a superclass using the keyword extends. The superclass can be referred as super in the subclass. Subclasses can override instance methods, getters, and setters of superclasses. Overriding members should be annotated with the @ override annotation.

Abstract classes are defined using the abstract modifier. Abstract classes cannot be instantiated. Abstract methods in abstract classes don't have implementations and must be implemented by non-abstract subclasses.

In Listing 3-18, the class Shape is abstract with an abstract method area(). Classes Rectangle and Circle both extend from Shape and implement the abstract method area().

Listing 3-18. Inheritance

```dart
import 'dart:math' show pi;

abstract class Shape {
  double area();
}

class Rectangle extends Shape {
  double width, height;
  Rectangle(this.width, this.height);

  @override
  double area() {
    return width * height;
  }
}

class Square extends Rectangle {
  Square(double width) : super(width, width);
}

class Circle extends Shape {
  double radius;
  Circle(this.radius);

  @override
  double area() {
    return pi * radius * radius;
  }
}
```

```
void main() {
  var rect = Rectangle(100, 50);
  var square = Square(50);
  var circle = Circle(50);
  print(rect.area());
  print(square.area());
  print(circle.area());
}
```

3-10. Adding Features to a Class
Problem

You want to reuse a class's code but are limited by single inheritance of Dart.

Solution

Use mixins.

Discussion

Inheritance is a common way to reuse code. Dart only supports single inheritance, that is, a class can have at most one superclass. If you want to reuse code from multiple classes, mixins should be used. A class can declare multiple mixins using the keyword with. A mixin is a class that extends from Object and declares on constructors. A mixin can be declared as a regular class using class or as a dedicated mixin using mixin. In Listing 3-19, CardHolder and SystemUser are mixins. The class Assistant extends from Student and has the mixin SystemUser, so we can use the useSystem() method of Assistant instances.

Listing 3-19. Mixins

```dart
class Person {
  String name;

  Person(this.name);
}

class Student extends Person with CardHolder {
  Student(String name) : super('Student: $name') {
    holder = this;
  }
}

class Teacher extends Person with CardHolder {
  Teacher(String name) : super('Teacher: $name') {
    holder = this;
  }
}

mixin CardHolder {
  Person holder;

  void swipeCard() {
    print('${holder.name} swiped the card');
  }
}

mixin SystemUser {
  Person user;

  void useSystem() {
    print('${user.name} used the system.');
  }
}
```

```dart
class Assistant extends Student with SystemUser {
  Assistant(String name) : super(name) {
    user = this;
  }
}

void main() {
  var assistant = Assistant('Alex');
  assistant.swipeCard();
  assistant.useSystem();
}
```

3-11. Using Interfaces

Problem

You want to have a contract for classes to follow.

Solution

Use implicit interface of a class.

Discussion

You should be familiar with interfaces as the contract of classes. Unlike other object-oriented programming languages, Dart has no concept of interfaces. Every class has an implicit interface that contains all the instance members of this class and the interfaces it implements. You can use implements to declare that a class implements the API of another class. In Listing 3-20, class CachedDataLoader implements the implicit interface of class DataLoader.

Listing 3-20. Interfaces

```dart
class DataLoader {
  void load() {
    print('load data');
  }
}

class CachedDataLoader implements DataLoader {
  @override
  void load() {
    print('load from cache');
  }
}

void main() {
  var loader = CachedDataLoader();
  loader.load();
}
```

3-12. Using Generics

Problem

You want to have type safety when your code is designed to work with different types.

Solution

Use generic classes and generic methods.

Discussion

Generics are not a strange concept to developers, especially for Java and C# developers. With generics, we can add type parameters to classes and methods. Generics are usually used in collections to create type-safe collections. Listing 3-21 shows the usage of generic collections in Dart. Dart generic types are reified, which means type information are available at runtime. That's why the type of names is List<String>.

Listing 3-21. Generic collections

```
var names = <String>['a', 'b', 'c'];
print(names is List<String>);
var values = <String, int>{'a': 1, 'b': 2, 'c': 3};
print(values.values.toList());
```

We can use generics to create classes that deal with different types. In Listing 3-22, Pair<F, S> is a generic class with two type parameters F and S. Use extends to specify the upper bound of a generic type parameter. The type parameter P in CardHolder has an upper bound of type Person, so that CardHolder<Student> is valid.

Listing 3-22. Generic types

```
class Pair<F, S> {
  F first;
  S second;

  Pair(this.first, this.second);
}

class Person {}

class Teacher extends Person {}
```

```
class Student extends Person {}

class CardHolder<P extends Person> {
  P holder;
  CardHolder(this.holder);
}

void main() {
  var pair = Pair('a', 1);
  print(pair.first);
  var student = Student();
  var cardHolder = CardHolder(student);
  print(cardHolder is CardHolder<Student>);
  print(cardHolder);
}
```

Generic methods can be added to regular classes. In Listing 3-23, the regular class Calculator has two generic methods add and subtract.

Listing 3-23. Generic methods

```
class Calculator {
  T add<T extends num>(T v1, T v2) => v1 + v2;
  T subtract<T extends num>(T v1, T v2) => v1 - v2;
}

void main() {
  var calculator = Calculator();
  int r1 = calculator.add(1, 2);
  double r2 = calculator.subtract(0.1, 0.2);
  print(r1);
  print(r2);
}
```

3-13. Using Libraries

Problem

You want to reuse libraries from Dart SDK or the community.

Solution

Use `import` to import libraries to use them in your app.

Discussion

When developing non-trivial Dart apps, it's inevitable to use libraries. These can be built-in libraries in Dart SDK or libraries contributed by the community. To use these libraries, we need to import them with `import` first. `import` has only one argument to specify the URI of the library. Built-in libraries have the URI scheme `dart:`, for example, `dart:html` and `dart:convert`. Community packages have the URI scheme `package:` and are managed by the Dart `pub` tool. Listing 3-24 shows examples of importing libraries.

Listing 3-24. Import libraries

```
import 'dart:html';
import 'package:meta/meta.dart';
```

It's possible that two libraries export the same identifiers. To avoid conflicts, we can use `as` to provide prefixes for one of the libraries or both. In Listing 3-25, both `lib1.dart` and `lib2.dart` export the class `Counter`. After assigning different prefixes to these two libraries, we can use the prefix to access the class `Counter`.

Listing 3-25. Rename libraries

```
import 'lib1.dart' as lib1;
import 'lib2.dart' as lib2;

lib1.Counter counter;
```

You don't need to import all members of a library. Use show to explicitly include members. Use hide to explicitly exclude members. In Listing 3-26, when importing the library dart:math, only Random is imported; when importing the library dart:html, only Element is excluded.

Listing 3-26. Show and hide members

```
import 'dart:math' show Random;
import 'dart:html' hide Element;
```

3-14. Using Exceptions
Problem

You want to deal with failures in Dart apps.

Solution

Report failures using throw. Handle exceptions using try-catch-finally.

Discussion

Code fails. It's natural for code to report failures and handle them. Dart has a similar exception mechanism as Java, except that all exceptions in Dart are unchecked exceptions. Methods in Dart don't declare exceptions they may throw, so it's not required to catch exceptions. However, uncaught exceptions cause the isolate to suspend and may result in program termination. Proper failure handing is also a key characteristic of robust apps.

Report Failures

We can use `throw` to throw exceptions. In fact, all non-`null` objects can be thrown, not only types that implement types `Error` or `Exception`. It's recommended to only throw objects of types `Error` and `Exception`.

An `Error` object represents a bug in the code that should not happen. For example, if a list only contains three elements, trying to access the fourth element causes a `RangeError` to be thrown. Unlike Exceptions, Errors are not intended to be caught. When an error occurred, the safest way is to terminate the program. `Errors` carry clear information about why they happen.

Comparing to `Errors`, `Exceptions` are designed to be caught and handled programmatically. For example, sending HTTP requests may not succeed, so we need to handle exceptions in the code to deal with failures. `Exceptions` usually carry useful data about the failures. We should create custom types that extend from `Exception` to encapsulate necessary data.

Catch Exceptions

When an exception is thrown, you can catch it to stop it from propagating, unless you rethrow it. The goal to catch an exception is to handle it. You shouldn't catch an exception if you don't want to handle it. Exceptions are caught using `try`, `catch`, and `on`. If you don't need to access the exception object, using `on` is enough. With `catch`, you can access the exception object and the stack trace. Use `on` to specify the type of exception to be caught.

When you catch an exception, you should handle it. However, sometimes you may only want to partially handle it. In this case, you should use `rethrow` to rethrow the exception. It's a bad practice to catch an exception but not handle it completely.

If you want some code to run whether or not an exception is thrown, you can put the code in a `finally` clause. If no exception is thrown, `finally` clause runs after the `try` block. If an exception is thrown, `finally` clause runs after the matching `catch` clause.

In Listing 3-27, the function `getNumber()` throws a custom exception type `ValueTooLargeException`. In the function `main()`, the exception is caught and rethrown.

Listing 3-27. Use exceptions

```dart
import 'dart:math' show Random;

var random = Random();

class ValueTooLargeException implements Exception {
  int value;
  ValueTooLargeException(this.value);

  @override
  String toString() {
    return 'ValueTooLargeException{value: $value}';
  }
}

int getNumber() {
  var value = random.nextInt(10);
  if (value > 5) {
    throw ValueTooLargeException(value);
  }
  return value;
}
```

```
void main() {
  try {
    print(getNumber());
  } on ValueTooLargeException catch (e) {
    print(e);
    rethrow;
  } finally {
    print('in finally');
  }
}
```

3-15. Summary

Learning a new programming language is not an easy task. Even though Dart looks similar with other programming languages, there are still some unique features in Dart. This chapter only provides a brief introduction of important features in Dart.

CHAPTER 4

Widget Basics

When building Flutter apps, most of the time you are dealing with widgets. This chapter provides basic background information about widgets in Flutter. It also covers several basic widgets that display texts, images, icons, buttons, and placeholders.

4-1. Understanding Widgets

Problem

You want to know how to use components in Flutter.

Solution

Widgets are everywhere in Flutter.

Discussion

If you have been involved in development of user interface, you should be familiar with concepts like widgets or components. These concepts represent reusable building blocks to create user interface. A good user interface library should have a large number of high-quality and easy-to-use components. Buttons, icons, images, menus, dialogs, and form inputs are all examples of components. Components can be big or small. Complicated components are usually composed of small components. You can create your own components by following the component model. You can also

F. Cheng, *Flutter Recipes*, https://doi.org/10.1007/978-1-4842-4982-6_4

choose to share your components to the community. A good eco-system of components is a key factor for a user interface library to be successful.

Flutter uses widgets to describe reusable building blocks in the user interface. Comparing to other libraries, widget in Flutter is a much broader concept. Not only common components like buttons and form inputs are widgets, layout constraints are also expressed as widgets in Flutter. For example, if you want to place a widget in the center of a box, you simply wrap the widget into a Center widget. Widgets are also used to retrieve context data. For example, DefaultTextStyle widget gets the TextStyle applies to un-styled Text widgets.

Widget in Flutter is an immutable description of a part of the user interface. All fields of a widget class are final and set in the constructor. Widget constructors only have named parameters. A widget can have one or many widgets as the children. Widgets of a Flutter app creates a tree-like hierarchy. The main() method of a Flutter app's entry point file uses the runApp() method to start the app. The only parameter of runApp() is a Widget object. This Widget object is the root of the app's widgets tree. Widgets are only static configurations that describe how to configure a subtree in the hierarchy. To actually run the app, we need a way to manage instantiation of widgets.

Flutter uses Element to represent an instantiation of a Widget at a particular location in the tree. A Widget can be instantiated zero or many times. The process to turn Widgets to Elements is called inflation. Widget class has a createElement() method to inflate the widget to a concrete instance of Element. Flutter framework is responsible for managing the lifecycle of elements. The widget associated with an element may change over time. The framework updates the element to use the new configuration.

When running the app, Flutter framework is responsible for rendering elements to create a render tree, so the end user can actually see the user interface. A render tree is composed of RenderObjects with the root of a RenderView. If you are using Android Studio, you can actually see the widgets tree and the render tree in **Flutter Inspector** view. Select View ➤ Tool Windows ➤ Flutter Inspector to open the Flutter Inspector view.

Figure 4-1 shows the widgets tree in Flutter Inspector. The top panel shows the widgets tree, while the bottom panel shows the details of a widget.

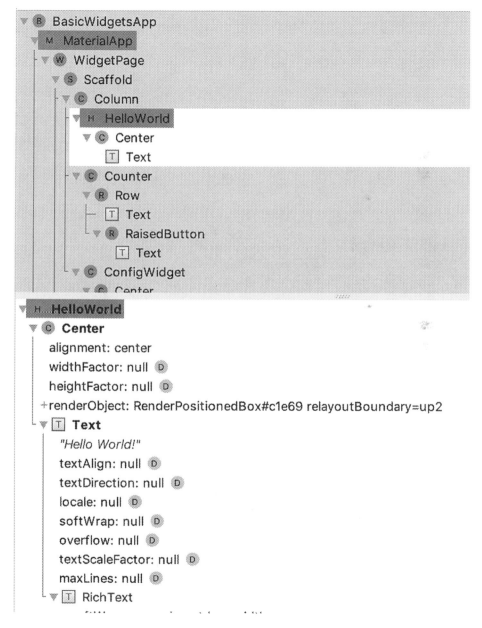

Figure 4-1. *Widgets tree in Flutter Inspector*

Figure 4-2 shows the render tree in Flutter Inspector. The root is a
`RenderView`.

Figure 4-2. *Render tree in Flutter Inspector*

4-2. Understanding BuildContext

Problem

You want to access information related to a widget in the widgets tree.

Solution

WidgetBuilder functions have a BuildContext parameter to access information related to a widget in the widgets tree. You can see BuildContext in StatelessWidget.build() and State.build() methods.

Discussion

When building a widget, the location of the widget in the widgets tree may determine its behavior, especially when it has an InheritedWidget as its ancestor. BuildContext class provides methods to access information related to the location; see Table 4-1.

Table 4-1. *Methods of BuildContext*

Name	Description
ancestorInheritedElement ForWidgetOfExactType	Get the InheritedElement corresponding to the nearest ancestor widget of the given type of InheritedWidget.
ancestorRender ObjectOfType	Get the RenderObject of the nearest ancestor RenderObjectWidget widget.
ancestorStateOfType	Get the State object of the nearest ancestor StatefulWidget widget.
rootAncestorStateOfType	Get the State object of the furthest ancestor StatefulWidget widget.
ancestorWidgetOfExactType	Get the nearest ancestor Widget.
findRenderObject	Get the current RenderObject for the widget.

(continued)

Table 4-1. (*continued*)

Name	Description
inheritFromElement	Register this BuildContext with the given ancestor InheritedElement such that this BuildContext is rebuilt when the ancestor's widget changes.
inheritFromWidgetOf ExactType	Get the nearest InheritedWidget of the given type and register this BuildContext such that this BuildContext is rebuilt when the widget changes.
visitAncestorElements	Visit ancestor elements.
visitChildElements	Visit children elements.

BuildContext is actually the interface of Element class. In StatelessWidget.build() and State.build() methods, the BuildContext object represents the location where the current widget is inflated. In Listing 4-1, ancestorWidgetOfExactType() method is used to get the ancestor widget of type Column.

Listing 4-1. Use BuildContext

```
class WithBuildContext extends StatelessWidget {
  @override
  Widget build(BuildContext context) {
    Column column = context.ancestorWidgetOfExactType(Column);
    return Text(column.children.length.toString());
  }
}
```

4-3. Understanding Stateless Widget

Problem

You want to create a widget that has no mutable state.

Solution

Extend from StatelessWidget class.

Discussion

When using a widget to describe a part of user interface, if the part can be fully described using the configuration information of the widget itself and the BuildContext in which it's inflated, then this widget should extend from StatelessWidget. When creating a StatelessWidget class, you need to implement the build() method which accepts a BuildContext and returns a Widget. In Listing 4-2, HelloWorld class extends from StatelessWidget class and returns a Center widget in the build() method.

Listing 4-2. Example of StatelessWidget

```
class HelloWorld extends StatelessWidget {
  const HelloWorld({Key key}) : super(key: key);

  @override
  Widget build(BuildContext context) {
    return Center(
      child: Text('Hello World!'),
    );
  }
}
```

4-4. Understanding Stateful Widget

Problem

You want to create a widget that has mutable state.

Solution

Extend from StatefulWidget class.

Discussion

If a part of user interface may change dynamically, you need to extend from StatefulWidget class. StatefulWidgets themselves are immutable with states managed in State objects created by them. A StatefulWidget subclass needs to implement the createState() method that returns a State<StatefulWidget> object. When the state changes, the State object should call setState() method to notify the framework to trigger the update. In Listing 4-3, _CounterState class is the State object of the Counter widget. When the button is pressed, the value is updated in the setState() method, which updates the _CounterState widget to show the new value.

Listing 4-3. Example of StatefulWidget

```
class Counter extends StatefulWidget {
  @override
  _CounterState createState() => _CounterState();
}

class _CounterState extends State<Counter> {
  int value = 0;

  @override
  Widget build(BuildContext context) {
```

```
    return Row(
      children: <Widget>[
        Text('$value'),
        RaisedButton(
          child: Text('+'),
          onPressed: () {
            setState(() {
              value++;
            });
          },
        ),
      ],
    );
  }
}
```

4-5. Understanding Inherited Widget

Problem

You want to propagate data down the widgets tree.

Solution

Extend from InheritedWidget class.

Discussion

When building a subtree of widgets, you may need to propagate data down the widgets tree. For example, your root widget of a subtree may define some context data, for example, configuration data retrieved from the server. Other widgets in the subtree may also need to access the context

113

data. One possible way is to add the context data to a widget's constructor, then propagate the data as constructor parameter of children widgets. The major drawback of this solution is that you need to add the constructor parameter to all widgets in the subtree. Even though some widgets may not actually need the data, they still need to have the data to pass to their children widgets.

A better approach is to use InheritedWidget class. BuildContext class has an inheritFromWidgetOfExactType() method to get the nearest instance of a particular type of InheritedWidget. With InheritedWidget, you can store the context data in an InheritedWiget instance. If a widget needs to access the context data, you can use inheritFromWidgetOfExactType() method to get the instance and access the data. If an inherited widget changes state, it will cause its consumers to rebuild.

In Listing 4-4, ConfigWidget class has the data config. The static of() method gets the nearest ancestor ConfigWidget instance for the config value. The method updateShouldNotify() determines when the consumer widgets should be notified.

Listing 4-4. Example of InheritedWidget

```
class ConfigWidget extends InheritedWidget {
  const ConfigWidget({
    Key key,
    @required this.config,
    @required Widget child,
  })  : assert(config != null),
        assert(child != null),
        super(key: key, child: child);

  final String config;

  static String of(BuildContext context) {
    final ConfigWidget configWidget =
```

114

```
      context.inheritFromWidgetOfExactType(ConfigWidget);
    return configWidget?.config ?? ";
  }

  @override
  bool updateShouldNotify(ConfigWidget oldWidget) {
    return config != oldWidget.config;
  }
}
```

In Listing 4-5, ConfigUserWidget class uses the ConfigWidget.of() method to get the config value.

Listing 4-5. Use of ConfigWidget

```
class ConfigUserWidget extends StatelessWidget {
  @override
  Widget build(BuildContext context) {
    return Text('Data is ${ConfigWidget.of(context)}');
  }
}
```

In Listing 4-6, ConfigWidget instance has a config value of "Hello!" and a descendant ConfigUserWidget instance.

Listing 4-6. Complete example

```
ConfigWidget(
  config: 'Hello!',
  child: Center(
    child: ConfigUserWidget(),
  ),
);
```

4-6. Displaying Text

Problem

You want to display some text.

Solution

Use the Text and RichText widgets.

Discussion

Almost all apps need to display some text to the end users. Flutter provides several classes related to text. Text and RichText are the two widgets to display text. In fact, Text uses RichText internally. The build() method of Text widget returns a RichText instance. The difference between Text and RichText is that Text uses the style from the closest enclosing DefaultTextStyle object, while RichText requires explicit style.

Text

Text has two constructors. The first constructor Text() accepts a String as the text to display. Another constructor Text.rich() accepts a TextSpan object to represent both text and style. The simplest form to create a Text widget is Text('Hello world'), which displays text using the style from the closest enclosing DefaultTextStyle object. Both Text() and Text.rich() constructors have several named parameters to customize them; see Table 4-2.

Table 4-2. *Named parameters of Text() and Text.rich()*

Name	Type	Description
style	TextStyle	Style of the text.
textAlign	TextAlign	How text should be aligned horizontally.
textDirection	TextDirection	Direction of text.
locale	Locale	Locale to select font based on Unicode.
softWrap	bool	Whether to break text at soft line breaks.
overflow	TextOverflow	How to handle text overflow.
textScaleFactor	double	The factor to scale the text.
maxLines	int	The maximum number of lines. If the text exceeds the limit, it will be truncated according to the strategy specified in overflow.
semanticsLabel	String	Semantics label for the text.

TextAlign is an enum type with values shown in Table 4-3.

Table 4-3. *TextAlign values*

Name	Description
left	Align text on the left edge of its container.
right	Align text on the right edge of its container.
center	Align text in the center of its container.
justify	For lines of text end with soft line breaks, stretch these lines to fill the width of the container; for lines of text end with hard line breaks, align them toward the start edge.
start	Align text on the leading edge of its container. The leading edge is the left edge for left-to-right text, while it's the right edge for right-to-left text.
end	Align text on the trailing edge of its container. The trailing edge is the opposite of the leading edge.

It's recommended to always use TextAlign values start and end instead of left and right to better handle bidirectional text. TextDirection is an enum type with values ltr and rtl. TextOverflow is an enum type with values shown in Table 4-4.

Table 4-4. *TextOverflow values*

Name	Description
clip	Clip the overflowing text.
fade	Fade the overflowing text to be transparent.
ellipsis	Add an ellipsis after the overflowing text.

DefaultTextStyle is an InheritedWidget that has properties style, textAlign, softWrap, overflow, and maxLines which have the same meaning as named parameters shown in Table 4-2. If a named parameter is provided in the constructors Text() and Text.rich(), then the provided value overrides the value in the nearest ancestor DefaultTextStyle object. Listing 4-7 shows several examples of using Text widget.

Listing 4-7. Examples of Text

```
Text('Hello World')

Text(
  'Bigger Bold Text',
  style: TextStyle(fontWeight: FontWeight.bold),
  textScaleFactor: 2.0,
);

Text(
  'Lorem ipsum dolor sit amet, consectetur adipiscing elit, sed
  do eiusmod tempor incididunt',
  maxLines: 1,
  overflow: TextOverflow.ellipsis,
);
```

TextSpan

The constructor Text.rich() takes a TextSpan object as the required parameter. TextSpan represents an immutable span of text. TextSpan() constructor has four named parameters; see Table 4-5. TextSpans are organized in a hierarchy. A TextSpan object may have many TextSpan objects as the children. Children TextSpans can override styles from their parent.

Table 4-5. *Named parameters of TextSpan()*

Name	Type	Description
style	TextStyle	Style of the text and children.
text	String	Text in the span.
children	List<TextSpan>	TextSpans as children of this span.
recognizer	GestureRecognizer	A gesture recognizer to receive events.

Listing 4-8 shows the example of using Text.rich(). This example displays the sentence "The quick brown fox jumps over the lazy dog" using different styles.

Listing 4-8. Example of Text.rich()

```
Text.rich(TextSpan(
  style: TextStyle(
    fontSize: 16,
  ),
  children: [
    TextSpan(text: 'The quick brown '),
    TextSpan(
        text: 'fox',
        style: TextStyle(
          fontWeight: FontWeight.bold,
          color: Colors.red,
        )),
    TextSpan(text: ' jumps over the lazy '),
    TextSpan(
        text: 'dog',
        style: TextStyle(
```

```
            color: Colors.blue,
        )),
    ],
));
```

RichText

RichText always uses TextSpan objects to represent text and styles. RichText() constructor has a required named parameter text of the type TextSpan. It also has optional named parameters textAlign, textDirection, softWrap, overflow, textScaleFactor, maxLines, and locale. These optional named parameters have the same meaning as Text() constructor shown in Table 4-2.

Text displayed in RichText requires explicit styling. You can use DefaultTextStyle.of() to get the default style from the BuildContext object. This is exactly what Text does internally. Text widget gets the default style and merges with the style provided in the style parameter, then creates a RichText with a TextSpan wrapping the text and merged style. If you find out that you do need to use the default style as the base, you should use Text directly instead of RichText. Listing 4-9 shows an example of using RichText.

Listing 4-9. Example of RichText

```
RichText(
  text: TextSpan(
    text: 'Level 1',
    style: TextStyle(color: Colors.black),
    children: [
      TextSpan(
        text: 'Level 2',
        style: TextStyle(fontWeight: FontWeight.bold),
```

121

```
      children: [
        TextSpan(
          text: 'Level 3',
          style: TextStyle(color: Colors.red),
        ),
      ],
    ),
  ],
),
);
```

4-7. Applying Styles to Text

Problem

You want the displayed text to have different styles.

Solution

Use TextStyle to describe styles.

Discussion

TextStyle describes styles applied to text. TextStyle() constructor has many named parameters to describe the style; see Table 4-6.

Table 4-6. *Named parameters of TextStyle()*

Name	Type	Description
color	Color	Color of the text.
fontSize	Double	Size of font.
fontWeight	FontWeight	Typeface thickness.
fontStyle	FontStyle	Typeface variant.
letterSpacing	Double	Space between each letter.
wordSpacing	Double	Space between each word.
textBaseLine	TextBaseLine	Common baseline to align this text span and its parent span.
height	Double	Height of the text.
locale	Locale	Locale to select region-specific glyphs.
foreground	Paint	Foreground for the text.
background	Paint	Background for the text.
shadows	List<Shadow>	Shadows painted underneath the text.
decoration	TextDecoration	Decoration of the text.
decorationColor	Color	Color of text decorations.
decorationStyle	TextDecorationStyle	Style of text decorations.
debugLabel	String	Description of the style for debugging.
fontFamily	String	Name of the font.
package	String	Use with fontFamily if the font is defined in a package.

FontWeight class defines values w100, w200, w300, w400, w500, w600, w700, w800, and w900. FontWeight.w100 is the thinnest, while w900 is the thickest. FontWeight.bold is an alias of FontWeight.w700, while FontWeight.normal is an alias of FontWeight.w400. FontStyle is an enum type with two values italic and normal. TextBaseline is an enum type with values alphabetic and ideographic.

TextDecoration class defines different types of text decorations. You can also use constructor TextDecoration.combine() to create a new TextDecoration instance by combing a list of TextDecoration instances. For example, TextDecoration.combine([TextDecoration.underline, TextDecoration.overline]) instance draws lines underneath and above text. Table 4-7 shows constants in TextDecoration.

Table 4-7. *TextDecoration constants*

Name	Description
none	No decoration.
underline	Draw a line underneath text.
overline	Draw a line above text.
lineThrough	Draw a line through text.

TextDecorationStyle is an enum type with values shown in Table 4-8. TextDecorationStyle defines the style of lines created by TextDecoration.

Table 4-8. *TextDecorationStyle values*

Name	Description
solid	Draw a solid line.
double	Draw two lines.
dotted	Draw a dotted line.
dashed	Draw a dashed line.
wavy	Draw a sinusoidal line.

Listing 4-10 shows an example of using TextDecoration and TextDecorationStyle.

Listing 4-10. Example of using TextDecoration and TextDecorationStyle

```
Text(
  'Decoration',
  style: TextStyle(
    fontWeight: FontWeight.w900,
    decoration: TextDecoration.lineThrough,
    decorationStyle: TextDecorationStyle.dashed,
  ),
);
```

If you want to create a copy of a TextStyle instance with some properties updated, use the copyWith() method. The apply() method also creates a new TextStyle instance, but it allows updating some properties using factor and delta. For example, the named parameters fontSizeFactor and fontSizeDelta can update the font size. The updated value of fontSize is calculated with "fontSize * fontSizeFactor + fontSizeDelta". You can also update values of height, letterSpacing, and wordSpacing using the same pattern. For fontWeight, only

125

fontWeightDelta is supported. In Listing 4-11, the TextStyle applied to the text has updated values of fontSize and decoration.

Listing 4-11. Update TextStyle

```
Text(
  'Scale',
  style: DefaultTextStyle.of(context).style.apply(
        fontSizeFactor: 2.0,
        fontSizeDelta: 1,
        decoration: TextDecoration.none,
      ),
);
```

4-8. Displaying Images
Problem

You want to display images loaded from network.

Solution

Use Image.network() with the image URL to load and display an image.

Discussion

If you have images hosted in your own servers or other places, you can display them using the Image.network() constructor. Image.network() constructor only requires the URL of the image to load. An image widget should be given specific dimension using the named parameters width and height or placed in a context that sets tight layout constraints. This is because the dimension of the image may change when the image is loaded. Without a strict size constraint, the image widget may affect layout of other widgets. In Listing 4-12, the size of the image widget is specified with named parameters `width` and `height`.

Listing 4-12. Example of Image.network()

```
Image.network(
  'https://picsum.photos/400/300',
  width: 400,
  height: 300,
);
```

All downloaded images are cached regardless of HTTP headers. This means that all HTTP cache control headers will be ignored. You can use cache buster to force cached images to refresh. For example, you can add a random string to the image URL.

If extra HTTP headers are required to load the image, you can specify the `headers` parameter of type `Map<String, String>` to provide these headers. A typical use case is to load protected images that require HTTP headers for authentication.

If an image cannot cover the whole area of a box, you can use the `repeat` parameter of type `ImageRepeat` to specify how images are repeated. `ImageRepeat` is an enum type with values shown in Table 4-9. The default value is `noRepeat`.

Table 4-9. *ImageRepeat values*

Name	Description
Repeat	Repeat in both x and y directions.
repeatX	Repeat only in the x direction.
repeatY	Repeat only in the y direction.
noRepeat	No repeat. The uncovered area will be transparent.

In Listing 4-13, the image is placed into a SizedBox which is larger than the image. By using ImageRepeat.repeat, the box is filled with this image.

Listing 4-13. Repeated images

```
SizedBox(
  width: 400,
  height: 300,
  child: Image.network(
    'https://picsum.photos/300/200',
    alignment: Alignment.topLeft,
    repeat: ImageRepeat.repeat,
  ),
);
```

4-9. Displaying Icons

Problem

You want to use icons.

Solution

Use Icon to show icons from Material Design or icon packs from community.

Discussion

Icons are used extensively in mobile apps. Comparing to text, icons take less screen estate to express the same semantics. Icons can be created from font glyphs or images. The Icon widget is drawn with a font glyph. A font glyph is described with IconData class. To create an IconData instance, the Unicode code point of this icon in the font is required.

Icons class has a number of predefined IconData constants for icons in Material Design (https://material.io/tools/icons/). For example, Icons.call is the IconData constant for the icon named "call". If the app uses Material Design, then these icons can be used out of box. CupertinoIcons class has a number of predefined IconData constants for iOS-style icons.

Icon() constructor has named parameters size and color to specify the size and color of the icon, respectively. Icons are always square with width and height both equal to size. The default value of size is 24. Listing 4-14 creates a red Icons.call icon of size 100.

Listing 4-14. Example of Icon()

```
Icon(
  Icons.call,
  size: 100,
  color: Colors.red,
);
```

To use the popular Font Awesome icons, you can use the package font_awesome_flutter (https://pub.dartlang.org/packages/font_awesome_flutter). After adding the package dependency to pubspec.yaml file, you can import the file to use FontAwesomeIcons class. Similar with Icons class, FontAwesomeIcons class has a number of IconData constants for different icons in Font Awesome. Listing 4-15 creates a blue FontAwesomeIcons.angry icon of size 80.

Listing 4-15. Use Font Awesome icon

```
Icon(
  FontAwesomeIcons.angry,
  size: 80,
  color: Colors.blue,
);
```

4-10. Using Buttons with Text

Problem

You want to use buttons with text.

Solution

Use button widgets FlatButton, RaisedButton, OutlineButton, and CupertinoButton.

Discussion

Flutter has different types of buttons for Material Design and iOS. These button widgets all have a required parameter onPressed to specify the handler function when pressed. If the onPressed handler is null, the button is disabled. The content of a button is specified with the parameter child of type Widget. FlatButton, RaisedButton, and OutlineButton have different styles and behaviors reacting to touches:

- A FlatButton has zero elevation and no visible borders. It reacts to touches by filling with color specified by highlightColor.

- A RaisedButton has elevation and is filled with color. It reacts to touches by increasing elevation to highlightElevation.

- An OutlineButton has borders, an initial elevation of 0.0, and transparent background. It reacts to touches by making its background opaque with the color and increasing its elevation to highlightElevation.

FlatButtons should be used on toolbars, in dialogs, in cards, or inline with other content where there is enough space to make buttons' presence obvious. RaisedButtons should be used where using space is not enough to make the buttons stand out. OutlineButton is the cross between RaisedButton and FlatButton. OutlineButtons can be used when neither FlatButtons nor RaisedButtons are appropriate.

If you prefer the iOS-style button, you can use the CupertinoButton widget. CupertinoButton reacts to touches by fading out and in. Listing 4-16 shows examples of creating different types of buttons.

Listing 4-16. Different types of buttons

```
FlatButton(
  child: Text('Flat'),
  color: Colors.white,
  textColor: Colors.grey,
  highlightColor: Colors.red,
  onPressed: () => {},
);

RaisedButton(
  child: Text('Raised'),
  color: Colors.blue,
  onPressed: () => {},
);

OutlineButton(
  child: Text('Outline'),
  onPressed: () => {},
);

CupertinoButton(
  child: Text('Cupertino'),
  color: Colors.green,
  onPressed: () => {},
);
```

4-11. Using Buttons with Icons

Problem

You want to use buttons with icons.

Solution

Use IconButton widget, FlatButton.icon(), RaisedButton.icon(), and OutlineButton.icon().

Discussion

There are two ways to create a button with an icon. If only the icon is enough, use IconButton widget. If both the icon and text are required, use constructors FlatButton.icon(), RaisedButton.icon(), or OutlineButton.icon().

IconButton constructor requires the icon parameter to specify the icon. FlatButton.icon(), RaisedButton.icon(), and OutlineButton. icon() use the parameters icon and label to specify the icon and text, respectively. Listing 4-17 shows examples of using IconButton() and RaisedButton.icon().

Listing 4-17. Examples of IconButton() and RaisedButton.icon()

```
IconButton(
  icon: Icon(Icons.map),
  iconSize: 50,
  tooltip: 'Map',
  onPressed: () => {},
);
```

```
RaisedButton.icon(
  icon: Icon(Icons.save),
  label: Text('Save'),
  onPressed: () => [],
);
```

4-12. Adding Placeholders

Problem

You want to add placeholders to represent widgets that will be added later.

Solution

Use Placeholder.

Discussion

Before implementing the interface of an app, you usually have a basic idea about how the app looks like. You can start by breaking down the interface into many widgets. You can use placeholders to represent unfinished widgets during development, so you can test the layout of other widgets. For example, if you need to create two widgets, one displays at the top, while the other one displays at the bottom. If you choose to create the bottom widget first and use a placeholder for the top widget, you can see the bottom widget in its desired position.

The Placeholder() constructor takes named parameters color, strokeWidth, fallbackWidth, and fallbackHeight. The placeholder is drawn as a rectangle and two diagonals. The parameters color and strokeWidth specify color and width of the lines, respectively. By default, the placeholder fits its container. However, if the placeholder's container is unbounded, it uses the given fallbackWidth and fallbackHeight to determine the size. Both fallbackWidth and fallbackHeight have the default value 400.0. Listing 4-18 shows an example of Placeholder widget.

Listing 4-18. Example of Placeholder

```
Placeholder(
  color: Colors.red,
  strokeWidth: 1,
  fallbackHeight: 200,
  fallbackWidth: 200,
);
```

4-13. Summary

Widgets are everywhere in Flutter apps. This chapter provides basic introduction of widgets in Flutter, including StatelessWidget, StatefulWidget, and InheritedWidget. This chapter also covers usage of common basic widgets to display text, images, icons, buttons, and placeholders. The next chapter will discuss layout in Flutter.

CHAPTER 5

Layout Widgets

Layout is always a challenging task when building user interface. When it comes to mobile apps, layout is much more complicated considering the large number of different screen resolutions for devices. This chapter covers recipes related to layout in Flutter.

5-1. Understanding Layout in Flutter

Problem

You want to know how layout works in Flutter.

Solution

Layout in Flutter is implemented by a set of widgets. These layout widgets wrap other widgets to apply different layout constraints.

Discussion

For mobile apps, the layout must be responsive to work with different screen resolutions without writing a lot of hard-to-maintain code. Luckily, with the evolution of layout techniques, it's now easier to build responsive layout. If you have experiences with web development with CSS, you may have heard CSS Flexible Box Layout Module specification by W3C (`https://www.w3.org/TR/css-flexbox-1/`). The flex layout model is

© Fu Cheng 2019
F. Cheng, *Flutter Recipes*, https://doi.org/10.1007/978-1-4842-4982-6_5

powerful because it allows developers to express what the layout should be, instead of how to implement the actual layout. This declarative approach shifts the heavy lifting work to the underlying framework. The result layout code is easier to understand and maintain.

For example, if you want to place a box in the center of a container, the old approach may require calculating the size of the box and container to determine the position of the box. When using flex layout, the layout can be simplified as CSS code in Listing 5-1.

Listing 5-1. CSS code to center an item

```css
.container {
  display: flex;
  width: 400px;
  height: 400px;
  justify-content: center;
  align-items: center;
  border: 1px solid green;
}
.item {
  width: 200px;
  height: 200px;
  border: 1px solid red;
}
```

The idea of flex layout has now been used not only in web design but also in mobile apps. React Native uses flex layout (https://facebook.github. io/react-native/docs/flexbox). Flutter also uses the idea of flex layout. As discussed in Recipe 4-1, layout is implemented as widgets. You can see widget classes like Flex, Row, Column, and Flexible in Flutter, which have names derived from flex layout concepts. The flex layout model in CSS is out of the scope of this book. However, it's still valuable to understand this W3C specification, which can help you better understand flex layout in Flutter.

RenderObject

The layout algorithm in Flutter is responsible for determining the dimension and position for each RenderObject instance in the render tree. RenderObject class is very flexible to work with any coordinate system or layout protocol. RenderObject class defines the basic layout protocol with the layout() method. The layout() method has one required positional parameter of type Constraints. Constraints class specifies the layout constraints that children must obey. For a particular Constraints instance, there may be multiple results that can satisfy it. The child is free to use any of these results as long as it's permissible. Sometimes, a Constraints instance may only leave one valid result to the child. This kind of Constraints instances are said to be tight. Tight constraints are generally less flexible, but they offer better performance as widgets with tight constraints don't need to relayout.

The layout() method has a named parameter parentUsesSize to specify whether the parent needs to use the layout information computed by the child. If parentUsesSize is true, it means the layout of the parent depends on the layout of the child. In this case, whenever the child needs to lay out, the parent may also need to lay out. After the layout is done, each RenderObject instance will have some fields set to include the layout information. The actual stored information depends on the layout implementation. This piece of layout information is stored in the parentData property.

By default, Flutter uses a 2D Cartesian coordinate system implemented with the RenderBox class. RenderBox class implements the box layout model with BoxConstraints class. In the box layout model, each RenderBox instance is treated as a rectangle with the size specified as a Size instance. Each box has its own coordinate system. The coordinate of the upper left corner is (0,0), while the lower right corner has the coordinate (width, height). RenderBox class uses BoxParentData as the type of layout data. The BoxParentData.offset property specifies the offset to paint the child in the parent's coordinate system.

137

BoxConstraints

A BoxConstraints instance is specified by four named double parameters: minWidth, maxWidth, minHeight, and maxHeight. The values of these must satisfy the following rules. double.infinity is a valid value for constraints:

- 0.0 <= minWidth <= maxWidth <= double.infinity

- 0.0 <= minHeight <= maxHeight <= double.infinity

After the box layout, the size of a RenderBox instance must satisfy constraints of the BoxConstraints instance applied to it:

- minWidth <= Size.width <= maxWidth

- minHeight <= Size.height <= maxHeight.

If the minimum constraint and the maximum constraint are the same in an axis, then this axis is tightly constrained. For example, if the values of minWidth and maxWidth are the same, then width is tight. A BoxConstraints instance is said to be tight when both width and height are tight. If the minimum constraint is 0.0 in an axis, then this axis is loose. If the maximum constraint is not infinite in an axis, then this axis is bounded; otherwise, this axis is unbounded.

Layout Algorithm

In the box layout model, layout is done in one pass with the render tree. It first walks down the render tree by passing constraints. In this phase, render objects are laid out using constraints passed by their parents. In the second phase, it walks up the render tree by passing concrete results that determine the size and offset of each render object.

Layout Widgets

Flutter provides a set of layout widgets for different layout requirements. There are two categories of these widgets. The first category is for widgets that contain a single child, which are descendant classes of SingleChildRenderObjectWidget class. The second category is for widgets that can contain multiple children, which are descendant classes of MultiChildRenderObjectWidget class. Constructors of these widgets have a similar pattern. The first named parameter is key of type Key. The last named parameter of single child layout widget constructors is child of type Widget, while the last named parameter of multiple children layout widget constructor is children of type List<Widget>.

These layout widgets are subclasses of RenderObjectWidget class. RenderObjectWidget class is used to configure RenderObjectElements. RenderObjectElements wrap RenderObjects.

5-2. Placing Widgets in the Center

Problem

You want to place a widget in the center of another widget.

Solution

Wrap the widget with a Center widget.

Discussion

To place a widget in the center of another widget, you can simply wrap the widget in a Center widget. This widget will be placed in the center of the Center widget both horizontally and vertically. This Center widget will be the child of the original parent widget. Center constructor has two named parameters widthFactor and heightFactor to specify the size factor for width and height, respectively. Listing 5-2 shows an example of using Center widget.

Listing 5-2. Example of Center widget

```
Center(
  widthFactor: 2.0,
  heightFactor: 2.0,
  child: Text("Center"),
)
```

Center widget is actually a subclass of Align widget with alignment set of Alignment.center. The behavior of Center widget is the same as Align widget discussed in Recipe 5-3.

5-3. Aligning Widgets

Problem

You want to align a widget in different position of its parent widget.

Solution

Wrap the widget with an Align widget.

Discussion

With Align widget, you can align a child widget in different position. Align widget constructor has the named parameter alignment of type AlignmentGeometry to specify the alignment. Center widget is actually a special kind of Align widget with alignment always set to Alignment.

center. Align widget constructor also has the named parameters widthFactor and heightFactor.

AlignmentGeometry class has two subclasses to be used in different situations. Alignment class represents alignment in visual coordinates. Alignment has two properties x and y to represent the position in the rectangle of the 2D coordinate system. The properties x and y specify the position in the horizontal and vertical direction, respectively. Alignment(0.0, 0.0) means the center of the rectangle. A unit of 1.0 means the distance from the center to one side of the rectangle. A unit of 2.0 means the length of the rectangle in a particular direction. For example, the value 2.0 of x means the width of the rectangle. Positive values of x mean positions to the right of the center, while negative values of x mean positions to the left. The same rule also applies to values of y. Align has several constants for commonly used positions; see Table 5-1.

Table 5-1. *Alignment constants*

Name	Value	Description
bottomCenter	Alignment(0.0, 1.0)	Center point of the bottom edge.
bottomLeft	Alignment(-1.0, 1.0)	Leftmost point of the bottom edge.
bottomRight	Alignment(1.0, 1.0)	Rightmost point of the bottom edge.
center	Alignment(0.0, 0.0)	Center point both horizontally and vertically.
centerLeft	Alignment(-1.0, 0.0)	Center point of the left edge.
centerRight	Alignment(1.0, 0.0)	Center point of the right edge.
topCenter	Alignment(0,0, -1.0)	Center point of the top edge.
topLeft	Alignment(-1.0, -1.0)	Leftmost point of the top edge.
topRight	Alignment(1.0, -1.0)	Rightmost point of the top edge.

If you want to consider text direction in alignment, you need to use AlignmentDirectional class instead of Alignment class. AlignmentDirectional class has the property start instead of x. The start value grows in the same direction as the text direction. The value of start has the same meaning of x in Alignment when the text direction is left-to-right. If the text direction is right-to-left, the value of start is the opposite of x in Alignment. AlignmentDirectional class also has several constants for commonly used positions; see Table 5-2. These constants use start and end instead of left and right to represent different directions.

Table 5-2. *AlignmentDirectional constants*

Name	Value	Description
bottomCenter	AlignmentDirectional (0.0, 1.0)	Center point of the bottom edge.
bottomStart	AlignmentDirectional (-1.0, 1.0)	Bottom corner on the start side.
bottomEnd	AlignmentDirectional (1.0, 1.0)	Bottom corner on the end side.
center	AlignmentDirectional (0.0, 0.0)	Center point both horizontally and vertically.
centerStart	AlignmentDirectional (-1.0, 0.0)	Center point of the start edge.
centerEnd	AlignmentDirectional (1.0, 0.0)	Center point of the end edge.
topCenter	AlignmentDirectional (0,0, -1.0)	Center point of the top edge.
topStart	AlignmentDirectional (-1.0, -1.0)	Top corner on the start side.
topEnd	AlignmentDirectional (1.0, -1.0)	Top corner on the end side.

The resolve() method of AlignmentGeometry takes a parameter of type TextDirection and returns an Alignment instance. You can use this method to convert an AlignmentDirectional instance to an Alignment instance.

The constrained passed to its child is the result of calling the loosen() method on this widget's constraints object. This means the child can choose a size not exceeding this widget. The size of the widget itself depends on values of parameters widthFactor and heightFactor and its constraints object. For the width, if widthFactor is not null or constraints.maxWidth is double.infinity, then the width is the closest value to childWidth * (widthFactory ?? 1.0) constrained by the constraints. Otherwise, the width is determined by the constraints. The same rule applies to the height.

Listing 5-3 shows an example of using Align widget.

Listing 5-3. Example of Align widget

```
Align(
  alignment: Alignment.topLeft,
  child: SizedBox(
    width: 200,
    height: 200,
    child: Center(
      child: Text("TopLeft"),
    ),
  ),
)
```

5-4. Imposing Constraints on Widgets

Problem

You want to impose layout constraints on widgets.

Solution

Use `ConstrainedBox` or `SizedBox`.

Discussion

As discussed in Recipe 5-1, `Constraints` and `BoxContraints` instances
are usually used in the `layout()` method of `RenderObject` and `RenderBox`,
respectively. When building the widgets tree, you may also want to impose
layout constraints on widgets. In this case, you can use `ConstrainedBox`
widget. `ConstrainedBox` constructor has a required named parameter
constraints of type `BoxConstraints` to specify the constraints to impose on
the child.

   `SizedBox` widget can be treated as a special kind of `ConstrainedBox`.
`SizedBox` has named parameters `width` and `height` which are used to
create a tight constraint using `BoxConstraints.tightFor()` method.
`SizedBox(width: width, height: height, child: child)` is the same
as `ConstrainedBox(constraints: BoxConstraints.tightFor(width:
width, height: height), child: child)`. If you want to impose tight
constraints, then `SizedBox` is more convenient than `ConstrainedBox`.
`SizedBox` has other named constructors for other common use cases; see
Table 5-3.

Table 5-3. *SizedBox constructors*

Name	Meaning	Description
SizedBox. expand()	SizedBox(width: double. infinity, height: double. infinity)	As large as its parent allows.
SizedBox. shrink()	SizedBox(width: 0.0, height: 0.0)	As small as its parent allows.
SizedBox. fromSize()	SizedBox(width: size.width; height: size.height)	A box with the specified size.

The actual constraints applied to the child widget is the combination of provided constraints parameter and the constraints provided by the parent of ConstrainedBox or SizedBox. The combination is done by calling providedContraints.enforce(parentContraints). The result constraints respect the parent constraints and are as close as possible to the provided constraints. The size of ConstrainedBox or SizedBox is the size of the child widget after layout.

Listing 5-4 shows four examples of using ConstrainedBox and SizedBox. The first example is a typical usage pattern of SizedBox. The second example with SizedBox.shrink() causes the image not to be displayed. The third example is a typical usage pattern of ConstrainedBox. The last example shows how a ConstrainedBox instance respects constraints from parent.

Listing 5-4. Examples of ConstrainedBox and SizedBox

```
SizedBox(
  width: 100,
  height: 100,
  child: Text('SizedBox'),
)
```

```
SizedBox.shrink(
  child: Image.network('https://picsum.photos/50'),
)

ConstrainedBox(
  constraints: BoxConstraints(
    maxWidth: 50,
    minHeight: 50,
  ),
  child: Text('ConstrainedBox'),
)

ConstrainedBox(
  constraints: BoxConstraints(
    maxWidth: 200,
  ),
  child: ConstrainedBox(
    constraints: BoxConstraints(
      maxHeight: 200,
    ),
    child: Image.network('https://picsum.photos/300'),
  ),
)
```

5-5. Imposing No Constraints on Widgets

Problem

You want to impose constraints on widgets to allow them to render at natural size.

Solution

Use UnconstrainedBox.

Discussion

UnconstrainedBox is the opposite of ConstrainedBox in Recipe 5-4. UnconstrainedBox imposes no constraints on its child. The child can render freely on the unlimited space provided by the UnconstrainedBox instance. UnconstrainedBox will try to use the child widget's size to determine its own size by following the limitations of its own constraints.

If the child widget's size is bigger than the maximum size of UnconstrainedBox can provide, the child widget will be clipped. Otherwise, the child widget is aligned based on the value of the parameter alignment of type AlignmentGeometry. If the child overflows the parent, a warning is displayed in debug mode. When using UnconstrainedBox, it's still possible to add constraints to one axis using the parameter constrainedAxis of type Axis. Then the child is only allowed to render unconstrained on the other axis.

In Listing 5-5, the UnconstrainedBox widget is placed in a SizedBox widget with fixed width and height. The UnconstrainedBox widget is constrained on the horizontal axis, which means the minimum and maximum width are both 100px. The image's width is 200px, so it's scaled down to 100px to meet the width constraint. This causes the image height to scale down to 150px, which exceeds the maximum height 100px of the parent SizedBox widget. When running in debug mode, you can see warning messages that the top and bottom are overflowed by 25px.

Listing 5-5. Example of UnconstrainedBox

```
SizedBox(
  width: 100,
  height: 100,
```

```
  child: UnconstrainedBox(
    constrainedAxis: Axis.horizontal,
    child: Image.network('https://picsum.photos/200/300'),
  ),
)
```

5-6. Imposing Constraints on Widgets when Ignoring Parents

Problem

You want to impose constraints no matter where a widget is placed.

Solution

Use OverflowBox.

Discussion

When imposing constraints on widgets, constraints from the parent widget are generally respected. Respecting parent constraints makes a widget's layout flexible to adapt different use cases. Sometimes you may want a widget to only respect explicitly provided constraints and ignore parent's constraints. In this case, you can use OverflowBox.

OverflowBox constructor has named parameters alignment, minWidth, maxWidth, minHeight, and maxHeight. If any of the constraints related parameter is null, the corresponding value from parent's constraints is used. If you provide non-null values to all four constraints related parameters, the layout of OverflowBox's child is completely irrelevant to the current widget.

In Listing 5-6, the `OverflowBox` widget is created with non-null values of all four constraints related parameters, so even though it's placed inside of a `SizedBox` widget, its size is always `Size(200, 200)`.

Listing 5-6. Example of OverflowBox

```
SizedBox(
  width: 100,
  height: 100,
  child: OverflowBox(
    minWidth: 200,
    minHeight: 200,
    maxWidth: 200,
    maxHeight: 200,
    child: Image.network('https://picsum.photos/300'),
  ),
)
```

5-7. Limiting Size to Allow Child Widget to Overflow

Problem

You want a widget to have a size and allow child widget to overflow.

Solution

Use `SizedOverflowBox`.

Discussion

SizedOverflowBox is created with a size. The widget's actual size respects its constraints and is as close as possible to the requested size. The child's layout only uses SizedOverflowBox widget's constraints.

In Listing 5-7, the SizedOverflowBox widget is placed in a ConstrainedBox widget with constraints BoxConstraints. loose(Size(100, 100)). The requested size of SizedOverflowBox widget is Size(50, 50). The actual size of SizedOverflowBox is also Size(50, 50). The child Image widget only uses the constraints of SizedOverflowBox. The result is the image widget has a size of Size(100, 100), which overflows its parent.

Listing 5-7. Example of SizedOverflowBox

```
ConstrainedBox(
  constraints: BoxConstraints.loose(Size(100, 100)),
  child: SizedOverflowBox(
    size: Size(50, 50),
    child: Image.network('https://picsum.photos/400'),
  ),
)
```

5-8. Limiting Widgets Size when Unbounded

Problem

You have a widget that normally matches its parent's size, but you want it to be used in other places where size constraints are required.

Solution

Use LimitedBox.

Discussion

Some widgets are normally designed to be as big as possible to match their parents' size. But these widgets need to be constrained in other places. For example, when these widgets are added to a vertical list, the height need to be limited. LimitedBox constructor has named parameters maxWidth and maxHeight to specify the limitations. If a LimitedBox widget's maximum width is unbounded, then its child's width is limited to maxWidth. If this LimitedBox's maximum height is unbounded, then its child's height is limited to maxHeigth.

In Listing 5-8, the maxHeight of a LimitedBox widget is set to 100, so the child's maximum height is 100px.

Listing 5-8. Example of LimitedBox

```
LimitedBox(
  maxHeight: 100,
  child: Image.network('https://picsum.photos/400'),
)
```

5-9. Scaling and Positioning Widgets

Problem

You want to scale and position a widget.

Solution

Use FittedBox with different fit mode and alignment.

Discussion

Align widget in Recipe 5-3 can position its child using different alignments. FittedBox widget supports scaling and positioning of its child. The fit mode is specified using the parameter fit of type BoxFit. BoxFit is an enum type with values shown in Table 5-4.

Table 5-4. *BoxFit values*

Name	Description
fill	Fill the target box. Source's aspect ratio is ignored.
contain	As large as possible to contain the source entirely in the target box.
cover	As small as possible to cover the entire target box.
fitWidth	Only make sure the full width of the source is shown.
fitHeight	Only make sure the full height of the source is shown.
none	Align the source within the target box and discard anything outside the box.
scaleDown	Align the source with the target box and scale down when necessary to ensure the source fits in the box. If the source is shrunk, this is the same as contain; otherwise, it is the same as none.

FittedBox is usually used when displaying images. Listing 5-9 shows an example to demonstrate different values of BoxFit. ImageBox widget uses a SizedBox widget to limit its size and places the image inside of a FittedBox widget. The DecoratedBox widget creates a red border to show the boundary of ImageBox widget.

Listing 5-9. Different values of BoxFit

```
class FitPage extends StatelessWidget {
  @override
  Widget build(BuildContext context) {
    return Scaffold(
      appBar: AppBar(
        title: Text('Fit'),
      ),
      body: Center(
        child: Wrap(
          spacing: 20,
          runSpacing: 20,
          alignment: WrapAlignment.spaceAround,
          children: <Widget>[
            ImageBox(fit: BoxFit.fill),
            ImageBox(fit: BoxFit.contain),
            ImageBox(fit: BoxFit.cover),
            ImageBox(fit: BoxFit.fitWidth),
            ImageBox(fit: BoxFit.fitHeight),
            ImageBox(fit: BoxFit.none),
            ImageBox(fit: BoxFit.scaleDown),
          ],
        ),
      ),
    );
  }
}

class ImageBox extends StatelessWidget {
  const ImageBox({
    Key key,
```

```
    this.boxWidth = 150,
    this.boxHeight = 170,
    this.imageWidth = 200,
    this.fit,
  });

  final double boxWidth;
  final double boxHeight;
  final double imageWidth;
  final BoxFit fit;

  @override
  Widget build(BuildContext context) {
    return DecoratedBox(
      decoration: BoxDecoration(border: Border.all(color:
      Colors.red)),
      child: SizedBox(
        width: boxWidth,
        height: boxHeight,
        child: FittedBox(
          fit: fit,
          child: SizedBox(
            width: imageWidth,
            height: imageWidth,
            child: Image.network('https://dummyimage.
            com/${imageWidth.toInt()}'
                '&text=${fit.toString().substring(7)}'),
          ),
        ),
      ),
    );
  }
}
```

Figure 5-1 shows the screenshot of code in Listing 5-9. Text in an image shows the BoxFit value used in this ImageBox widget.

Figure 5-1. *Different values of BoxFit*

5-10. Rotating Widgets

Problem

You want to rotate a widget.

Solution

Use RotatedBox.

Discussion

RotatedBox widget rotates its child before layout. Rotation is specified by an int type of clockwise quarter turns with quarterTurns parameter. The value 1 of quarterTurns parameter means rotating 90 degrees clockwise.

In Listing 5-10, the Text widget is rotated one quarter turn.

Listing 5-10. Example of RotatedWidget

```
RotatedBox(
  quarterTurns: 1,
  child: Text(
    'Hello World',
    textScaleFactor: 2,
  ),
)
```

5-11. Adding Padding when Displaying Widgets

Problem

You want to add padding around a widget.

Solution

Use Padding.

Discussion

Padding widget creates empty space around its child. The layout constraints passed to its child are the widget's constraints after shrinking by the padding, which causes the child to lay out at a smaller size. The padding is specified in the required padding parameter of type EdgeInsetsGeometry.

Similar with AlignmentGeometry, EdgeInsetsGeometry has two subclasses EdgeInsets and EdgeInsetsDirectional. EdgeInsets class expresses offsets in visual coordinates. Offsets values are specified for left, right, top, and bottom edges. Table 5-5 shows constructors of EdgeInsets class.

Table 5-5. *EdgeInsets constructors*

Name	Description
EdgeInsets.all()	All the offsets have the given value.
EdgeInsets.fromLTRB()	Specify values of offsets for left, top, right, and bottom edges.
EdgeInsets.only()	It has named parameters left, top, right, and bottom with default value of 0.0.
EdgeInsets.symmetric()	It has named parameters vertical and horizontal to create symmetrical offsets.

To consider text direction, EdgeInsetsDirectional class should be used instead of EdgeInsets. EdgeInsetsDirectional class uses start and end instead of left and right. It has EdgeInsetsDirectional.fromSTEB() constructor to create insets from offsets of start, top, end, and bottom. The EdgeInsetsDirectional.only() constructor is similar with EdgeInsets. only().

Listing 5-11 shows an example of Padding widget.

Listing 5-11. Example of Padding

```
Padding(
  padding: EdgeInsets.all(20),
  child: Image.network('https://picsum.photos/200'),
)
```

5-12. Sizing Widgets to Aspect Ratio
Problem

You want to size widgets to maintain a specific aspect ratio.

Solution

Use AspectRatio.

Discussion

AspectRatio constructor has the required parameter aspectRatio to specify the aspect ratio value of width/height. For example, a 4:3 aspect ratio uses the value of 4.0/3.0. AspectRatio widget tries to find the best size to maintain the aspect ratio while respecting its layout constraints.

The process starts from setting the width to the maximum width of the constraints. If the maximum width is finite, then the height is calculated by width / aspectRatio. Otherwise, the height is set to the maximum height of the constraints and width is set to height * aspectRatio. There may be extra steps to make sure the result width and height meet the layout constraints. For example, if the height is less than the minimum height of the constraints, then height is set to this minimum value and width is calculated based on the height and aspect ratio. The general rule is to check width before height and maximum value before minimum value. The final size may not meet the ratio requirement, but it must meet the layout constraints.

In Listing 5-12, AspectRatio widget is placed in a ConstrainedBox with a loose constraints of Size(200, 200). The aspect ratio is 4.0/3.0, so the height is calculated based on 200 / (4.0 / 3.0) = 150.0. The result size of ApsectRatio is Size(200.0, 150.0).

Listing 5-12. Example of AspectRatio

```
ConstrainedBox(
  constraints: BoxConstraints.loose(Size(200, 200)),
  child: AspectRatio(
    aspectRatio: 4.0 / 3.0,
    child: Image.network('https://picsum.photos/400/300'),
  ),
)
```

5-13. Transforming Widgets

Problem

You want to apply a transformation on a widget.

Solution

Use Transform.

Discussion

Transform widget can apply a transformation on its child before painting it. Transformations are expressed using Matrix4 instances. Transform constructor has named parameters shown in Table 5-6.

Table 5-6. *Named parameters of Transform*

Name	Type	Description
transform	Matrix4	Matrix to transform the child.
origin	Offset	Origin of the coordinate system to apply the transform.
alignment	AlignmentGeometry	Alignment of the origin.
transformHitTests	bool	Should the transform be applied when performing hit tests.

Transform class has other constructors to create common transformations:

- Tranform.rotate() – Transform the child by rotating specified angle.

- Transform.scale() – Transform the child by scaling uniformly with specified scale factor.

- Transform.translate() – Transform the child by translating specified offset.

Listing 5-13 shows examples of using Transform's named constructors.

Listing 5-13. Examples of Transform

```
Transform.rotate(
  angle: pi / 4.0,
  origin: Offset(10, 10),
  child: Text('Hello World'),
)

Transform.translate(
  offset: Offset(50, 50),
  child: Text('Hello World'),
)
```

5-14. Controlling Different Layout Aspects on a Widget

Problem

You want to define different layout aspects for a widget.

Solution

Use Container.

Discussion

Flutter has many widgets to control different aspects of layout. For example, SizedBox widget controls the size, while Align widget controls the alignment. If you want to control different layout aspects on the same widget, you can wrap these widgets in a nested way. Actually, Flutter provides a Container widget to make it easier to define different layout aspects.

Table 5-7 shows the named parameters of Container constructor. You cannot provide non-null values to both color and decoration, because color is just a shorthand to create decoration with value BoxDecoration(color: color). If width or height is not null, their values are used to tighten the constraints.

***Table** 5-7. Named parameters of Container*

Name	Type	Description
alignment	AlignmentGeometry	Alignment of the child.
padding	EdgeInsetsGeometry	Empty space inside the decoration.
color	Color	Background color.
decoration	Decoration	Decoration to paint behind the child.
foreground Decoration	Decoration	Decoration to paint in front of the child.
width	double	Width of the child.
height	double	Height of the child.
constraints	BoxConstraints	Additional constraints.
margin	EdgeInsetsGeometry	Empty space to surround the decoration.
transform	Matrix4	Transformation applied to the container.

Container is a composition of different widgets based on the values of parameters. Listing 5-14 shows the nesting structure of different widgets used by Container and the parameters these widgets may use. If the value of a parameter is null, then the corresponding widget may not exist.

Listing 5-14. Structure of Container

```
Transform (transform)
  - Padding (margin)
    - ConstrainedBox (constraints, width, height)
      - DecoratedBox (foregroundDecoration)
        - DecoratedBox (decoration, color)
          - Padding (padding, decoration)
            - Align (alignment)
              - child
```

Listing 5-15 shows an example of Container widget that uses all named parameters.

Listing 5-15. Example of Container

```
Container(
  alignment: Alignment.bottomRight,
  padding: EdgeInsets.all(16),
  color: Colors.red.shade100,
  foregroundDecoration: BoxDecoration(
    image: DecorationImage(
      image: NetworkImage('https://picsum.photos/100'),
    ),
  ),
  width: 300,
  height: 300,
  constraints: BoxConstraints.loose(Size(400, 400)),
  margin: EdgeInsets.all(32),
  transform: Matrix4.rotationZ(0.1),
  child: Text(
```

```
    'Hello World',
    textScaleFactor: 3,
  ),
)
```

Figure 5-2 shows the structure of the Container widget in Listing 5-15. You can see clearly how these widgets are nested.

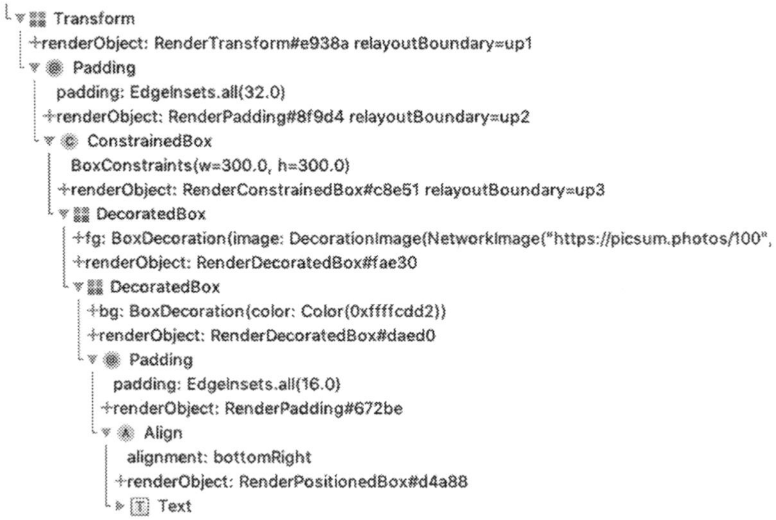

Figure 5-2. *Structure of Container*

5-15. Implementing Flex Box Layout

Problem

You have multiple widgets to lay out, and you want them to be able to take extra space.

Solution

Use Flex, Column, Row, Flexible, and Expanded.

Discussion

To lay out multiple widgets using the flex box model, you can use a set of widgets provided by Flutter, including Flex, Column, Row, Flexible, Expanded, and Spacer. In fact, only Flex and Flexible widgets are important to understand. Flex widget is used as the layout container, while Flexible widget is used to wrap children widgets inside the container. Flex widget displays its children in one-dimension array. It supports layout of children in two directions, horizontal and vertical. Row and Column are subclasses of Flex that only places children in the horizontal and vertical direction, respectively. Flexible widget of a Flex container can control how a child flexes to take extra space. Children of Flex widget can be flexible or not. If you want a child to be flexible, you can simply wrap it in a Flexible widget.

Same as CSS flex box layout, Flex widget uses two axes for layout. The axis where children are placed along is the *main axis*. The other axis is the *cross axis*. The main axis is configured using the direction parameter of type Axis. If the value is Axis.horizontal, then the main axis is horizontal axis, while the cross axis is vertical axis. If the value is Axis.vertical, then the main axis is vertical axis, while the cross axis is horizontal axis. Row widget always uses horizontal axis as the main axis, and Column widget always uses vertical axis as the main axis. If the main axis is known, then Row or Column widget should be used instead of Flex widget.

Flex Box Layout Algorithm

Layout of Flex children is complicated and done in multiple steps. The first step is to lay out each child with a null or zero flex factor. These are non-flexible children. The constraints used to lay out these children depend on the value of crossAxisAlignment. If the value of crossAxisAlignment is CrossAxisAlignment.stretch, then the constraints will be tight cross-axis constraints of the maximum size on the cross axis. Otherwise, the constraints only set the maximum value for the cross axis. For example, if the direction is Axis.horizontal and crossAxisAlignment is CrossAxisAlignment.stretch, then the constraints for these non-flexible children set both minHeight and maxHeight to maxHeight of the Flex's constraints. This makes these children take all space on the cross axis. During the first step, the total allocated size for these children and the maximum value of cross-axis size are recorded.

The second step is to lay out each child with a flex factor. These are flexible children. From the first step, the allocated size of main axis is known. The free space can be calculated based on the max size and allocated size of main axis. The free space is distributed among all flexible children based on the flex factor. A child with a flex factor of 2.0 will receive twice the amount of free space as a child with a flex factor of 1.0. Suppose there are three children with flex factors 1.0, 2.0, and 3.0, if the free space is 120px, then these children will receive space of 20px, 40px, and 60px, respectively. The calculated value based on flex factor for each child will be the maximum constraints on the main axis. The minimum constraints on the main axis depends on the value of FlexFit for the child. If fit value is FlexFit.tight, then the minimum value is the same as the maximum, which creates tight constraints on the main axis. If fit value is FlexFit.loose, then the minimum value is 0.0, which creates loose constraints on the main axis. The constraints on the cross axis are the same as Flex widget's constraints. The final constraints are used to lay out these flex children.

The third step is to determine the extent of main and cross axis. If the value of mainAxisSize is MainAxisSize.max, then the main-axis extent is the maximum constraints of current Flex widget. Otherwise, the main-axis extent is the allocated size for all children. The extent of cross axis is the maximum value of cross-axis constraints of all children.

The last step is to determine the position of each child based on the value of mainAxisAlignment and crossAxisAlignment.

Table 5-8 shows values of the enum MainAxisAlignment.

Table 5-8. *MainAxisAlignment values*

Name	Description
start	Place the children close to the start of the main axis. The start position is determined by TextDirection for horizontal direction and VerticalDirection for vertical direction.
end	Place the children close to the end of the main axis. The end position is determined using the same way as start.
center	Place the children close to the middle.
spaceBetween	Distribute the free space evenly between the children.
spaceAround	Distribute the free space evenly between the children with half of the space before and after the first and last child.
spaceEvenly	Distribute the free space evenly between the children including before and after the first and last child.

Table 5-9 shows values of the enum CrossAxisAlignment.

Table 5-9. *CrossAxisAlignment values*

Name	Description
start	Place the children with start edge aligned with the start side of the cross axis. The start position is determined by TextDirection for horizontal direction and VerticalDirection for vertical direction.
end	Place the children with end edge aligned with the end side of the cross axis. The end position is determined using the same way as start.
center	Place the children with center aligned with the middle of the cross axis.
stretch	Require the children to fill the cross axis.
baseline	Match baselines of children on the cross axis.

Flexible

Flexible has the flex parameter to specify the flex factor and fit parameter to specify the BoxFit value. The default value of flex parameter is 1, while the default value of fit is BoxFit.loose. Expanded is a subclass of Flexible with fit parameter set to BoxFit.tight.

In Listing 5-16, Column widget is placed in a LimitedBox widget to limit its height. All children of Column widget are non-flexible.

Listing 5-16. Flex widget with non-flexible children

```
LimitedBox(
  maxHeight: 320,
  child: Column(
    crossAxisAlignment: CrossAxisAlignment.end,
    mainAxisAlignment: MainAxisAlignment.spaceAround,
    children: <Widget>[
      Image.network('https://picsum.photos/50'),
      Image.network('https://picsum.photos/70'),
      Image.network('https://picsum.photos/90'),
    ],
  ),
)
```

In Listing 5-17, Column widget has both flexible and non-flexible children. Flexible widgets can be created by wrapping with Flexible or Expanded widgets.

Listing 5-17. Flex widget with flexible and non-flexible children

```
LimitedBox(
  maxHeight: 300,
  child: Column(
    mainAxisAlignment: MainAxisAlignment.spaceBetween,
```

```
  children: <Widget>[
    Flexible(
      child: Image.network('https://picsum.photos/50'),
    ),
    Image.network('https://picsum.photos/40'),
    Expanded(
      child: Image.network('https://picsum.photos/50'),
    ),
    Expanded(
      flex: 2,
      child: Image.network('https://picsum.photos/50'),
    ),
  ],
),
)
```

5-16. Displaying Overlapping Widgets
Problem

You want to lay out widgets that may overlap with each other.

Solution

Use Stack or IndexedStack.

Discussion

Children of Stack widget can be positioned or non-positioned. Positioned children are wrapped in a Positioned widget with at least one non-null property. Size of a Stack widget is determined by all the non-positioned children. The layout process has two phases.

The first phase is to lay out all non-positioned children. The constraints used for non-positioned children depend on the value of fit property of type StackFit:

- StackFit.loose – Loose constraints created by constraints.loosen()

- StackFilt.expand – Tight constraints created by BoxConstraints.tight(constraints.biggest)

- StackFilt.passthrough – The same constraints as Stack widget

Size of the Stack widget is determined by the maximum size of all non-positioned children.

In the second phase, all non-positioned children are positioned according to the alignment property. The constraints used for positioned children are determined by the size of Stack widget and their properties. Positioned widget has six properties: left, top, right, bottom, width, and height. Properties left, right, and width are used to determine the tight width constraint. Properties top, bottom, and height are used to determine the tight height constraint. For example, if both left and right values are not null, the tight width constraint is widthOfStack – right – left. The positioned child is then positioned based on the left, right, top, and bottom values in two axes. If all these values are null, it's positioned based on the alignment.

Children of Stack are painted in the order with the first child being at the bottom. The order in the children array determines how children overlap with each other.

IndexedStack class is a subclass of Stack. An IndexedStack instance only shows a single child from a list of children. IndexedStack constructor not only has the same parameters as Stack constructor but also includes a parameter index of type int to specify the index of child to display. If the value of parameter index is null, then nothing will be displayed. The layout of IndexedStack is the same as Stack. IndexedStack class simply has a different way to paint itself. This means even though only one child is displayed, all the children still need to lay out the same way as Stack.

Listing 5-18 shows an example of Stack widget with positioned child.

Listing 5-18. Example of Stack

```
Stack(
  children: <Widget>[
    Image.network('https://picsum.photos/200'),
    Image.network('https://picsum.photos/100'),
    Positioned(
      right: 0,
      bottom: 0,
      child: Image.network('https://picsum.photos/150'),
    ),
  ],
)
```

5-17. Displaying Widgets in Multiple Runs

Problem

You want to display widgets in multiple horizontal or vertical runs.

Solution

Use Wrap.

Problem

Flex widget doesn't allow size of children to exceed the size of the main axis. Wrap widget creates new runs; there is no enough space to fit the children. Table 5-10 shows named parameters of Wrap constructor.

Table 5-10. Named parameters of Wrap

Name	Value	Default value	Description
direction	Axis	Axis.horizontal	Direction of the main axis.
alignment	WrapAlignment	WrapAlignment.start	Alignment of children within a run in the main axis.
spacing	Double	0.0	Space between children in a run in the main axis.
runAlignment	WrapAlignment	WrapAlignment.start	Alignment of runs in the cross axis.
runSpacing	Double	0.0	Space between runs in the cross axis.
crossAxisAlignment	WrapCrossAlignment	WrapCrossAlignment. start	Alignment of children within a run in the cross axis.
textDirection	TextDirection		Order to lay out children horizontally.
verticalDirection	VerticalDirection	VerticalDirection.down	Order to lay out children vertically.
children	List<Widget>	[]	Children.

WrapAlignment enum has the same values as MainAxisAlignment. WrapCrossAlignment enum only has values start, end, and center.

Listing 5-19 shows an example of Wrap widget by wrapping ten Image widgets.

Listing 5-19. Example of Wrap

```
Wrap(
  spacing: 10,
  runSpacing: 5,
  crossAxisAlignment: WrapCrossAlignment.center,
  children: List.generate(
    10,
    (index) => Image.network('https://picsum.photos/${50 +
    index * 10}'),
  ),
)
```

5-18. Creating Custom Single Child Layout

Problem

You want to create a custom layout for a single child.

Solution

Use CustomSingleChildLayout.

Discussion

If those built-in layout widgets for a single child cannot meet your requirement, you can create a custom layout using CustomSingleChildLayout. CustomSingleChildLayout widget simply delegates the layout to a SingleChildLayoutDelegate instance. You need to create your own subclass of SingleChildLayoutDelegate to implement methods shown in Table 5-11.

Table 5-11. *Methods of SingleChildLayoutDelegate*

Name	Description
getConstraintsForChild (BoxConstraints constraints)	Get the constraints for the child.
getPositionForChild(Size size, Size childSize)	Get the position of the child based on the size of this widget and child.
getSize(BoxConstraints constraints)	Get the size of this widget.
shouldRelayout()	Should relayout.

The size of this widget is the result of the size returned by delegate's getSize() method after applying the constraints. Layout of child is done using the constraints returned by delegate's getConstraintsForChild() method. Finally the position of child is updated with the value returned by delegate's getPositionForChild() method.

In Listing 5-20, FixedPositionLayoutDelegate class overrides getSize() method to provide the size of the parent widget. It also overrides getPositionForChild() methods to provide the position of the child. The getConstraintsForChild() method is also overridden to return tighten constraints.

Listing 5-20. Custom single child layout delegate

```
class FixedPositionLayoutDelegate extends SingleChildLayout
Delegate {
  @override
```

```
bool shouldRelayout(SingleChildLayoutDelegate oldDelegate) {
  return false;
}

@override
Size getSize(BoxConstraints constraints) {
  return constraints.constrain(Size(300, 300));
}

@override
BoxConstraints getConstraintsForChild(BoxConstraints
constraints) {
  return constraints.tighten(width: 300, height: 300);
}

@override
Offset getPositionForChild(Size size, Size childSize) {
  return Offset(50, 50);
}
}
```

Listing 5-21 shows how to use FixedPositionLayoutDelegate.

Listing 5-21. Example of FixedPositionLayoutDelegate

```
CustomSingleChildLayout(
  delegate: FixedPositionLayoutDelegate(),
  child: Image.network('https://picsum.photos/100'),
)
```

5-19. Creating Custom Multiple Children Layout

Problem

You want to create a custom layout for multiple children.

Solution

Use CustomMultiChildLayout and MultiChildLayoutDelegate.

Discussion

If those built-in widgets for multiple children cannot meet your requirement, you can create a custom layout using CustomMultiChildLayout. Similar to CustomSingleChildLayout, CustomMultiChildLayout delegates the layout logic to a MultiChildLayoutDelegate instance. All children of CustomMultiChildLayout must be wrapped in a LayoutId widget to provide unique ids for them. Of all the methods shown in Table 5-12, performLayout() and shouldRelayout() methods must be implemented. All other methods have default implementation. In the implementation of performLayout() method, the layoutChild() method must be called exactly once for each child.

Table 5-12. *Methods of MultiChildLayoutDelegate*

Name	Description
hasChild(Object childId)	Check if a child with the given id exists.
layoutChild(Object childId, BoxConstraints constraints)	Layout the child with the provided constraints.
positionChild(Object childId, Offset offset)	Position the child with the given offset.
getSize(BoxConstraints constraints)	Get the size of this widget.
performLayout(Size size)	The actual layout logic.
shouldRelayout()	Should relayout.

Listing 5-22 shows a custom multiple children layout delegate. This delegate uses increasing int values as the layout id. Layout ids of children must start from 0. In the performLayout() method, layoutChild() method is called on each child, starting with the first child with loose constraints, which allows the first child to take the natural size. The actual size of the first child is recorded. Then positionChild() method is called with Offset. zero to place the first child at the top left corner. After the first child, layoutChild() and positionChild() methods are called on all the other children with increasing size and position offsets, respectively.

Listing 5-22. Custom multiple children layout delegate

```
class GrowingSizeLayoutDelegate extends MultiChildLayout
Delegate {
  @override
  void performLayout(Size size) {
    int index = 0;
```

```
    Size childSize = layoutChild(index, BoxConstraints.
    loose(size));
    Offset offset = Offset.zero;
    positionChild(index, offset);
    index++;

    while (hasChild(index)) {
      double sizeFactor = 1.0 + index * 0.1;
      double offsetFactor = index * 10.0;
      childSize = layoutChild(
          index,
          BoxConstraints.tight(Size(
              childSize.width * sizeFactor, childSize.height *
              sizeFactor)));
      offset = offset.translate(offsetFactor, offsetFactor);
      positionChild(index, offset);
      index++;
    }
  }

  @override
  bool shouldRelayout(MultiChildLayoutDelegate oldDelegate) {
    return false;
  }

  @override
  Size getSize(BoxConstraints constraints) =>
      constraints.constrain(Size(400, 400));
}
```

Listing 5-23 shows the usage of GrowingSizeLayoutDelegate. The children of CustomMultiChildLayout are six images nested in SizedBox. The wrapping LayoutId widget is required to pass the layout id to the delegate.

Listing 5-23. Example of GrowingSizeLayoutDelegate

```
CustomMultiChildLayout(
  delegate: GrowingSizeLayoutDelegate(),
  children: List.generate(
    6,
    (index) => LayoutId(
        id: index,
        child: DecoratedBox(
          decoration:
              BoxDecoration(border: Border.all(color: Colors.
              red)),
          child: SizedBox(
            width: 70,
            height: 70,
            child: Image.network(
                'https://dummyimage.com/${50 + index * 10}'),
          ),
        ),
      ),
    ),
  ),
)
```

Figure 5-3 shows the result of using GrowingSizeLayoutDelegate.

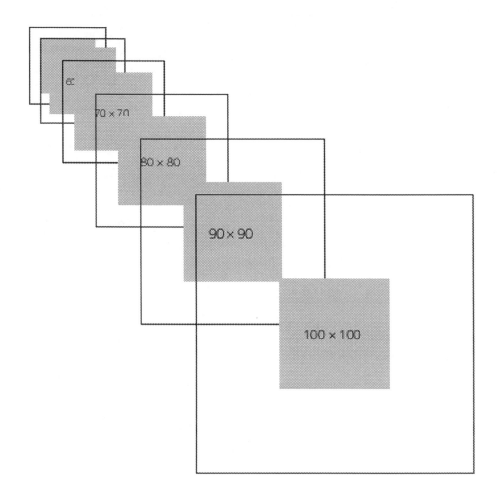

Figure 5-3. *Result of using GrowingSizeLayoutDelegate*

5-20. Summary

With the layout widgets in Flutter, it's easy to satisfy common layout requirements in build Flutter apps. This chapter covers many layout widgets for single child and multiple children. In the next chapter, we'll discuss form widgets.

CHAPTER 6

Form Widgets

Form controls are important in mobile apps to interact with the user. Flutter provides a set of form widgets for Material Design and iOS style. These form widgets generally have no internal state. Their appearance and behavior are purely defined by constructor parameters. With state maintained in ancestor widgets, form widgets are re-rendered to reflect to state changes. This chapter covers recipes related to basic usage of form widgets.

6-1. Collecting Text Inputs
Problem

You want to collect text inputs.

Solution

Use TextField for Material Design and CupertinoTextField for iOS style.

Discussion

To collect user inputs in Flutter apps, you can use TextField widget for Material Design or CupertinoTextField widget for iOS style. Both widgets have similar usage pattern and behavior. In fact, both widgets wrap the same EditableText which provides the basic text input capability with support for scrolling, selection, and cursor movement. EditableText is a

© Fu Cheng 2019
F. Cheng, *Flutter Recipes*, https://doi.org/10.1007/978-1-4842-4982-6_6

highly customizable widget with many named parameters. This recipe focuses on how to set the initial value of a TextField or CupertinoTextField widget and get the text from it.

The text of an EditableText widget is controlled by a TextEditingController instance. You can use the controller parameter to set a TextEditingController instance when creating a new EditableText widget. The controller maintains a bidirectional data binding with the corresponding EditableText widget. The controller has a text property to track the current editing text and a selection property of type TextSelection to track the currently selected text. Whenever the text in a EditableText widget is modified or selected by user, the text and selection properties of the associated TextEditingController instance will be updated. If you modify the text or selection properties of the TextEditingController instance, the EditableText widget will update itself. TextEditingController class is a subclass of ValueNotifier<TextEditingVa lue>, so you can add listeners to the controller to get notifications when the text or selection changes. When creating a new TextEditingController instance, you can pass some text with the text parameter, which becomes the initial text of the corresponding EditableText widget.

Let's see three different ways to get the text from EditableText widgets.

Using TextEditingController

The first way is using TextEditingController. The ReverseText widget in Listing 6-1 is used to reverse an input string. The TextEditingController instance is created with initial text "<input>". When the button is pressed, the _value is updated to the text retrieved from the controller. The reversed string is displayed.

Listing 6-1. Use TextEditingController to get text

```
class ReverseText extends StatefulWidget {
  @override
  _ReverseTextState createState() => _ReverseTextState();
}

class _ReverseTextState extends State<ReverseText> {
  final TextEditingController _controller =
TextEditingController(
    text: "<input>",
  );
  String _value;

  @override
  Widget build(BuildContext context) {
    return Column(
      crossAxisAlignment: CrossAxisAlignment.start,
      children: <Widget>[
        Row(
          children: <Widget>[
            Expanded(
              child: TextField(
                controller: _controller,
              ),
            ),
            RaisedButton(
              child: Text('Go'),
              onPressed: () {
                this.setState(() {
                  _value = _controller.text;
                });
              },
```

```
            ),
          ],
        ),
        Text( (_value ?? "). split(").reversed.join()),
      ],
    );
  }
}
```

Figure 6-1 shows the screenshot of code in Listing 6-1.

Hello World   Go
_____
dlroW olleH

Figure 6-1. *Use TextEditingController*

Using Listeners of TextEditingController

A TextEditingController instance is also an instance of ValueNotifier<Te
xtEditingValue>, so you can add listeners to it and react to notifications.
In Listing 6-2, the listener function _handleTextChanged calls setState()
function to update the state when receiving change notifications. The
listener is added in the initState() function and removed in the dispose()
function, which makes sure resource is properly cleaned up.

Listing 6-2. Use TextEditingController listener

```
class ReverseTextWithListener extends StatefulWidget {
  @override
  _ReverseTextWithListenerState createState() =>
      _ReverseTextWithListenerState();
}
```

```
class _ReverseTextWithListenerState extends
State<ReverseTextWithListener> {
  TextEditingController _controller;
  String _value;

  @override
  void initState() {
    super.initState();
    _controller = TextEditingController(
      text: "<input>",
    );
    _controller.addListener(_handleTextChanged);
  }

  @override
  Widget build(BuildContext context) {
    return Column(
      crossAxisAlignment: CrossAxisAlignment.start,
      children: <Widget>[
        TextField(
          controller: _controller,
        ),
        Text( (_value ?? "). split(").reversed.join()),
      ],
    );
  }

  @override
  void dispose() {
    _controller.removeListener(_handleTextChanged);
    super.dispose();
  }
```

```
  void _handleTextChanged() {
    this.setState(() {
      this._value = _controller.text;
    });
  }
}
```

Figure 6-2 shows the screenshot of code in Listing 6-2.

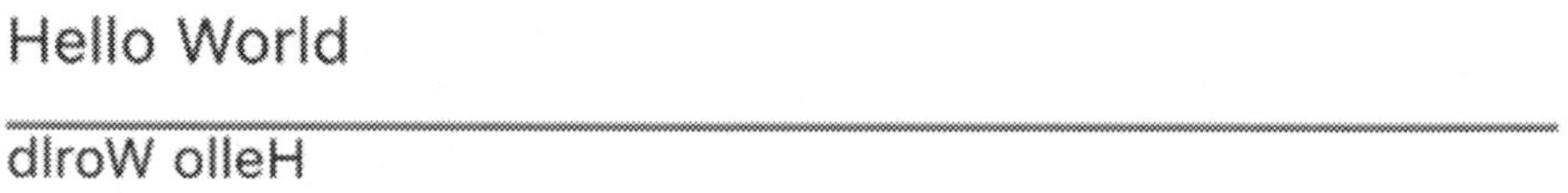

Hello World

dlroW olleH

Figure 6-2. *Use TextEditingController listener*

Using Callbacks

The last way to get text from EditableText widgets is using the callbacks.
There are three types of callbacks related to text editing; see Table 6-1.

Table 6-1. *EditableText callbacks*

Name	Type	Description
onChanged	ValueChanged<String>	Called when text changed.
onEditingComplete	VoidCallback	Called when user submits the text.
onSubmitted	ValueChanged<String>	Called when user finishes editing the text.

If you want to actively watch for text changes, you should use
onChanged callback. When user finishes editing the text, both
onEditingComplete and onSubmitted callbacks will be invoked.

The difference is that onEditingComplete callback doesn't provide access to the submitted text.

In Listing 6-3, different messages are logged in different callbacks. All the log messages are displayed in a RichText widget.

Listing 6-3. EditableText callbacks

```
class TextFieldCallbacks extends StatefulWidget {
  @override
  _TextFieldCallbacksState createState() =>
  _TextFieldCallbacksState();
}

class _TextFieldCallbacksState extends
State<TextFieldCallbacks> {
  List<String> _logs = List();

  void _log(String value) {
    this.setState(() {
      this._logs.add(value);
    });
  }

  @override
  Widget build(BuildContext context) {
    return Column(
      crossAxisAlignment: CrossAxisAlignment.start,
      children: <Widget>[
        TextField(
          onChanged: (text) => _log('changed: $text'),
          onEditingComplete: () => _log('completed'),
          onSubmitted: (text) => _log('submitted: $text'),
        ),
```

```
    Text.rich(TextSpan(
      children: this._logs.map((log) => TextSpan(text:
      '$log\n')).toList(),
    )),
  ],
);
}
}
```

Figure 6-3 shows the screenshot of code in Listing 6-3.

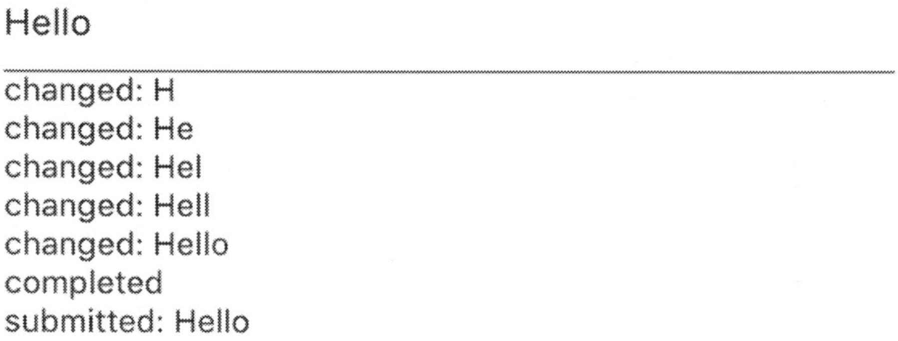

Hello

changed: H
changed: He
changed: Hel
changed: Hell
changed: Hello
completed
submitted: Hello

Figure 6-3. *EditableText callbacks*

Although examples in Listings 6-1, 6-2, and 6-3 use TextField, the same pattern can also be applied to CupertinoTextField.

6-2. Customizing Keyboard for Text Input
Problem

You want to customize the keyboard used to edit the text.

Solution

Use keyboardType, textInputAction, and keyboardAppearance parameters.

Discussion

EditableText widget allows customization of the keyboard used for editing the text. You can use keyboardType parameter of type TextInputType class to set a keyboard type suitable for the text. For example, if the EditableText widget is used to edit phone numbers, then TextInputType.phone is a better choice for the keyboardType parameter. Table 6-2 shows constants in TextInputType. TextInputType.number constant is used for unsigned numbers without a decimal point. For other types of numbers, you can use TextInputType.numberWithOptions({bool signed: false, bool decimal: false }) constructor to set whether the numbers should be signed or a decimal point should be included.

Table 6-2. *TextInputType constants*

Name	Description
text	Plain text.
multiline	Multi-line text.
number	Unsigned number without a decimal point.
phone	Phone numbers.
datetime	Date and time.
emailAddress	Email addresses.
url	URLs.

The textInputAction parameter of type TextInputAction enum sets the logic action to perform when user is submitting the text. For example, if the text field is for use to input search queries, then the TextInputAction.search value makes the keyboard to display the text "Search". The user can expect a search action to perform after tapping the action button. TextInputAction enum defined a set of actions. The buttons for these actions may have different appearances on different platforms or different versions of the same platform. Most of these actions are supported by both Android and iOS. They are mapped to IME input types on Android and keyboard return types on iOS. Table 6-3 shows values of TextInputAction and their mappings on Android and iOS. Some actions may only be supported on Android or iOS. Using an unsupported action will cause an error to be thrown in the debug mode. However, in the release mode, an unsupported action will be mapped to IME_ACTION_UNSPECIFIED on Android and UIReturnKeyDefault on iOS, respectively.

Table 6-3. *TextInputAction values*

Name	Android IME input type	iOS keyboard return type
none	IME_ACTION_NONE	N/A
unspecified	IME_ACTION_UNSPECIFIED	UIReturnKeyDefault
done	IME_ACTION_DONE	UIReturnKeyDone
search	IME_ACTION_SEARCH	UIReturnKeySearch
send	IME_ACTION_SEND	UIReturnKeySend
next	IME_ACTION_NEXT	UIReturnKeyNext
previous	IME_ACTION_PREVIOUS	N/A
continueAction	N/A	UIReturnKeyContinue
join	N/A	UIReturnKeyJoin
route	N/A	UIReturnKeyRoute
emergencyCall	N/A	UIReturnKeyEmergencyCall
newline	IME_ACTION_NONE	UIReturnKeyDefault

The last keyboardAppearance parameter of type Brightness sets the appearance of the keyboard. Brightness enum has two values, dark and light. The parameter is only used for iOS.

Listing 6-4 shows the usage of textInputAction and last keyboardAppearance parameters.

Listing 6-4. *keyboardType and keyboardAppearance parameters*

```
TextField(
  keyboardType: TextInputType.phone,
)

TextField(
  keyboardType: TextInputType.numberWithOptions(
    signed: true,
    decimal: true,
  ),
)

TextField(
  textInputAction: TextInputAction.search,
  keyboardAppearance: Brightness.dark,
)
```

6-3. Add Decorations to Text Input in Material Design

Problem

You want to add decorations like prefix and suffix to text fields in Material Design.

Solution

Use the decoration parameter of type InputDecoration.

Discussion

TextField widget supports adding different decorations to present various information to user. For example, if the value of text input is invalid, you can add a red border and some text below the text input to indicate that. You can also add text or icons as the prefix or suffix. If the TextField widget is for editing currency value, you can add a currency symbol as the prefix. The decoration parameter of type InputDecoration of TextField is used to add this information. InputDecoration class has many named parameters, which we will review next.

Borders

Let's start from adding borders to text input widgets. InputDecoration constructor has several parameters of type InputBorder that are related to borders, including errorBorder, disabledBorder, focusedBorder, focusedErrorBorder, and enabledBorder. The names of these parameters indicate when these borders will be displayed based on the state. There is also a border parameter, but this parameter is only used to provide the shape of the border.

InputBorder class is abstract, so one of its subclasses UnderlineInputBorder or OutlineInputBorder should be used. UnderlineInputBorder class only has a border at the bottom side. UnderlineInputBorder constructor has parameters borderSide of type BorderSide and borderRadius of type BorderRadius. BorderSide class defines color, width, and style of one side of a border. A border's style is defined by BorderStyle enum which has values none and solid. A BorderSide with style BorderStyle.none won't be rendered. BorderRadius class defines a set of radii for each corner of a rectangle.

The radius for a corner is created using Radius class. The shape of a radius can be circular or elliptical. Circular or elliptical radii can be created using constructors Radius.circular(double radius) and Radius.elliptical(double x, double y), respectively. BorderRadius has topLeft, topRight, bottomLeft, and bottomRight properties of type Radius to represent radii of these four corners. You can use BorderRadius.only() to specify different Radius instances for each corner or use BorderRadius.all() to use a single Radius instance for all corners.

OutlineInputBorder class draws a rectangle around the widget. OutlineInputBorder constructor also has parameters borderSide and borderRadius. It also has the gapPadding parameter to specify the horizontal padding for the label text displayed in a gap of the border.

In Listing 6-5, both TextField widgets declare borders that are rendered when they gain focus using focusedBorder parameter.

Listing 6-5. Examples of InputDecoration

```
TextField(
  decoration: InputDecoration(
    enabledBorder: UnderlineInputBorder(
      borderSide: BorderSide(color: Colors.red),
      borderRadius: BorderRadius.all(Radius.elliptical(5, 10)),
    ),
  ),
)

TextField(
  decoration: InputDecoration(
    labelText: 'Username',
    focusedBorder: OutlineInputBorder(
      borderSide: BorderSide(color: Colors.blue),
      borderRadius: BorderRadius.circular(10),
```

```
      gapPadding: 2,
    ),
  ),
)
```

Figure 6-4 shows the screenshot of code in Listing 6-5. The second TextField is focused, so the focused border is displayed.

Figure 6-4. *Borders*

Prefix and Suffix

Prefix and suffix in a text input can provide information and actions that are useful when editing text. Prefix and suffix can both be plain text or widgets. When using text, you can customize the style of the text. InputDecoration constructor has parameters prefix, prefixIcon, prefixText, and prefixStyle to customize the prefix. It also has parameters suffix, suffixIcon, suffixText, and suffixStyle to customize the suffix. You cannot specify non-null values to both prefix and prefixText. This restriction also applies to suffix and suffixText. You can only provide a widget or text, but not both at the same time.

Listing 6-6. Example of prefix and suffix

```
TextField(
  decoration: InputDecoration(
    prefixIcon: Icon(Icons.monetization_on),
```

```
    prefixText: 'Pay ',
    prefixStyle: TextStyle(fontStyle: FontStyle.italic),
    suffixText: '.00',
  ),
)
```

Figure 6-5 shows the screenshot of Listing 6-6.

 Pay 150| .00

***Figure 6-5.** Prefix and suffix*

Text

You can add different types of text as the decorations and customize their styles. There are five types of text shown in Table 6-4.

***Table 6-4.** Different types of text*

Type	Text	Style	Description
Label	labelText	labelStyle	Labels are displayed above the input field.
Helper	helperText	helperStyle	Helper text are displayed below the input field.
Hint	hintText	hintStyle	Hints are displayed in the input field when it's empty.
Error	errorText	errorStyle	Errors are displayed below the input field.
Counter	counterText	counterStyle	Counters are displayed below the input field but aligned to the right.

If errorText value is not null, the input field is set to the error state.

195

Listing 6-7. Example of text

```
TextField(
  keyboardType: TextInputType.emailAddress,
  decoration: InputDecoration(
    labelText: 'Email',
    labelStyle: TextStyle(fontWeight: FontWeight.bold),
    hintText: 'Email address for validation',
    helperText: 'For receiving validation emails',
    counterText: '10',
  ),
)
```

Figure 6-6 shows the screenshot of code in Listing 6-7.

Email
Email address for validation
_____

For receiving validation emails   10

Figure 6-6. *Text of TextField*

6-4. Setting Text Limits
Problem

You want to control the length of text.

Solution

Use maxLength parameter.

Discussion

To set the maximum length of text in TextField and CupertinoTextField, you can use the maxLength parameter. The default value of maxLength parameter is null, which means there is no restriction on the number of characters. If maxLength parameter is set, a character counter is displayed below the text input, which shows the number of characters entered and the number of allowed characters. If maxLength parameter is set to TextField.noMaxLength, then only the number of characters entered is displayed. When maxLength is set, if the characters reach the limit, the behavior depends on the value of maxLengthEnforced parameter. If maxLengthEnforced is true, which is the default value, no more characters can be entered. If maxLengthEnforced is false, additional characters can be entered, but the widget switches to the error style.

Listing 6-8. Examples of maxLength

```
TextField(
  maxLength: TextField.noMaxLength,
)

TextField(
  maxLength: 10,
  maxLengthEnforced: false,
)

CupertinoTextField(
  maxLength: 10,
)
```

Figure 6-7 shows the screenshot of two TextField widgets in Listing 6-8.

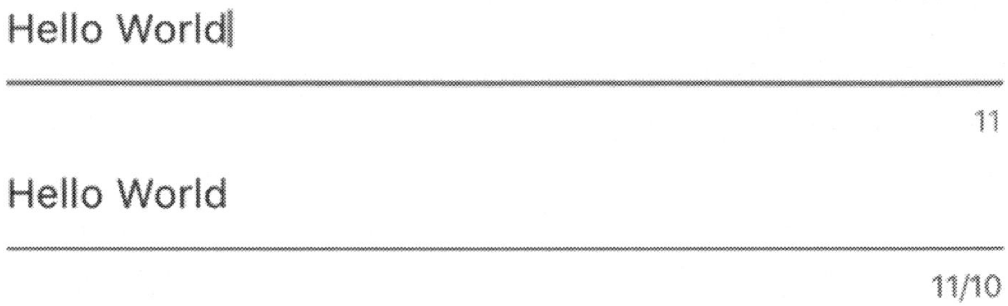

Hello World|

11

Hello World

11/10

Figure 6-7. *Text limits*

6-5. Selecting Text

Problem

You want to select some text in the text input.

Solution

Use selection property of TextEditingController.

Discussion

In Recipe 6-1, you have seen the example of using TextEditingController
to get and set the text of widgets using EditableText. TextEditingController
can also be used to get the text selection by user and select text. This
is done by getting or setting the value of selection property of type
TextSelection.

TextSelection is a subclass of TextRange. You can use TextRange.
textInside() to get the selected text. TextSelection class uses baseOffset
and extentOffset properties to represent the position which the selection
originates and terminates, respectively. The value of baseOffset may be
larger than, smaller than, or equal to extentOffset. If baseOffset equals to

extentOffset, the selection is collapsed. Collapsed text selection contains zero characters, but they are used to represent text insertion points. TextSelection.collapsed() constructor can create a collapsed selection at specified offset.

In Listing 6-9, when text selection changes, the selected text is displayed. The first button selected the text in the range [0, 5], while thp7;e second button moves the cursor to offset 1.

Listing 6-9. Text selection

```
class TextSelectionExample extends StatefulWidget {
  @override
  _TextSelectionExampleState createState() =>
  _TextSelectionExampleState();
}

class _TextSelectionExampleState extends
State<TextSelectionExample> {
  TextEditingController _controller;
  String _selection;

  @override
  void initState() {
    super.initState();
    _controller = new TextEditingController();
    _controller.addListener(_handleTextSelection);
  }

  @override
  void dispose() {
    _controller.removeListener(_handleTextSelection);
    super.dispose();
  }
```

```
  @override
  Widget build(BuildContext context) {
    return Column(
      crossAxisAlignment: CrossAxisAlignment.start,
      children: <Widget>[
        TextField(
          controller: _controller,
        ),
        Row(
          children: <Widget>[
            RaisedButton(
              child: Text('Select text [0, 5]'),
              onPressed: () {
                setState(() {
                  _controller.selection =
                      TextSelection(baseOffset: 0,
                      extentOffset: 5);
                });
              },
            ),
            RaisedButton(
              child: Text('Move cursor to offset 1'),
              onPressed: () {
                setState(() {
                  _controller.selection = TextSelection.
                  collapsed(offset: 1);
                });
              },
            ),
          ],
        ),
```

```
      Text.rich(TextSpan(
        children: [
          TextSpan(
            text: 'Selected:',
            style: TextStyle(fontWeight: FontWeight.bold),
          ),
          TextSpan(text: _selection ?? "),
        ],
      )),
    ],
  );
}

_handleTextSelection() {
  TextSelection selection = _controller.selection;
  if (selection != null) {
    setState(() {
      _selection = selection.textInside(_controller.text);
    });
  }
}
}
}
```

Figure 6-8 shows the screenshot of code in Listing 6-9.

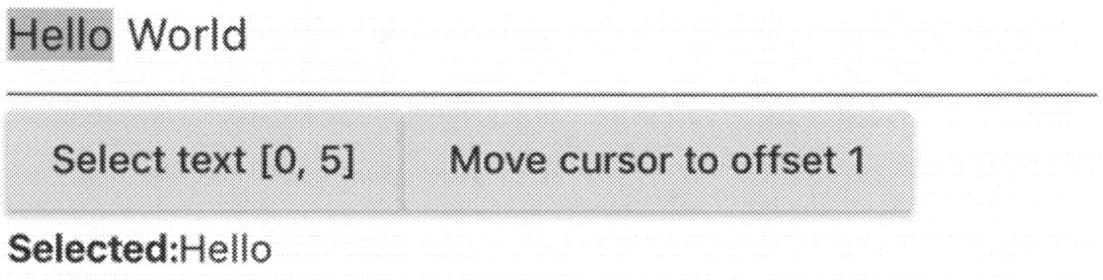

Figure 6-8. *Text selection*

6-6. Formatting Text

Problem

You want to format the text.

Solution

Use TextInputFormatter with EditableText.

Discussion

When the user is typing in a text input, you may want to validate and format the entered text. A common requirement is to remove characters in a blacklist. This is done by providing a list of TextInputFormatter instances as the inputFormatters parameter of TextField and CupertinoTextField.

TextInputFormatter is an abstract class with only formatEditUpdate (TextEditingValue oldValue, TextEditingValue newValue) to implement. The oldValue and newValue parameters represent the previous text and new text, respectively. The return value is another TextEditingValue instance representing the formatted text. TextInputFormatter instances can be chained. When chained, the value of oldValue to invoke formatEditUpdate method is always the previous text, but the value of newValue is the return value of invoking the formatEditUpdate method of previous TextInputFormatter instance in the chain.

There are already three built-in implementation classes of TextInputFormatter shown in Table 6-5. These classes are used in implementation of TextField and CupertinoTextField. For example, when the value of maxLines parameter is 1, BlacklistingTextInputFormatter. singleLineFormatter is added to the list of TextInputFormatter instances to filter out the "\n" character.

Table 6-5. *Implementations of TextInputFormatter*

Name	Description
LengthLimitingText InputFormatter	Limit the number of characters can be entered.
BlacklistingText InputFormatter	Replace characters matching regular expression pattern with given string.
WhitelistingText InputFormatter	Allow only characters matching given regular expression pattern.

Instead of declaring new subclasses of TextInputFormatter, an easier way is to use TextInputFormatter.withFunction() method with a function matching the type of formatEditUpdate() method.

In Listing 6-10, the input text is formatted to use uppercase.

Listing 6-10. Format text

```
TextField(
  inputFormatters: [
    TextInputFormatter.withFunction((oldValue, newValue) {
      return newValue.copyWith(text: newValue.text?.
      toUpperCase());
    }),
  ],
)
```

6-7. Selecting a Single Value

Problem

You want to select a single value from a list of values.

Solution

Use a group of Radio widgets.

Discussion

Radio buttons are commonly used for scenarios requiring single selections. Only one radio button in a group can be selected. Radio class has a type parameter T representing the type of values. When creating Radio instances, you need to provide required parameters including value, groupValue, and onChanged. A Radio widget doesn't maintain any state. Its appearance is purely determined by value and groupValue parameters. When the selection of a radio group is changed, onChanged listener is invoked with the selected value. Table 6-6 shows the named parameters of Radio constructor.

Table 6-6. *Named parameters of Radio*

Name	Type	Description
value	T	Value of this radio button.
groupValue	T	Selected value of this group of radio buttons. The radio button with groupValue is in selected state.
onChanged	ValueChanged<T>	Listener function when selection changed.
activeColor	Color	Color when this radio button is selected.

In Listing 6-11, Fruit.allFruits variable is a list of all Fruit instances. _selectedFruit is the currently selected Fruit instance. For each Fruit instance, a Radio<Fruit> widget is created with the groupValue set to _selectedFruit.

Listing 6-11. Example of using Radio

```
class FruitChooser extends StatefulWidget {
  @override
  _FruitChooserState createState() => _FruitChooserState();
}

class _FruitChooserState extends State<FruitChooser> {
  Fruit _selectedFruit;

  @override
  Widget build(BuildContext context) {
    return Column(
      crossAxisAlignment: CrossAxisAlignment.start,
      children: <Widget>[
        Column(
          children: Fruit.allFruits.map((fruit) {
            return Row(
              children: <Widget>[
                Radio<Fruit>(
                  value: fruit,
                  groupValue: _selectedFruit,
                  onChanged: (value) {
                    setState(() {
                      _selectedFruit = value;
                    });
                  },
                ),
                Expanded(
                  child: Text(fruit.name),
                ),
              ],
            );
          }).toList(),
```

```
      ),
      Text(_selectedFruit != null ? _selectedFruit.name : ")
    ],
  );
  }
}
```

Figure 6-9 shows the screenshot of the example in Listing 6-11.

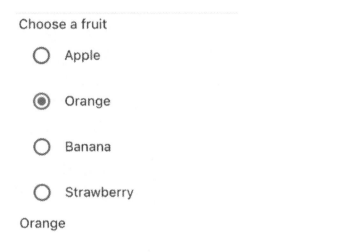

Figure 6-9. *Radio widgets*

6-8. Selecting a Single Value from Dropdown

Problem

You want to select a single value from a dropdown list.

Solution

Use DropdownButton.

Discussion

A DropdownButton widget shows a list of items when tapped.
DropdownButton class is generic with the type parameter representing
the type of values. The list of items is specified using the items parameter
of type List< DropdownMenuItem<T>>. DropdownMenuItem widget is
a simple wrapper with the value and a child widget. When the selection
is changed, the onChanged callback will be invoked with the value of
selected item. Value of the selected item is passed as value parameter.
If value is null, the hint widget is displayed instead.

In Listing 6-12, each Fruit instance is mapped to a
DropdownMenuItem widget.

Listing 6-12. Example of DropdownButton

```
class FruitChooser extends StatefulWidget {
  @override
  _FruitChooserState createState() => _FruitChooserState();
}

class _FruitChooserState extends State<FruitChooser> {
  Fruit _selectedFruit;

  @override
  Widget build(BuildContext context) {
    return Column(
      crossAxisAlignment: CrossAxisAlignment.start,
      children: <Widget>[
        DropdownButton(
          value: _selectedFruit,
          items: Fruit.allFruits.map((fruit) {
            return DropdownMenuItem(
              value: fruit,
              child: Text(fruit.name),
```

207

```
      );
    }).toList(),
    onChanged: (fruit) {
      setState(() {
        _selectedFruit = fruit;
      });
    },
    hint: Text('Select a fruit'),
  ),
  ],
  );
 }
}
```

Figure 6-10 shows the screenshot of an expanded DropdownButton.

Figure 6-10. *Expanded DropdownButton*

6-9. Selecting Multiple Values

Problem

You want to select multiple values.

Solution

Use Checkbox widget.

Discussion

Checkboxes are commonly used to allow multiple selections. A checkbox can display three values, true, false, and null, if this checkbox is created with parameter tristate set to true. Otherwise, only values true and false are allowed. If the value is null, a dash is displayed. A checkbox itself doesn't maintain any state. Its appearance is purely determined by the value parameter. When the value of a checkbox is changed, the onChanged callback is invoked with the value of the new state.

In Listing 6-13, selected fruits are maintained in a List<Fruit> instance. Each Fruit instance is mapped to a Checkbox widget. The value of a Checkbox depends on whether corresponding Fruit instance is in the _selectedFruits list.

Listing 6-13. Example of Checkbox

```
class FruitSelector extends StatefulWidget {
  @override
  _FruitSelectorState createState() => _FruitSelectorState();
}

class _FruitSelectorState extends State<FruitSelector> {
  List<Fruit> _selectedFruits = List();

  @override
  Widget build(BuildContext context) {
```

```
  return Column(
    crossAxisAlignment: CrossAxisAlignment.start,
    children: <Widget>[
      Column(
        children: Fruit.allFruits.map((fruit) {
          return Row(
            children: <Widget>[
              Checkbox(
                value: _selectedFruits.contains(fruit),
                onChanged: (selected) {
                  setState(() {
                    if (selected) {
                      _selectedFruits.add(fruit);
                    } else {
                      _selectedFruits.remove(fruit);
                    }
                  });
                },
              ),
              Expanded(
                child: Text(fruit.name),
              )
            ],
          );
        }).toList(),
      ),
      Text(_selectedFruits.join(', ')),
    ],
  );
 }
}
```

Figure 6-10 shows the screenshot of the example in Listing 6-13.

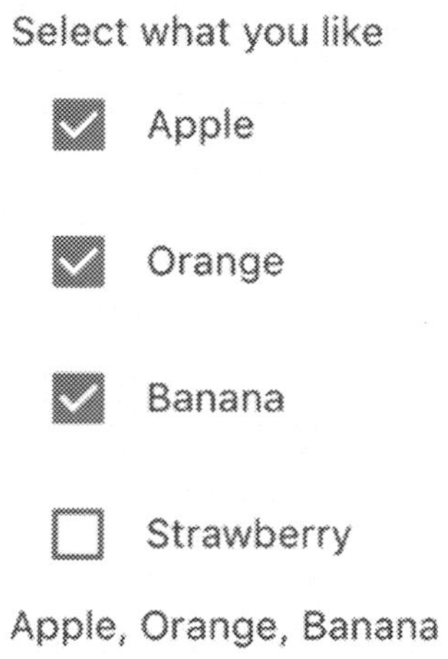

Select what you like

☑ Apple

☑ Orange

☑ Banana

☐ Strawberry

Apple, Orange, Banana

Figure 6-11. *Checkbox*

6-10. Toggling On/Off State

Problem

You want to toggle the on/off state.

Solution

Use Switch for Material Design and CupertinoSwitch for iOS style.

Discussion

Switch is a commonly used UI control to toggle the on/off state of a setting. Switch widget is used for Material Design. A Switch widget can be in two states, active and inactive. A Switch widget itself doesn't maintain any state. Its behavior and appearance are purely determined by values of constructor parameters. If the value parameter is true, then Switch widget is in active state; otherwise, it's in inactive state. When the on/off state of a Switch widget is changed, the onChanged callback is invoked with the new state to be. You can customize the appearance of a Switch widget in different states using parameters activeColor, activeThumbImage, activeTrackColor, inactiveThumbColor, inactiveThumbImage, and inactiveTrackColor.

In Listing 6-14, the Switch widget is used to control the state of another TextField widget.

Listing 6-14. Example of Switch

```
class NameInput extends StatefulWidget {
  @override
  _NameInputState createState() => _NameInputState();
}

class _NameInputState extends State<NameInput> {
  bool _useCustomName = false;

  _buildNameInput() {
    return TextField(
      decoration: InputDecoration(labelText: 'Name'),
    );
  }

  _buildToggle() {
    return Row(
      children: <Widget>[
        Switch(
          value: _useCustomName,
          onChanged: (value) {
            setState(() {
              _useCustomName = value;
            });
          },
```

```
      activeColor: Colors.green,
      inactiveThumbColor: Colors.grey.shade200,
    ),
    Expanded(
      child: Text('Use custom name'),
    ),
  ],
 );
}

@override
Widget build(BuildContext context) {
  return Column(
    crossAxisAlignment: CrossAxisAlignment.start,
    children: _useCustomName
        ? [_buildToggle(), _buildNameInput()]
        : [_buildToggle()],
  );
 }
}
```

Figure 6-12 shows the screenshot of example in Listing 6-14.

Name

Figure 6-12. Switch

CupertinoSwitch widget creates an iOS-style switch and it works the same way as Switch, but it only supports customization of the active color. Switch widget has the constructor Switch.adaptive() to create either a Switch widget or CupertinoSwitch widget depends on the target platform. When a CupertinoSwitch widget is created using Switch.adaptive(), only constructor parameters accepted by CupertinoSwitch() are used; other parameters are ignored.

Listing 6-15 shows examples of using CupertinoSwitch and Switch. adaptive().

Listing 6-15. Example of CupertinoSwitch

```
CupertinoSwitch(
  value: true,
  onChanged: (value) => {},
  activeColor: Colors.red.shade300,
)

Switch.adaptive(
  value: true,
  onChanged: (value) => {},
)
```

6-11. Selecting from a Range of Values
Problem

You want to select from a range of continuous or a discrete set of values.

Solution

Use Slider for Material Design or CupertinoSlider for iOS style.

Discussion

A slider is commonly used to select from a range of continuous or a discrete set of values. You can use Slider widget for Material Design or CupertinoSlider for iOS style. These two widgets have the same behavior but different visual appearance. When creating sliders, you need to provide a valid range of the values using min and max parameters. If non-null value is used for divisions parameter, a set of discrete values will be the selections. Otherwise, a continuous range of values will be the selections. For example, if value in min is 0.0 and max is 10.0, with the divisions set to 5, then values of selections are 0.0, 2.0, 4.0, 6.0, 8.0, and 10.0. A slider widget doesn't maintain any state. Its behavior and appearance are purely determined by constructor parameters. When the value of a slider is changed, the onChanged callback is invoked with the selected value. You can also use onChangeStart and onChangeEnd callbacks to get notifications when the value starts to change and it's done changing, respectively. You can further customize a slider's appearance using label, activeColor, and inactiveColor. Only activeColor parameter is supported by CupertinoSlider. The slider widget will be disabled if onChanged is null or if the range is empty.

In Listing 6-16, a Slider widget is created with the given value of divisions parameter and shows the current value.

Listing 6-16. Example of Slider

```
class SliderValue extends StatefulWidget {
  SliderValue({Key key, this.divisions}) : super(key: key);

  final int divisions;

  @override
  _SliderValueState createState() =>
  _SliderValueState(divisions);
}
```

```
class _SliderValueState extends State<SliderValue> {
  _SliderValueState(this.divisions);

  final int divisions;
  double _value = 0.0;

  @override
  Widget build(BuildContext context) {
    return Row(
      children: <Widget>[
        Expanded(
          child: Slider(
            value: _value,
            min: 0.0,
            max: 10.0,
            divisions: divisions,
            onChanged: (value) {
              setState(() {
                _value = value;
              });
            },
          ),
        ),
        Text(_value.toStringAsFixed(2)),
      ],
    );
  }
}
```

The usage of CupertinoSlider is similar with Slider. You can simply replace Slider with CupertinoSlider in Listing 6-16. Figure 6-13 shows screenshot of Slider and CupertinoSlider.

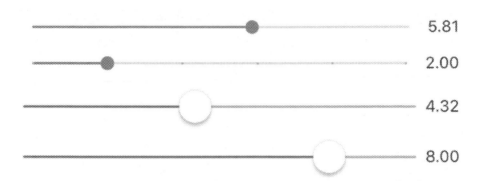

Figure 6-13. *Slider and CupertinoSlider*

6-12. Using Chips

Problem

You want to have compact alternatives to represent different types of entities.

Solution

Use different types of Chips.

Discussion

When space is limited, traditional widget like buttons, radio buttons, and checkboxes may not be suitable. Chips in Material Design can be used in this case to represent the same semantic but use less space.

Chip widget is the generic chip implementation that has a required label and an optional avatar. It can also include a delete button when setting a non-null onDeleted callback.

InputChip widget is more powerful than Chip widget. An InputChip widget can be selectable by setting the onSelected callback and pressable by setting the onPressed callback. However, you cannot set non-null values

217

to both onSelected and onPressed callbacks. When using onSelected, an InputChip widget behaves like a checkbox. You can use the selected parameter to set the state. When using onPressed, an InputChip widget behaves like a button.

A ChoiceChip widget behaves like a radio button with selected parameter to set its state and onSelected callback to notify state changes. However, ChoiceChip widget doesn't have a parameter similar with groupValue in Radio widget, so you have to set the selected state manually.

A FilterChip widget behaves like a checkbox. FilterChip constructor has the same parameters as ChoiceChip constructor.

An ActionChip widget behaves like a button with the onPressed parameter. The difference between action chips and buttons is that action chips cannot be disabled by setting onPressed parameter to null. Action chips should be removed if their actions are not applicable. This behavior is consistent with the goal to using chips for reducing space.

In fact, all these chip widgets wrap RawChip widgets by using only a subset of parameters supported by RawChip constructor.

In Listing 6-17, ChoiceChip widget is used to implement single selection.

Listing 6-17. Example of ChoiceChip

```
class FruitChooser extends StatefulWidget {
  @override
  _FruitChooserState createState() => _FruitChooserState();
}

class _FruitChooserState extends State<FruitChooser> {
  Fruit _selectedFruit;

  @override
  Widget build(BuildContext context) {
```

```
  return Column(
    crossAxisAlignment: CrossAxisAlignment.start,
    children: <Widget>[
      Wrap(
        spacing: 5,
        children: Fruit.allFruits.map((fruit) {
          return ChoiceChip(
            label: Text(fruit.name),
            selected: _selectedFruit == fruit,
            onSelected: (selected) {
              setState(() {
                _selectedFruit = selected ? fruit : null;
              });
            },
            selectedColor: Colors.red.shade200,
          );
        }).toList(),
      ),
      Text(_selectedFruit != null ? _selectedFruit.name : ")
    ],
  );
 }
}
```

In Listing 6-18, FilterChip widget is used to implement multiple selections.

Listing 6-18. Example of FilterChip

```
class FruitSelector extends StatefulWidget {
  @override
  _FruitSelectorState createState() => _FruitSelectorState();
}
```

```
class _FruitSelectorState extends State<FruitSelector> {
  List<Fruit> _selectedFruits = List();

  @override
  Widget build(BuildContext context) {
    return Column(
      crossAxisAlignment: CrossAxisAlignment.start,
      children: <Widget>[
        Wrap(
          spacing: 5,
          children: Fruit.allFruits.map((fruit) {
            return FilterChip(
              label: Text(fruit.name),
              selected: _selectedFruits.contains(fruit),
              onSelected: (selected) {
                setState(() {
                  if (selected) {
                    _selectedFruits.add(fruit);
                  } else {
                    _selectedFruits.remove(fruit);
                  }
                });
              },
              selectedColor: Colors.blue.shade200,
            );
          }).toList(),
        ),
        Text(_selectedFruits.join(', ')),
      ],
    );
  }
}
```

Figure 6-14 shows the screenshot of examples in Listings 6-17 and 6-18.

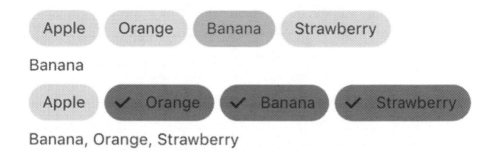

Figure 6-14. *ChoiceChip and FilterChip*

6-13. Selecting Date and Time
Problem

You want to select date and time.

Solution

Use showDatePicker() and showTimePicker() functions for Material Design or CupertinoDatePicker and CupertinoTimerPicker for iOS style.

Discussion

For Material Design, you can use widgets like YearPicker, MonthPicker, and DayPicker or showDatePicker() function to allow user to pick dates. The showTimePicker() function is used to pick times. Widgets are rarely used to pick dates. Most of the time, showDatePicker() and showTimePicker() functions are used to show dialogs.

YearPicker widget shows a list of years to pick. When creating YearPicker widgets, you need to provide DateTime instances for selected date, earliest date, and latest date using selectedDate, firstDate, and lastDate parameters, respectively. When the selection is changed, the onChanged callback is invoked with the selected DateTime instance.

MonthPicker widget shows a list of months to pick. MonthPicker constructor has the same parameters selectedDate, firstDate, lastDate, and onChanged as YearPicker. It also has a predicate function selectableDayPredicate to customize which days are selectable.

DayPicker widget shows the days of a given month to pick. DayPicker constructor has all the parameters of MonthPicker and the displayedMonth parameter to set the month to pick for days.

If you want to show a dialog for user to select dates, showDatePicker() function is easier to use than creating your own dialogs. You need to pass DateTime instances for parameters initialDate, firstDate, and lastDate. The context parameter of type BuildContext is also required. This function can work in two modes defined in the DatePickerMode enum. DatePickerMode.day means choosing a month a day, while DatePickerMode.year means choosing a year. The return value of showDatePicker() function is a Future<DateTime> representing the selected date.

In Listing 6-19, the TextField widget has an IconButton as the suffix. When the button is pressed, showDatePicker() function is invoked to show the date picker dialog. The selected date is displayed in the TextField widget.

Listing 6-19. Pick date

```
class PickDate extends StatefulWidget {
  @override
  _PickDateState createState() => _PickDateState();
}

class _PickDateState extends State<PickDate> {
  DateTime _selectedDate = DateTime.now();
  TextEditingController _controller = TextEditingController();
```

```
  @override
  Widget build(BuildContext context) {
    return TextField(
      controller: _controller,
      decoration: InputDecoration(
        labelText: 'Date',
        suffix: IconButton(
          icon: Icon(Icons.date_range),
          onPressed: () {
            showDatePicker(
              context: context,
              initialDate: _selectedDate,
              firstDate: DateTime.now().subtract(Duration(days:
              30)),
              lastDate: DateTime.now().add(Duration(days: 30)),)
            .then((selectedDate) {
              if (selectedDate != null) {
                _selectedDate = selectedDate;
                _controller.text = DateFormat.yMd().format(_
                selectedDate);
              }
            });
          },
        ),
      ),
    );
  }
}
```

The showTimePicker() function shows a dialog to pick times. You need to pass the initialTime parameter of type TimeOfDay as the initial time to show. The return value is a Future<TimeOfDay> instance representing the selected time. The code in Listing 6-20 uses the similar pattern as Listing 6-19 to show the time picker dialog.

Listing 6-20. Pick time

```
class PickTime extends StatefulWidget {
  @override
  _PickTimeState createState() => _PickTimeState();
}

class _PickTimeState extends State<PickTime> {
  TimeOfDay _selectedTime = TimeOfDay.now();
  TextEditingController _controller = TextEditingController();

  @override
  Widget build(BuildContext context) {
    return TextField(
      controller: _controller,
      decoration: InputDecoration(
          labelText: 'Time',
          suffix: IconButton(
            icon: Icon(Icons.access_time),
            onPressed: () {
              showTimePicker(
                context: context,
                initialTime: _selectedTime,
              ).then((selectedTime) {
                if (selectedTime != null) {
                  _selectedTime = selectedTime;
                  _controller.text = _selectedTime.
                  format(context);
                }
              });
```

```
        },
      )),
   );
  }
}
```

For iOS style, you can use CupertinoDatePicker and CupertinoTimerPicker widgets to pick date and time, respectively. A CupertinoDatePicker can have different modes based on the mode parameter of enum CupertinoDatePickerMode, including date, time, and dateAndTime. Similar to widgets in Material Design, CupertinoDatePicker constructor has parameters initialDateTime, minimumDate, maximumDate, and onDateTimeChanged. A CupertinoTimerPicker can also have different modes based on the mode parameter of enum CupertinoTimerPickerMode, including hm, ms, and hms. The difference is that CupertinoTimerPicker uses Duration instances to set the initial value and as the value in onTimerDurationChanged callback.

6-14. Wrapping Form Fields

Problem

You want to wrap form widgets as form fields.

Solution

Use FormField or TextFormField.

Discussion

Form widgets can be used as normal widgets. However, these form widgets don't maintain any state; you always need to wrap them in stateful widgets to keep the state. A typical usage pattern is to use the onChanged callback to update the state and trigger the rebuild of the form widget. Since this is a typical pattern of using form widgets, Flutter has a built-in FormField widget to maintain the current state of a form widget. It handles the updates and validation errors.

FormField class is generic with type parameter T representing the type of value. A FormField can be used as a standalone widget or be part of a Form widget. This recipe only discusses the standalone usage. Table 6-7 shows the named parameters of FormField constructor.

Table 6-7. *Named parameters of FormField*

Name	Type	Description
builder	FormFieldBuilder<T>	Build the widget representing this form field.
onSaved	FormFieldSetter<T>	Callback when the form is saved.
validator	FormFieldValidator<T>	Validator of the form field.
initialValue	T	Initial value.
autovalidate	boolean	Whether to validate automatically after every change.
enabled	boolean	Whether this form field is enabled.

FormFieldBuilder<T> type is a typedef in the form of Widget (FormFieldState<T> field). FormFieldState<T> class extends from State class and represents the current state of the form field. FormFieldBuilder is responsible for building the widget based on the state. From FormFieldState, you can get the current value and error text of the form field. You can also use methods of FormFieldState in Table 6-8. FormFieldValidator<T> is also a typedef in the form of String(T value). It takes the current value as the input and returns a non-null string as the error message if the validation fails. FormFieldSetter<T> type is a typedef in the form of void(T newValue).

Table 6-8. *Methods in FormFieldState*

Name	Description
save()	Call the onSaved() method with the current value.
validate()	Call the validator and set the errorText if validation fails.
didChange(T value)	Update the field's state to the new value.
reset()	Reset the field to its initial value.

When wrapping TextFields inside of FormFields, it's better to use the built-in TextFormField. TextFormField widget already handles setting text using TextEditingController and using the error text returned by FormFieldValidator to update the input decoration. TextFormField constructor supports parameters from TextField and FormField constructors. TextFormField in Listing 6-21 has a validator to validate text length.

Listing 6-21. TextFormField

```
class NameInput extends StatelessWidget {
  @override
  Widget build(BuildContext context) {
    return TextFormField(
      decoration: InputDecoration(
        labelText: 'Name',
      ),
      validator: (value) {
        if (value == null || value.isEmpty) {
          return 'Name is required.';
        } else if (value.length < 6) {
          return 'Minimum length is 6.';
```

```
      } else {
        return null;
      }
    },
    autovalidate: true,
  );
  }
}
```

Figure 6-15 shows the screenshot of code in Listing 6-21.

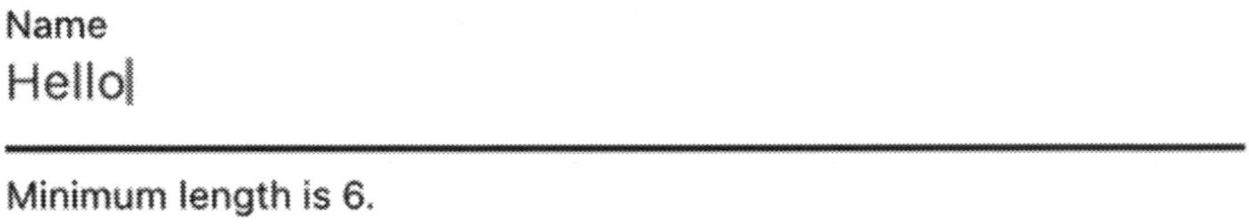

Name
Hello|

_____

Minimum length is 6.

Figure 6-15. *TextFormField*

FormFieldState instances are only accessible in the builder function of FormField. If you need to access the state from other places, you can pass a GlobalKey as the key parameter of FormField, then use the currentState property to access the current state.

In Listing 6-22, the state of FormField is a List<PizzaTopping> instance. With the GlobalKey, the current value can be retrieved when the button is pressed.

Listing 6-22. FormField

```
class PizzaToppingsSelector extends StatelessWidget {
  final GlobalKey<FormFieldState<List<PizzaTopping>>>
  _formFieldKey =
      GlobalKey();
```

```
@override
Widget build(BuildContext context) {
  return Column(
    children: <Widget>[
      FormField<List<PizzaTopping>>(
        key: _formFieldKey,
        initialValue: List(),
        builder: (state) {
          return Wrap(
            spacing: 5,
            children: PizzaTopping.allPizzaToppings.
            map((topping) {
              return ChoiceChip(
                label: Text(topping.name),
                selected: state.value.contains(topping),
                onSelected: state.value.length < 2 ||
                      state.value.contains(topping)
                  ? (selected) {
                      List<PizzaTopping> newValue = List.
                      of(state.value);
                      if (selected) {
                        newValue.add(topping);
                      } else {
                        newValue.remove(topping);
                      }
                      state.didChange(newValue);
                    }
                  : null,
              );
            }).toList(),
          );
```

```
            },
        ),
        RaisedButton(
          child: Text('Get toppings'),
          onPressed: () => print(_formFieldKey.currentState?.
          value),
        ),
      ],
    );
  }
}
```

6-15. Creating Forms
Problem

You want to create a form with multiple form fields.

Solution

Use Form.

Discussion

When using form fields, generally you're trying to build a form with multiple form fields. Managing form fields separately is a tedious task when dealing with multiple form fields. Form is a convenient wrapper for multiple form fields. You need to wrap all form fields in FormField widgets and use a Form widget as the common ancestor of all these FormField widgets. Form widget is a stateful widget with state managed by associated FormState instance. FormState class has methods save(), validate(), and reset(). These methods call corresponding functions on all FormFieldState instances of descendant FormField widgets.

There are two ways to get the FormState instance depends on the location of the widget wants to use FormState. If the widget is a descendant of the Form widget, using Form.of(BuildContext context) is an easy way to get the closest FormState instance. The second way is to use GlobalKey instance when creating the Form widget, then use GlobalKey.currentState to get the FormState.

Listing 6-23 shows the code of a login form. Two TextFormField widgets are created with GlobalKey instances.

Listing 6-23. Login form

```
class LoginForm extends StatefulWidget {
  @override
  _LoginFormState createState() => _LoginFormState();
}

class _LoginFormState extends State<LoginForm> {
  final GlobalKey<FormFieldState<String>> _usernameFormFieldKey
  = GlobalKey();
  final GlobalKey<FormFieldState<String>> _passwordFormFieldKey
  = GlobalKey();

  _notEmpty(String value) => value != null && value.isNotEmpty;

  get _value => ({
        'username': _usernameFormFieldKey.currentState?.value,
        'password': _passwordFormFieldKey.currentState?.value
      });

  @override
  Widget build(BuildContext context) {
    return Form(
```

```
    child: Column(
      children: <Widget>[
        TextFormField(
          key: _usernameFormFieldKey,
          decoration: InputDecoration(
            labelText: 'Username',
          ),
          validator: (value) =>
              !_notEmpty(value) ? 'Username is required' :
              null,
        ),
        TextFormField(
          key: _passwordFormFieldKey,
          obscureText: true,
          decoration: InputDecoration(
            labelText: 'Password',
          ),
          validator: (value) =>
              !_notEmpty(value) ? 'Password is required' :
              null,
        ),
        Builder(builder: (context) {
          return Row(
            mainAxisAlignment: MainAxisAlignment.end,
            children: <Widget>[
              RaisedButton(
                child: Text('Log In'),
                onPressed: () {
                  if (Form.of(context).validate()) {
                    print(_value);
                  }
```

```
            },
          ),
          FlatButton(
            child: Text('Reset'),
            onPressed: () => Form.of(context).reset(),
          )
        ],
      );
    }),
  ],
 ),
 );
 }
}
```

Figure 6-16 shows the screenshot of the login form.

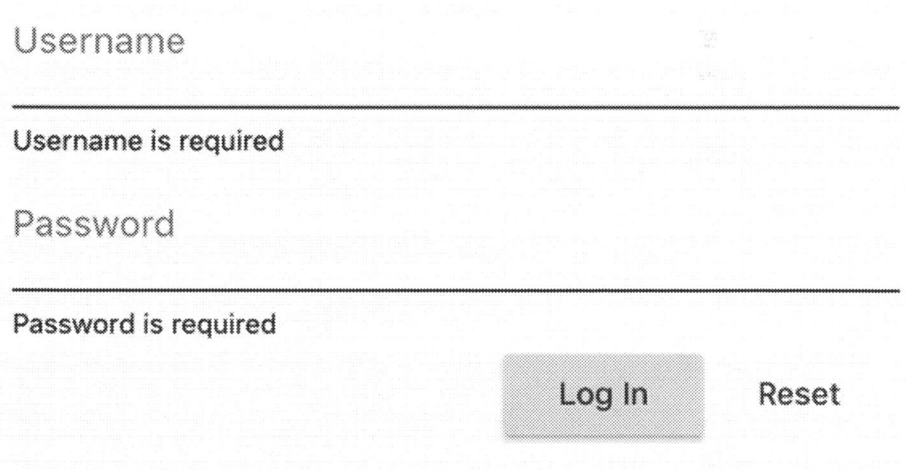

Username
_____
Username is required
Password
....
Password is required

                                    Log In   Reset

Figure 6-16. *Login form*

6-16. Summary

Form widgets are important to interact with user. This chapter covers form widgets for Material Design and iOS style, including text input, radio button, checkbox, dropdown, switch, chip, and slider. In the next chapter, we'll discuss widgets for application scaffolding.

CHAPTER 7

Common Widgets

In Flutter apps, some widgets are widely used for different purposes. This chapter discusses some common widgets.

7-1. Displaying a List of Items

Problem

You want to display a scrollable list of items.

Solution

Use ListView widget as the container of items.

Discussion

Flutter layout widgets like Flex, Row, and Column don't support scrolling, and these widgets are not designed to be used to display items when scrolling is required. If you want to display a large number of items, you should use ListView widget. You can think ListView as the scrollable counterpart of Flex widget.

© Fu Cheng 2019
F. Cheng, *Flutter Recipes*, https://doi.org/10.1007/978-1-4842-4982-6_7

There are three different ways to create ListView widgets using different constructors:

- Create from a static list of children widgets.

- Create by building children on demand based on the scrolling position.

- Create a custom implementation.

- This recipe focuses on the first two ways.

ListView with Static Children

If you have a static list of children that may exceed the size of their parent widget, you can wrap them in a ListView widget to enable scrolling. This is done by invoking the ListView() constructor with the children parameter of type Widget[]. The scrolling direction is determined by the scrollDirection parameter of type Axis. The default scroll direction is Axis.vertical. If you want to display the children in a reverse order, you can set the reverse parameter to true. Listing 7-1 shows a ListView widget with three children.

Listing 7-1. ListView with static children

```
ListView(
  children: <Widget>[
    ExampleWidget(name: 'Box 1'),
    ExampleWidget(name: 'Box 2'),
    ExampleWidget(name: 'Box 3'),
  ],
)
```

The default ListView() constructor should only be used when you have a small number of children. All children will be created, even though some of them are not visible in the viewport. This is likely to have performance impact.

ListView with Item Builders

If you have a large number of items or items need to be dynamically created, you can use ListView.builder() and ListView.separated() constructors. Instead of a static list of widgets, you need to provide builder functions of type IndexedWidgetBuilder to build items on demand. IndexedWidgetBuilder is typedef of Widget (BuildContext context, int index). The index parameter is the index of the item to build. ListView widget determines the indices of items in the viewport and invokes the builder function to build the items to render. If the total number of items is known, you should pass this number as the itemCount parameter. If itemCount is non-null, the builder function will only be invoked with indices greater than or equal to zero and less than itemCount. If itemCount is null, the builder function needs to return null to indicate that no more items are available.

When using ListView.builder() constructor, you only need to provide the itemBuilder parameter of type IndexedWidgetBuilder. For ListView.separated() constructor, apart from the itemBuilder parameter, you also need to provide the separatorBuilder parameter of type IndexedWidgetBuilder to build the separators between items. When using ListView.separated(), the itemCount parameter is required. Listing 7-2 shows examples of using ListView.builder() and ListView.separated().

Listing 7-2. ListView with item builders

```
ListView.builder(
  itemCount: 20,
  itemBuilder: (context, index) {
    return ExampleWidget(name: 'Dynamic Box ${index + 1}');
  },
);
```

```
ListView.separated(
  itemBuilder: (context, index) {
    return ExampleWidget(name: 'Separated Box ${index + 1}');
  },
  separatorBuilder: (context, index) {
    return Divider(
      height: 8,
    );
  },
  itemCount: 20,
);
```

If the extent of an item in the scroll direction is known, you should pass this value as the itemExtent parameter. Non-null values of itemExtent parameter make the scrolling more efficient.

ListTile

You can use any widget as child of ListView. If you the item to include text, icon, and other control, you can use ListTile and its subclasses. A list tile contains one to three lines of text and leading and trailing widgets surrounding the text. Table 7-1 shows

Table 7-1. *Parameters of ListTile*

Name	Type	Description
title	Widget	Title of the list tile.
subtitle	Widget	Optional content displayed below the title.
isThreeLine	bool	Whether the list tile may have three lines of text.
leading	Widget	Widget displayed before the title.
trailing	Widget	Widget displayed after the title.
enabled	bool	Whether the list tile is enabled.
selected	bool	Whether the list tile is selected. When selected, icons and text are rendered with the same color.
onTap	GestureTapCallback	Callback when the title is tapped.
onLongPress	GestureLongPressCallback	Callback when the title is long pressed.
dense	bool	When true, the size of the tile is reduced.
contentPadding	EdgeInsetsGeometry	Padding inside of the tile.

Listing 7-3 shows an example of using ListTile.

Listing 7-3. Example of ListTile

```
ListTile(
  title: Text('Title'),
  subtitle: Text('Description'),
  leading: Icon(Icons.shop),
  trailing: Icon(Icons.arrow_right),
)
```

If you want to have a checkbox in a list tile, you can use CheckboxListTile widget which combines ListTile and Checkbox. CheckboxListTile constructor has the same parameters title, subtitle, isThreeLine, selected, and dense as ListTile constructor. It also has parameters value, onChanged, and activeColor used for Checkbox constructor.

Table 7-2. *Parameters of CheckboxListTile*

Name	Type	Description
secondary	Widget	Widget displayed on the opposite side of the tile.
controlAffinity	ListTileControlAffinity	Where to place the control in the tile.

ListTileControlAffinity enum defines the position of control in the list tile. It has three values, leading, trailing, and platform. When the position of control is specified, the secondary widget is always placed on the opposite side.

Listing 7-4. Example of CheckboxListTile

```
class CheckboxInListTile extends StatefulWidget {
  @override
  _CheckboxInListTileState createState() => _
CheckboxInListTileState();
}

class _CheckboxInListTileState extends
State<CheckboxInListTile> {
  bool _value = false;

  @override
  Widget build(BuildContext context) {
    return CheckboxListTile(
```

```
      title: Text('Checkbox'),
      subtitle: Text('Description'),
      value: _value,
      onChanged: (value) {
        setState(() {
          _value = value;
        });
      },
      secondary: Icon(_value ? Icons.monetization_on : Icons.
      money_off),
    );
  }
}
```

If you want to add a radio button in a list tile, you can use
RadioListTile<T> widget. For the parameters of RadioListTile constructor,
value, groupValue, onChanged, and activeColor have the same
meaning as in Radio constructor; title, subtitle, isThreeLine, dense,
secondary, selected, and controlAffinity have the same meaning as in
CheckboxListTile constructor. Listing 7-5 shows an example of using
RadioListTile.

Listing 7-5. Example of RadioListTile

```
enum CustomColor { red, green, blue }

class RadioInListTile extends StatefulWidget {
  @override
  _RadioInListTileState createState() => _
RadioInListTileState();
}
```

```
class _RadioInListTileState extends State<RadioInListTile> {
  CustomColor _selectedColor;

  @override
  Widget build(BuildContext context) {
    return Column(
      children: CustomColor.values.map((color) {
        return RadioListTile<CustomColor>(
          title: Text(color.toString()),
          value: color,
          groupValue: _selectedColor,
          onChanged: (value) {
            setState(() {
              _selectedColor = value;
            });
          },
        );
      }).toList(),
    );
  }
}
```

If you want to add switch to a list tile, you can use SwitchListTile. Some parameters of SwitchListTile constructor come from Switch constructor, while other parameters come from ListTile constructor. Listing 7-6 shows an example of using SwitchListTile.

Listing 7-6. Example of SwitchListTile

```
class SwitchInListTile extends StatefulWidget {
  @override
  _SwitchInListTileState createState() => _
SwitchInListTileState();
}
```

```
class _SwitchInListTileState extends State<SwitchInListTile> {
  bool _value = false;

  @override
  Widget build(BuildContext context) {
    return SwitchListTile(
      title: Text('Switch'),
      subtitle: Text('Description'),
      value: _value,
      onChanged: (value) {
        setState(() {
          _value = value;
        });
      },
    );
  }
}
```

Figure 7-1 shows the screenshot of different ListTiles.

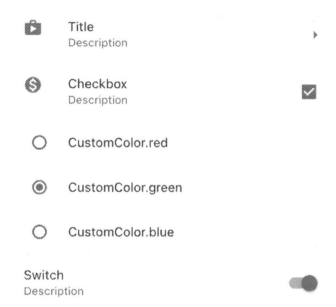

Figure 7-1. *ListTiles*

7-2. Displaying Items in a Grid

Problem

You want to display items in a grid.

Solution

Use GridView.

Discussion

ListView widget displays items in a linear array. To display widgets
in a two-dimensional array, you can use GridView. The actual
layout of children of GridView is delegated to an implementation of
SliverGridDelegate. Flutter provides two built-in implementations of

SliverGridDelegate, SliverGridDelegateWithFixedCrossAxisCount and
SliverGridDelegateWithMaxCrossAxisExtent. You can also create your own
implementations of SliverGridDelegate.

There are three ways to provide the children of the GridView.
You can provide a static list of widgets, or use builder function
of type IndexedWidgetBuilder, or provide an implementation of
SliverChildDelegate.

Depending on the choice of SliverGridDelegate and providing
children, you can use different GridView constructors. Table 7-3 shows the
usage of different constructors.

Table 7-3. *GridView constructors*

Name	Delegate	Children
GridView()	SliverGridDelegate	Widget[]
GridView.builder()	SliverGridDelegate	IndexedWidgetBuilder
GridView.count()	SliverGridDelegateWithFixedCross AxisCount	Widget[]
GridView.extent()	SliverGridDelegateWithMaxCross AxisExtent	Widget[]
GridView.custom()	SliverGridDelegate	SliverChildDelegate

SliverGridDelegateWithFixedCrossAxisCount class uses the
crossAxisCount parameter to specify the fixed number of tiles in the
cross axis. For example, if the scroll direction of GridView is vertical, the
crossAxisCount parameter specifies the number of columns. Listing 7-7
shows an example of using GridView.count() to create a grid with three
columns.

Listing 7-7. Example of using Gridview.count()

```
GridView.count(
  crossAxisCount: 3,
  children: List.generate(10, (index) {
    return ExampleWidget(
      name: 'Fixed Count ${index + 1}',
    );
  }),
);
```

SliverGridDelegateWithMaxCrossAxisExtent class uses the maxCrossAxisExtent parameter to specify the maximum extent in the cross axis. The actual cross-axis extent for tiles will be as large as possible to evenly divide the cross-axis extent of the GridView and won't exceed the specified maximum value. For example, if the cross-axis extent of the GridView is 400 and the value of maxCrossAxisExtent is 120, then the cross-axis extent for tiles is 100. If the GridView's scroll direction is vertical, it will have four columns. Listing 7-8 shows an example of using GridView. extent().

Listing 7-8. Example of using GridView.extent()

```
GridView.extent(
  maxCrossAxisExtent: 250,
  children: List.generate(10, (index) {
    return ExampleWidget(
      name: 'Max Extent ${index + 1}',
    );
  }),
);
```

To use a builder function to create children, you need to use GridView. builder() constructor with a SliverGridDelegate implementation.

246

Listing 7-9 shows an example of using GridView.builder() with
SliverGridDelegateWithFixedCrossAxisCount.

Listing 7-9. Example of using GridView.builder()

```
GridView.builder(
  itemCount: 32,
  gridDelegate:
      SliverGridDelegateWithFixedCrossAxisCount
      (crossAxisCount: 3),
  itemBuilder: (context, index) {
    return ExampleWidget(
      name: 'Builder ${index + 1}',
    );
  },
);
```

Both SliverGridDelegateWithFixedCrossAxisCount and
SliverGridDelegateWithMaxCrossAxisExtent classes have other named
parameters to configure the layout; see Table 7-4.

Table 7-4. *Parameters of built-in SliverGridDelegate*
implementations

Name	Type	Description
mainAxisSpacing	double	Spacing of tiles along the main axis.
crossAxisSpacing	double	Spacing of tiles along the cross axis.
childAspectRatio	double	Ratio of cross-axis to main-axis extent for the tiles.

When using these two SliverGridDelegate implementations, the
cross-axis extent of each tile is determined first, then the main-axis extent
is determined by the childAspectRatio parameter. If GridView is used

to display images with desired aspect ratio, you can use the same ratio as the value of childAspectRatio parameter. Both GridView.count() and GridView.extent() constructors have the same named parameters in Table 7-4 to pass these parameters to the underlying SliverGridDelegate implementations. Listing 7-10 shows an example of using childAspectRatio parameter when displaying images.

Listing 7-10. Using childAspectRatio parameter

```
GridView.count(
  crossAxisCount: 3,
  childAspectRatio: 4 / 3,
  children: List.generate(10, (index) {
    return Image.network('https://picsum.photos/400/300');
  }),
);
```

Just like using ListTiles in ListView, you can also use GridTiles in GridView. A grid tile has a required child widget and optional header and footer widgets. For header and footer of grid tiles, it's typical to use the GridTileBar widget. GridTileBar is similar with ListTile. GridTileBar constructor has parameters title, subtitle, leading, trailing, and backgroundColor.

Listing 7-11. Example of GridTile and GridTileBar

```
GridView.count(
  crossAxisCount: 2,
  children: <Widget>[
    GridTile(
      child: ExampleWidget(name: 'Simple'),
    ),
    GridTile(
```

```
    child: ExampleWidget(name: 'Header & Footer'),
    header: GridTileBar(
      title: Text('Header'),
      backgroundColor: Colors.red,
    ),
    footer: GridTileBar(
      title: Text('Footer'),
      subtitle: Text('Description'),
      backgroundColor: Colors.blue,
    ),
  )
 ],
);
```

Figure 7-2 shows the screenshot of code in Listing 7-11.

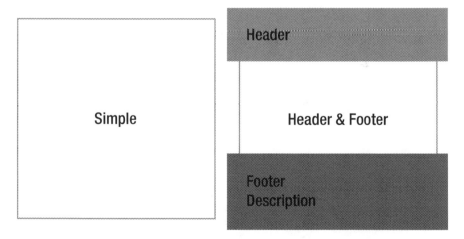

Figure 7-2. *GridTile and GridTileBar*

7-3. Displaying Tabular Data

Problem

You want to display tabular data or use table layout for children.

Solution

Use Table widget.

Discussion

If you want to display tabular data, using data tables is a natural choice. Tables can also be used for layout purpose to organize children. For these two usage scenarios, you can use the Table widget.

A Table widget may have multiple rows. A table row is represented with TableRow widget. Table widget constructor has the children parameter of type List<TableRow> to provide the list of rows. TableRow constructor also has the children parameter of type List<Widget> to provide the list of cells in this row. Every row in a table must have the same number of children.

The border of a table is defined using TableBorder class. TableBorder is similar with Border, but TableBorder has two extra sides:

- horizontalInside – The inner horizontal borders between rows

- verticalInside – The inner vertical borders between columns

Listing 7-12 shows an example of a simple table with three rows and four columns.

Listing 7-12. Simple table

```
Table(
  border: TableBorder.all(color: Colors.red.shade200),
  children: [
    TableRow(children: [Text('A'), Text('B'), Text('C'),
    Text('D')]),
    TableRow(children: [Text('E'), Text('F'), Text('G'),
    Text('H')]),
    TableRow(children: [Text('I'), Text('J'), Text('K'),
    Text('L')]),
  ],
);
```

Width of columns in a table is configured by TableColumnWidth implementations. The columnWidths parameter of type Map<int, TableColumnWidth> defines the mapping between column index and its TableColumnWidth implementation. Table 7-5 shows built-in TableColumnWidth implementations. MinColumnWidth and MaxColumnWidth classes combine other TableColumnWidth implementations. If no TableColumnWidth implementation is found for a column, the defaultColumnWidth parameter is used to get the default TableColumnWidth implementation. The default value of defaultColumnWidth is FlexColumnWidth(1.0), which means all columns share the same width.

Table 7-5. *TableColumnWidth implementations*

Name	Performance	Description
FixedColumnWidth	High	Use fixed number of pixels as the column width.
FlexColumnWidth	Medium	Use flex factor to divide remaining space once all the other non-flexible columns have been sized.
FractionColumnWidth	Medium	Use a fraction of the table's max width as the column width.
IntrinsicColumnWidth	Low	Use the intrinsic dimensions of all cells in a column to determine the column width.
MinColumnWidth		Minimum of two TableColumnWidth objects.
MaxColumnWidth		Maximum of two TableColumnWidth objects.

Listing 7-13 shows an example of a table with different column width.

Listing 7-13. Table with different column width

```
Table(
  border: TableBorder.all(color: Colors.blue.shade200),
  columnWidths: {
    0: FixedColumnWidth(100),
    1: FlexColumnWidth(1),
    2: FlexColumnWidth(2),
    3: FractionColumnWidth(0.2),
  },
  children: [
    TableRow(children: [Text('A'), Text('B'), Text('C'),
    Text('D')]),
```

```
      TableRow(children: [Text('E'), Text('F'), Text('G'),
      Text('H')]),
      TableRow(children: [Text('I'), Text('J'), Text('K'),
      Text('L')]),
    ],
);
```

The vertical alignment of cells is configured with values of
TableCellVerticalAlignment enum. TableCellVerticalAlignment
enum has values top, middle, bottom, baseline, and fill. The
defaultVerticalAlignment parameter of Table constructor specifies the
default TableCellVerticalAlignment value. If you want to customize vertical
alignment of a single cell, you can wrap the cell widget inside of TableCell
widget and specify the verticalAlignment parameter. Listing 7-14 shows an
example of specifying vertical alignment for cells.

Listing 7-14. Vertical alignment of table cells

```
class VerticalAlignmentTable extends StatelessWidget {
  @override
  Widget build(BuildContext context) {
    return Table(
      border: TableBorder.all(color: Colors.green.shade200),
      defaultVerticalAlignment: TableCellVerticalAlignment.
      bottom,
      children: [
        TableRow(children: [
          TextCell('A'),
          TableCell(
            verticalAlignment: TableCellVerticalAlignment.
            middle,
            child: Text('B'),
          ),
```

```
          Text('C'),
          Text('D'),
        ]),
        TableRow(children: [Text('E'), Text('F'), Text('G'),
        Text('H')]),
        TableRow(children: [Text('I'), Text('J'), Text('K'),
        Text('L')]),
      ],
    );
  }
}

class TextCell extends StatelessWidget {
  TextCell(this.text, {this.height = 50});

  final String text;
  final double height;

  @override
  Widget build(BuildContext context) {
    return ConstrainedBox(
      constraints: BoxConstraints(
        minHeight: height,
      ),
      child: Text(text),
    );
  }
}
```

Figure 7-3 shows the screenshot of different tables.

A	B	C	D
E	F	G	H
I	J	K	L

A	B	C		D
E	F	G		H
I	J	K		L

A				
	B			
		C		D
E	F	G		H
I	J	K		L

Figure 7-3. *Tables*

7-4. Scaffolding Material Design Pages

Problem

You want to scaffold Material Design pages.

Solution

Use Scaffold and other related widgets.

Discussion

Material Design apps have common layout structures. Scaffold widget puts together other common widgets to create the basic page structures. Table 7-6 shows the elements that can be included in a Scaffold widget. Widgets specified as drawer and endDrawer are initially hidden and can be revealed by swiping. The swiping direction depends on the text direction. The drawer widget uses the same direction as the text direction, while the endDrawer widget uses the opposite direction. For example, if the text direction is left-to-right, drawer widget is opened by swiping from left to right, and endDrawer widget is opened by swiping from right to left.

The second column in Table 7-6 only lists preferred widget types for these elements. Scaffold constructor actually accepts any type of widgets. For example, you can use ListView widget as the drawer. However, these preferred widgets are more suitable.

Table 7-6. *Scaffold elements*

Parameter	Widget	Description
appBar	AppBar	An app bar to display at the top.
floatingActionButton	FloatingActionButton	A button to float above the body in the bottom right corner.
drawer	Drawer	A hidden panel to display to the side of the body.
endDrawer	Drawer	A hidden panel to display to the side of the body.
bottomNavigationBar	BottomAppBar BottomNavigationBar	Navigation bar to display at the bottom.
bottomSheet	BottomSheet	Persistent bottom sheet.
persistentFooterButtons	List<Widget>	A set of buttons to display at the bottom.
body	Widget	Primary content.

App Bar

AppBar widget displays basic information of the current screen. It consists of a toolbar and other widgets. Table 7-7 shows the elements of an AppBar widget. These elements are also named parameters of AppBar constructor.

Table 7-7. *Parameters of AppBar*

Name	Description
title	Primary widget in the toolbar.
leading	Widget to display before the title.
actions	List of widgets to display after the title.
bottom	Widget to display at the bottom.
flexibleSpace	Widget to stack behind the toolbar and the bottom.

If the leading widget is null and automaticallyImplyLeading parameter is true, the actual leading widget is deduced from the state. If the Scaffold has a drawer, the leading widget is a button to open the drawer. If the nearest Navigator has previous routes, the leading widget is a BackButton to go back to previous route.

Widgets in the list of actions are usually IconButtons. If there is no enough space for these IconButtons, you can use a PopupMenuButton as the last action and put other actions in the popup menu. TabBar widget is usually used as the bottom widget. Listing 7-15 shows an example of using AppBar.

Listing 7-15. Example of AppBar

```
AppBar(
  title: Text('Scaffold'),
  actions: <Widget>[
    IconButton(
      icon: Icon(Icons.search),
      onPressed: () {},
    ),
  ],
);
```

Floating Action Button

FloatingActionButton widget is a special kind of buttons to provide quick access to primary action. A floating action button is a circular icon that usually displays at the bottom right corner of the screen. In the Gmail app, the email list screen has a floating action button to compose new emails.

There are two types of FloatingActionButtons. When using FloatingActionButton() constructor, you only need to provide the child widget and onPressed callback. When using FloatingActionButton. extend() constructor, you need to provide icon and label widgets and onPressed callback. For both constructors, foregroundColor and backgroundColor parameters can customize the colors. Listing 7-16 shows an example of using FloatingActionButton.

Listing 7-16. Example of FloatingActionButton

```
FloatingActionButton(
  child: Icon(Icons.create),
  onPressed: () {},
);
```

Drawer

Drawer widget is a convenient wrapper for the panel that displays at the edge of a Scaffold widget when sliding. Although you can use Drawer to wrap any widget, it's common to show app logo, information of current user, and links to app pages in the drawer. ListView widget is usually used as the child of Drawer widget to enable scrolling in the drawer.

To show app logo and information of current user, you can use the provided DrawerHeader widget and its subclass UserAccountsDrawerHeader. DrawerHeader widget wraps a child widget and has a predefined style. UserAccountsDrawerHeader is a specific widget to show user details. Table 7-8 shows sections that can be added in a UserAccountsDrawerHeader widget. You can also use onDetailsPressed parameter to add a callback when the area with account name and email is tapped.

Table 7-8. *Sections in UserAccountsDrawerHeader*

Name	Description
currentAccountPicture	Picture of the current user's account.
otherAccountsPictures	List of pictures of the current user's other accounts. You can only have up to three of these pictures.
accountName	Name of the current user's account.
accountEmail	Email of the current user's account.

Listing 7-17 shows an example of using Drawer with UserAccountsDrawerHeader.

Listing 7-17. Example of Drawer

```
Drawer(
  child: ListView(
    children: <Widget>[
      UserAccountsDrawerHeader(
        currentAccountPicture: CircleAvatar(
          child: Text('JD'),
        ),
        accountName: Text('John Doe'),
        accountEmail: Text('john.doe@example.com'),
      ),
      ListTile(
        leading: Icon(Icons.search),
        title: Text('Search'),
```

```
      ),
      ListTile(
        leading: Icon(Icons.history),
        title: Text('History'),
      ),
    ],
  ),
);
```

Bottom App Bar

BottomAppBar widget is a simplified version of AppBar that displays at the bottom of a Scaffold. It's common to only add icon buttons in the bottom app bar. If the scaffold also has a floating action button, the bottom app bar also creates the notch for the button to dock. Listing 7-18 shows an example of using BottomAppBar.

Listing 7-18. Example of BottomAppBar

```
BottomAppBar(
  child: Text('Bottom'),
  color: Colors.red,
);
```

Bottom Navigation Bar

BottomNavigationBar widget provides extra links to navigate between different views. Table 7-9 shows the parameters of BottomNavigationBar constructor.

Table 7-9. *Parameters of BottomNavigationBar*

Name	Type	Description
items	List < BottomNavigationBarItem>	List of items.
currentIndex	int	Index of the selected item.
onTap	ValueChanged<int>	Callback when selected item changed.
type	BottomNavigationBarType	Type of the navigation bar.
fixedColor	Color	Color of selected item when type if BottomNavigationBarType.fixed.
iconSize	double	Size of icons.

When an item is tapped, the onTap callback is invoked with index of the tapped item. Depending on the number of items, there can be different ways to show these items. The layout of items is defined by values of BottomNavigationBarType enum. If the value is fixed, these items have fixed width and always display text labels. If the value is shifting, location of items may change according to the selected item and only text label of selected item is displayed. BottomNavigationBar has a default strategy to select the type. When there are less than four items, BottomNavigationBarType.fixed is used; otherwise, BottomNavigationBarType.shifting is used. You can use the type parameter to override the default behavior.

Table 7-10 shows parameters of BottomNavigationBarItem constructor. Both icon and title parameters are required. If the type of BottomNavigationBar is BottomNavigationBarType.shifting, then the background of navigation bar is determined by the background color of selected item. You should specify the backgroundColor parameter to differentiate items.

Table 7-10. *Parameters of BottomNavigationBarItem*

Name	Type	Description
icon	Widget	Item's icon.
title	Widget	Item's title.
activeIcon	Widget	Icon to display when the item is selected.
backgroundColor	Color	Item's background color.

Listing 7-19 shows an example of using BottomNavigationBar and BottomNavigationBarItem.

Listing 7-19. Example of BottomNavigationBar

```
BottomNavigationBar(
  currentIndex: 1,
  type: BottomNavigationBarType.shifting,
  items: [
    BottomNavigationBarItem(
      icon: Icon(Icons.cake),
      title: Text('Cake'),
      backgroundColor: Colors.red.shade100,
    ),
    BottomNavigationBarItem(
      icon: Icon(Icons.map),
      title: Text('Map'),
      backgroundColor: Colors.green.shade100,
    ),
    BottomNavigationBarItem(
      icon: Icon(Icons.alarm),
      title: Text('Alarm'),
```

```
      backgroundColor: Colors.blue.shade100,
    ),
  ],
);
```

Bottom Sheet

BottomSheet widget displays at the bottom of the app to provide additional information. The system sharing sheet is a typical example of bottom sheet. There are two types of bottom sheets:

- Persistent bottom sheets are always visible. Persistent bottom sheets can be created using ScaffoldState. showBottomSheet function and bottomSheet parameter of Scaffold constructor.

- Modal bottom sheets behave like modal dialogs. Modal bottom sheets can be created using showModalBottomSheet function.

BottomSheet constructor uses a WidgetBuilder function to create the actual content. You also need to provide an onClosing callback that's invoked when the bottom sheet begins to close. Listing 7-20 shows an example of using BottomSheet.

Listing 7-20. Example of BottomSheet

```
BottomSheet(
  onClosing: () {},
  builder: (context) {
    return Text('Bottom');
  },
);
```

Scaffold State

Scaffold is a stateful widget. You can use Scaffold.of() method to get the ScaffoldState object of nearest Scaffold widget from the build context. ScaffoldState has different methods to interact with other components; see Table 7-11.

Table 7-11. *Methods of ScaffoldState*

Name	Description
openDrawer()	Open the drawer.
openEndDrawer()	Open the drawer on the end side.
showSnackBar(SnackBar snackbar)	Show the SnackBar.
hideCurrentSnackBar()	Hide the current SnackBar.
removeCurrentSnackBar()	Remove the current SnackBar.
showBottomSheet()	Show a persistent bottom sheet.

SnackBar

SnackBar widget shows a message with an optional action at the bottom of the screen. To create a SnackBar widget, the constructor requires the content parameter to specify the content. The duration parameter controls how long the snack bar is displayed. To add an action to the snack bar, you can use action parameter of type SnackBarAction. When an action is provided, the snack bar is dismissed when the action is pressed.

To create a SnackBarAction instance, you need to provide the label and onPressed callback. You can customize the button label color using textColor parameter. The button of a snack bar action can only be pressed once.

The showSnackBar() method of ScaffoldState shows a SnackBar widget. There can be at most one snack bar displayed at a time. If ScaffoldState() method is invoked when another snack bar is still visible, the given snack bar is added to a queue and will be displayed after other snack bars are dismissed. The return type of showSnackBar() method is ScaffoldFeatureController<SnackBar, SnackBarClosedReason>. SnackBarClosedReason is an enum that defines the reasons a snack bar may be closed.

Listing 7-21 shows an example of opening snack bar.

Listing 7-21. Example of SnackBar

```
Scaffold.of(context).showSnackBar(SnackBar(
  content: Text('This is a message.'),
  action: SnackBarAction(label: 'OK', onPressed: () {}),
));
```

7-5. Scaffolding iOS Pages
Problem

You want to scaffold iOS pages.

Solution

Use CupertinoPageScaffold.

Discussion

For iOS apps, you can use CupertinoPageScaffold widget to create the basic layout of pages. Comparing to Scaffold in Material Design, customizations provided by CupertinoPageScaffold are limited. You can only specify navigation bar, child, and background color.

CupertinoNavigationBar widget is similar with AppBar in Material Design, but CupertinoNavigationBar can only have leading, middle, and trailing widgets. The middle widget is centered between leading and trailing widgets. The leading widget can be automatically implied based on the navigation state when automaticallyImplyLeading parameter is true. The middle widget can also be automatically implied when automaticallyImplyMiddle parameter is true.

Listing 7-22 shows an example of using CupertinoPageScaffold and CupertinoNavigationBar.

Listing 7-22. Example of CupertinoPageScaffold

```
CupertinoPageScaffold(
  navigationBar: CupertinoNavigationBar(
    middle: Text('App'),
    trailing: CupertinoButton(
      child: Icon(CupertinoIcons.search),
      onPressed: () {},
    ),
  ),
  child: Container(),
);
```

7-6. Creating Tab Layout in Material Design
Problem

You want to create tab bars and tabs.

Solution

Use TabBar, Tab, and TabController.

Discussion

Tab layout is widely used in mobile apps to organize multiple sections in one page. To implement tab layout in Material Design, you need to work with several widgets. TabBar widget is the container of Tab widgets. TabController widget is responsible for coordinating TabBar and TabView.

A Tab widget must have at least some text, an icon, or a child widget, but it cannot have both text and child widget. To create a TabBar, you need to provide a list of tabs. You can choose to use an explicitly created TabController instance or use the shared DefaultTabController instance. DefaultTabController is an inherited widget. TabBar will try to look up an ancestor DefaultTabController instance if no TabController is provided.

You can choose to provide a TabController instance or use the inherited DefaultTabController. To create a TabController, you need to provide the number of tabs and a TickerProvider instance.

In Listing 7-23, the mixin SingleTickerProviderStateMixin of _TabPageState is an implementation of TickerProvider, so the current instance of _TabPageState is passed as the vsync parameter of TabController constructor. The TabController instance is shared by TabBar and TabBarView.

Listing 7-23. TabBar with provided TabController

```
class TabPage extends StatefulWidget {
  @override
  _TabPageState createState() => _TabPageState();
}

class _TabPageState extends State<TabPage> with
SingleTickerProviderStateMixin {
  final List<Tab> _tabs = [
    Tab(text: 'List', icon: Icon(Icons.list)),
    Tab(text: 'Map', icon: Icon(Icons.map)),
```

```
];
TabController _tabController;

@override
void initState() {
  super.initState();
  _tabController = TabController(length: _tabs.length, vsync:
  this);
}

@override
void dispose() {
  _tabController.dispose();
  super.dispose();
}

@override
Widget build(BuildContext context) {
  return Scaffold(
    appBar: AppBar(
      title: Text('Tab'),
      bottom: TabBar(
        tabs: _tabs,
        controller: _tabController,
      ),
    ),
    body: TabBarView(
      children: _tabs.map((tab) {
        return Center(
          child: Text(tab.text),
        );
      }).toList(),
      controller: _tabController,
```

```
      ),
    );
  }
}
```

If you don't need to interact with TabController, using DefaultTabController is a better choice. Code in Listing 7-24 uses DefaultTabController to implement the same functionality as code in Listing 7-23.

Listing 7-24. DefaultTabController

```
class DefaultTabControllerPage extends StatelessWidget {
  final List<Tab> _tabs = [
    Tab(text: 'List', icon: Icon(Icons.list)),
    Tab(text: 'Map', icon: Icon(Icons.map))
  ];

  @override
  Widget build(BuildContext context) {
    return DefaultTabController(
      length: _tabs.length,
      child: Scaffold(
        appBar: AppBar(
          bottom: TabBar(tabs: _tabs),
        ),
        body: TabBarView(
          children: _tabs.map((tab) {
            return Center(
              child: Text(tab.text),
            );
          }).toList(),
        ),
```

```
      ),
   );
 }
}
```

7-7. Implementing Tab Layout in iOS

Problem

You want to implement tab layout in iOS apps.

Solution

Use CupertinoTabScaffold, CupertinoTabBar, and CupertinoTabView.

Discussion

Tab layout can also be implemented for iOS apps with widgets
CupertinoTabScaffold, CupertinoTabBar, and CupertinoTabView. When
creating CupertinoTabScaffold, you should use CupertinoTabBar as the
value of tabBar parameter. Tabs in CupertinoTabBar are represented as
BottomNavigationBarItem widgets. The tabBuilder parameter specifies
the builder function to build the view for each tab. Listing 7-25 shows an
example of implementing tab layout.

Listing 7-25. Tab layout for iOS style

```
class CupertinoTabPage extends StatelessWidget {
  @override
  Widget build(BuildContext context) {
    return CupertinoTabScaffold(
      tabBar: CupertinoTabBar(items: [
```

```
    BottomNavigationBarItem(icon: Icon(CupertinoIcons.
    settings)),
    BottomNavigationBarItem(icon: Icon(CupertinoIcons.
    info)),
  ]),
  tabBuilder: (context, index) {
    return CupertinoTabView(
      builder: (context) {
        return Center(
          child: Text('Tab $index'),
        );
      },
    );
  },
);
}
}
```

7-8. Summary

This chapter discusses common widgets in Flutter, including list view, grid view, table layout, page scaffolding, and tab layout. These widgets create the basic structure of pages in Flutter. In the next chapter, we'll discuss page navigation in Flutter apps.

CHAPTER 8

Page Navigation

Flutter apps may have multiple screens or pages. Pages are groups of functionalities. The user navigates between different pages to use different functionalities. Concepts like pages are called routes in Flutter. Routes not only include full-screen pages but also modal dialogs and popups. Routes are managed by Navigator widget. This chapter discusses recipes related to page navigation in Flutter.

8-1. Implementing Basic Page Navigation
Problem

You want to have basic page navigation support.

Solution

Use Navigator.push() to navigate to a new route and Navigator.pop() to navigate to the previous route.

Discussion

Routes are managed by Navigator widget. The navigator manages a stack of routes. Routes can be pushed on the stack using push() method and popped off the stack using pop() method. The top element in the stack is the currently active route. Navigator is a stateful widget with

© Fu Cheng 2019
F. Cheng, *Flutter Recipes*, https://doi.org/10.1007/978-1-4842-4982-6_8

NavigatorState as its state. To interact with the navigator, you can use the static methods of Navigator or get an instance of NavigatorState. By using Navigator.of() method, you can get the nearest enclosing NavigatorState instance of the given build context. You can explicitly create Navigator widgets, but most of the time you'll use the Navigator widget created by WidgetsApp, MaterialApp, or CupertinoApp widget.

Routes are represented using implementations of abstract Route class. For example, PageRoute represents full-screen modal route, and PopupRoute represents modal routes that overlay a widget over the current route. Both PageRoute and PopupRoute classes are subclasses of ModalRoute class. For Material Design apps, the easiest way to create a full-screen page is using MaterialPageRoute class. MaterialPageRoute uses a WidgetBuilder function to build the content of the route.

In Listing 8-1, Navigator.of(context) gets the NavigatorState instance to work with. The new route pushed to the navigator is a MaterialPageRoute instance. The new route has a button that uses NavigatorState.pop() method to pop the current route off the navigator. In fact, when using Scaffold widget, a back button is added automatically in the app bar, so there is no need to use an explicit back button.

Listing 8-1. Page navigation using Navigator

```
class SimpleNavigationPage extends StatelessWidget {
  @override
  Widget build(BuildContext context) {
    return Scaffold(
      appBar: AppBar(
        title: Text('Simple Navigation'),
      ),
      body: Center(
        child: RaisedButton(
          child: Text('Show page'),
```

```
      onPressed: () {
        Navigator.of(context).
        push(MaterialPageRoute(builder: (context) {
          return Scaffold(
            appBar: AppBar(
              title: Text('New Page'),
            ),
            body: Center(
              child: Column(
                crossAxisAlignment: CrossAxisAlignment.
                center,
                children: <Widget>[
                  Text('A new page'),
                  RaisedButton(
                    child: Text('Go back'),
                    onPressed: () {
                      Navigator.of(context).pop();
                    },
                  ),
                ],
              ),
            ),
          );
        }));
      },
    ),
  ),
);
  }
}
```

Navigator class has static methods like push() and pop() which do the same thing as the same method in NavigatorState class, but these static methods require an extra BuildContext parameter. Navigator.push(context) is actually the same as Navigator.of(context).push(). You can choose to use either method.

8-2. Using Named Routes
Problem

You want to navigate to the same route from different places.

Solution

Use named routes with Navigator.pushNamed() method.

Discussion

When using Navigator.push() method to push new routes to the navigator, new routes are built on demand using builder functions. This approach doesn't work well when routes can be navigated from different places, because we don't want to duplicate the code of building the routes. In this case, using named routes is a better choice. A named route has a unique name. Navigator.pushNamed() method uses the name to specify the route to push to the navigator.

Named routes need to be registered before they can be navigated to. The easiest way to register named routes is using the routes parameter of WidgetsApp, MaterialApp, or CupertinoApp constructor. The routes parameter is a Map<String, WidgetBuilder> object with keys as the route names. Route names are usually in path-like format starting with "/". This is similar to how web apps organize the pages. For example, you can have route names like /log_in, /orders, and /orders/1234.

In Listing 8-2, pressing the "Sign Up" button pushes the named route /
sign_up to the navigator.

Listing 8-2. Use named route

```
class LogInPage extends StatelessWidget {
  @override
  Widget build(BuildContext context) {
    return Scaffold(
      appBar: AppBar(
        title: Text('Log In'),
      ),
      body: Center(
        child: RaisedButton(
          child: Text('Sign Up'),
          onPressed: () {
            Navigator.pushNamed(context, '/sign_up');
          },
        ),
      ),
    );
  }
}
```

In Listing 8-3, two named routes are registered in routes parameter.

Listing 8-3. Register named routes

```
class PageNavigationApp extends StatelessWidget {
  @override
  Widget build(BuildContext context) {
    return MaterialApp(
      title: 'Page Navigation',
```

```
    home: IndexPage(),
    routes: {
      '/sign_up': (context) => SignUpPage(),
      '/log_in': (context) => LogInPage(),
    },
  );
 }
}
```

8-3. Passing Data Between Routes

Problem

You want to pass data between different routes.

Solution

Pass data to routes using constructor parameters or RouteSettings objects
and pass data from routes using result parameter of Navigator.pop()
method.

Discussion

A route may require additional data when building its content. A route
may also return some data when popped off. For example, a route to edit
user details may need the current details as the input and return updated
details as the output. Depending on how routes are navigated to, there are
different ways to pass data between routes.

When using Navigator.push() method to push new routes, the easiest
way is to pass the data as constructor parameters of the widget returned
by WidgetBuilder function. When using Navigator.pop() method, you

can use the optional `result` parameter to pass return value to the previous route. The return value of `Navigator.push()` method is a `Future<T>` object. This `Future` object will be resolved when the newly pushed route is popped off. The resolved value is the return value passed when invoking `Navigator.pop()` method. If the route is popped off using the back button, then the resolved value is `null`.

In Listing 8-4, `UserDetails` class contains first name and last name of a user. `UserDetailsPage` displays the user's details. When the edit button is pressed, a new route is pushed to the navigator. Content of the new route is an `EditUserDetailsPage` widget with the `UserDetails` object as the constructor parameter. The return value of the new route is also a `UserDetails` object, which is used to update the state of `UserDetailsPage`.

Listing 8-4. User details page

```
class UserDetails {
  UserDetails(this.firstName, this.lastName);

  final String firstName;
  final String lastName;
}

class UserDetailsPage extends StatefulWidget {
  @override
  _UserDetailsPageState createState() =>
  _UserDetailsPageState();
}

class _UserDetailsPageState extends State<UserDetailsPage> {
  UserDetails _userDetails = UserDetails('John', 'Doe');

  @override
  Widget build(BuildContext context) {
    return Scaffold(
```

```
  appBar: AppBar(
    title: Text('User Details'),
  ),
  body: Column(
    children: <Widget>[
      Text('First name: ${_userDetails.firstName}'),
      Text('Last name: ${_userDetails.lastName}'),
      RaisedButton.icon(
        label: Text('Edit (route builder)'),
        icon: Icon(Icons.edit),
        onPressed: () async {
          UserDetails result = await Navigator.push(
            context,
            MaterialPageRoute<UserDetails>(
              builder: (BuildContext context) {
                return EditUserDetailsPage(_userDetails);
              },
            ),
          );
          if (result != null) {
            setState(() {
              _userDetails = result;
            });
          }
        },
      ),
    ],
  ),
);
  }
}
```

In Listing 8-5, EditUserDetailsPage uses two TextFormField widgets to edit user details. When the save button is pressed, the updated UserDetails object is returned using Navigator.pop() method.

Listing 8-5. Edit user details page

```
class EditUserDetailsPage extends StatefulWidget {
  EditUserDetailsPage(this.userDetails);
  final UserDetails userDetails;

  @override
  _EditUserDetailsPageState createState() =>
      _EditUserDetailsPageState(userDetails);
}

class _EditUserDetailsPageState extends
State<EditUserDetailsPage> {
  _EditUserDetailsPageState(this._userDetails);

  UserDetails _userDetails;
  final GlobalKey<FormFieldState<String>> _firstNameKey =
  GlobalKey();
  final GlobalKey<FormFieldState<String>> _lastNameKey =
  GlobalKey();

  @override
  Widget build(BuildContext context) {
    return Scaffold(
      appBar: AppBar(
        title: Text('Edit User Details'),
      ),
      body: Column(
        children: <Widget>[
          TextFormField(
```

```
        key: _firstNameKey,
        decoration: InputDecoration(
          labelText: 'First name',
        ),
        initialValue: _userDetails.firstName,
      ),
      TextFormField(
        key: _lastNameKey,
        decoration: InputDecoration(
          labelText: 'Last name',
        ),
        initialValue: _userDetails.lastName,
      ),
      RaisedButton(
        child: Text('Save'),
        onPressed: () {
          Navigator.pop(
              context,
              UserDetails(_firstNameKey.currentState?.
              value,
                _lastNameKey.currentState?.value));
        },
      )
    ],
  ),
  );
  }
}
```

If named routes are used, data can be passed to the route using the
arguments parameter of Navigator.pushNamed() method. In Listing 8-6,
pushNamed() method is used to navigate to the /edit_user route with
current UserDetails object.

Listing 8-6. Pass data to named route

```
UserDetails result = await Navigator.pushNamed(
  context,
  '/edit_user',
  arguments: _userDetails,
);
```

The named route /edit_user is registered in MaterialApp. The route parameters cannot be used, because you cannot access the data passed to the route in the builder function. The onGenerateRoute parameter of WidgetsApp, MaterialApp, or CupertinoApp should be used instead. The type of onGenerateRoute parameter is RouteFactory, which is a typedef of function type Route (RouteSettings settings). RouteSettings class contains data that may be required when creating the Route object. Table 8-1 shows properties of RouteSettings class.

Table 8-1. *Properties of RouteSettings*

Name	Type	Description
name	String	Name of the route.
arguments	Object	Data passed to the route.
isInitialRoute	bool	Whether this route is the first route pushed to the navigator.

When implementing the onGenerateRoute function, you need to return routes based on the provided RouteSettings object. In Listing 8-7, the name property is checked first, then a MaterialPageRoute is returned with EditUserDetailsPage as the content. The arguments property of RouteSettings is used in EditUserDetailsPage constructor. The value of arguments property is the UserDetails object passed in Listing 8-6.

Listing 8-7. Use onGenerateRoute

```
MaterialApp(
  onGenerateRoute: (RouteSettings settings) {
    if (settings.name == '/edit_user') {
      return MaterialPageRoute<UserDetails>(
        settings: settings,
        builder: (context) {
          return EditUserDetailsPage(settings.arguments);
        },
      );
    }
  },
);
```

8-4. Implementing Dynamic Route Matching

Problem

You want to use complicated logic to match route names.

Solution

Use onGenerateRoute parameter.

Discussion

When named routes are registered using the routes parameter of WidgetsApp, only the whole route name can be used to match the Route objects. If you want to use complicated logic to match Route objects with route names, you can use onGenerateRoute parameter and RouteSettings object. For example, you can match all route names start with /order to a single Route object.

In Listing 8-8, all route names starting with /order will navigate to a route using OrderPage.

Listing 8-8. Route matching

```
MaterialApp(
  onGenerateRoute: (RouteSettings settings) {
    if (settings.name.startsWith('/order')) {
      return MaterialPageRoute(
        settings: settings,
        builder: (context) {
          return OrderPage();
        },
      );
    }
  },
);
```

8-5. Handling Unknown Routes

Problem

You want to handle the case of navigating to an unknown route.

Solution

Use onUnknownRoute parameter of Navigator, WidgetsApp, MaterialApp, and CupertinoApp.

Discussion

It's possible that the navigator may be asked to navigate to an unknown route. This can be caused by programming errors in the app or external requests for route navigation. If onGenerateRoute function returns null for the given RouteSettings object, the onUnknownRoute function is invoked to provide a fallback route. This onUnknownRoute function is usually used for error handling, just like 404 pages in web apps. The type of onUnknownRoute is also RouteFactory.

In Listing 8-9, onUnknownRoute function returns the route that shows the NotFoundPage widget.

Listing 8-9. Use onUnknownRoute

```
MaterialApp(
  onUnknownRoute: (RouteSettings settings) {
    return MaterialPageRoute(
      settings: settings,
      builder: (BuildContext context) {
        return NotFoundPage(settings.name);
      },
    );
  },
);
```

8-6. Displaying Material Design Dialogs
Problem

You want to show Material Design dialogs.

Solution

Use showDialog() function and Dialog, SimpleDialog, and AlertDialog widgets.

Discussion

To use Material Design dialogs, you need to create dialog widgets and show them. Dialog class and its subclasses SimpleDialog and AlertDialog can be used to create dialogs.

SimpleDialog widget presents several options to the user. Options are represented using SimpleDialogOption class. A SimpleDialogOption widget can have a child widget and an onPressed callback. When creating SimpleDialog, you can provide a list of children and an optional title. AlertDialog widget presents content and a list of actions to the user. AlertDialog is used to acknowledge user or ask for confirmation.

To show dialogs, you should use showDialog() function. Invoking this function pushes dialog route to the navigator. Dialogs are closed using Navigator.pop() method. The showDialog() function uses a WidgetBuilder function to build the dialog content. The return value of showDialog() function is a Future<T> object which is actually the return value of Navigator.push() method.

In Listing 8-10, pressing the button shows a simple dialog with two options.

Listing 8-10. Show simple dialogs

```
RaisedButton(
  child: Text('Show SimpleDialog'),
  onPressed: () async {
    String result = await showDialog<String>(
        context: context,
```

```
      builder: (BuildContext context) {
        return SimpleDialog(
          title: Text('Choose Color'),
          children: <Widget>[
            SimpleDialogOption(
              child: Text('Red'),
              onPressed: () {
                Navigator.pop(context, 'Red');
              },
            ),
            SimpleDialogOption(
              child: Text('Green'),
              onPressed: () {
                Navigator.pop(context, 'Green');
              },
            ),
          ],
        );
      });
    print(result);
  },
);
```

Figure 8-1 shows the screenshot of code in Listing 8-10.

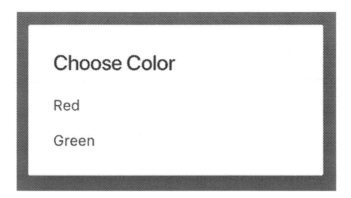

Figure 8-1. *Material Design simple dialog*

In Listing 8-11, pressing the button shows an alert dialog with two actions.

Listing 8-11. Show alert dialog

```
RaisedButton(
  child: Text('Show AlertDialog'),
  onPressed: () async {
    bool result = await showDialog<bool>(
      context: context,
      builder: (BuildContext context) {
        return AlertDialog(
          title: Text('Delete'),
          content: Text('Delete this item?'),
          actions: <Widget>[
            FlatButton(
              child: Text('Yes'),
              onPressed: () {
                Navigator.pop(context, true);
              },
            ),
```

```
            FlatButton(
              child: Text('No'),
              onPressed: () {
                Navigator.pop(context, false);
              },
            ),
          ],
        );
      },
    );
    print(result);
  },
);
```

Figure 8-2 shows the screenshot of code in Listing 8-11.

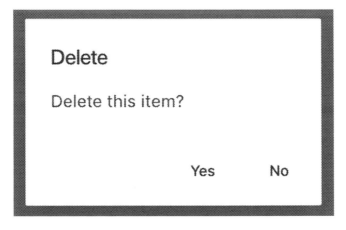

Figure 8-2. *Material Design alert dialog*

8-7. Displaying iOS Dialogs

Problem

You want to display iOS dialogs.

Solution

Use showCupertinoDialog() function and CupertinoAlertDialog and
CupertinoPopupSurface widgets.

Discussion

For iOS apps, you can use showCupertinoDialog() function and widgets
like CupertinoAlertDialog and CupertinoPopupSurface to show dialogs.
The showCupertinoDialog() function is similar with showDialog()
function for Material Design. This function also uses Navigator.push()
method to push dialog route to the navigator. CupertinoAlertDialog
is a built-in dialog implementation to acknowledge user or require for
confirmation. A CupertinoAlertDialog may have title, content, and a list
of actions. Actions are represented using CupertinoDialogAction widget.
Table 8-2 shows parameters of CupertinoDialogAction constructor.

Table 8-2. *Parameters of CupertinoDialogAction*

Name	Type	Description
child	Widget	Content of the action.
onPressed	VoidCallback	Action pressed callback.
isDefaultAction	bool	Whether this action is the default action.
isDestructiveAction	bool	Whether this action is destructive. Destructive actions have a different style.
textStyle	TextStyle	Text style applied to the action.

In Listing 8-12, pressing the button shows an iOS-style alert dialog.

Listing 8-12. Show iOS alert dialog

```
CupertinoButton(
  child: Text('Show Alert Dialog'),
  onPressed: () async {
    bool result = await showCupertinoDialog<bool>(
      context: context,
      builder: (BuildContext context) {
        return CupertinoAlertDialog(
          title: Text('Delete'),
          content: Text('Delete this item?'),
          actions: <Widget>[
            CupertinoDialogAction(
              child: Text('Delete'),
              onPressed: () {
                Navigator.pop(context, true);
              },
              isDestructiveAction: true,
            ),
            CupertinoDialogAction(
              child: Text('Cancel'),
              onPressed: () {
                Navigator.pop(context, false);
              },
            ),
          ],
        );
      },
    );
    print(result);
  },
);
```

Figure 8-3 shows the screenshot of code in Listing 8-12.

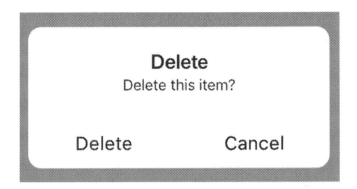

Figure 8-3. *iOS alert dialog*

If you want to create a custom dialog, you can use
CupertinoPopupSurface widget which creates rounded rectangle surface.

8-8. Displaying iOS Action Sheets
Problem

You want to present a set of actions for the user to choose in iOS apps.

Solution

Use showCupertinoModalPopup() function and CupertinoActionSheet
widget.

Discussion

If you want to present a set of actions for the user to choose in iOS
apps, you can use showCupertinoModalPopup() function to display
CupertinoActionSheet widgets. A CupertinoActionSheet can have a title,
a message, a cancel button, and a list of actions. Actions are represented

as CupertinoActionSheetAction widgets. CupertinoActionSheetAction
constructor has parameters child, onPressed, isDefaultAction,
and isDestructiveAction, which have the same meaning as in
CupertinoDialogAction constructor shown in Table 8-2.

In Listing 8-13, pressing the button shows an action sheet with three
actions and a cancel button.

Listing 8-13. Show iOS action sheet

```
CupertinoButton(
  child: Text('Show Action Sheet'),
  onPressed: () async {
    String result = await showCupertinoModalPopup<String>(
      context: context,
      builder: (BuildContext context) {
        return CupertinoActionSheet(
          title: Text('What to do'),
          message: Text('Please select an action'),
          actions: <Widget>[
            CupertinoActionSheetAction(
              child: Text('Duplicate'),
              isDefaultAction: true,
              onPressed: () {
                Navigator.pop(context, 'duplicate');
              },
            ),
            CupertinoActionSheetAction(
              child: Text('Move'),
              onPressed: () {
                Navigator.pop(context, 'move');
              },
            ),
```

```
          CupertinoActionSheetAction(
            isDestructiveAction: true,
            child: Text('Delete'),
            onPressed: () {
              Navigator.pop(context, 'delete');
            },
          ),
        ],
        cancelButton: CupertinoActionSheetAction(
          child: Text('Cancel'),
          onPressed: () {
            Navigator.pop(context);
          },
        ),
      );
    },
  );
  print(result);
  },
);
```

Figure 8-4 shows the screenshot of code in Listing 8-13.

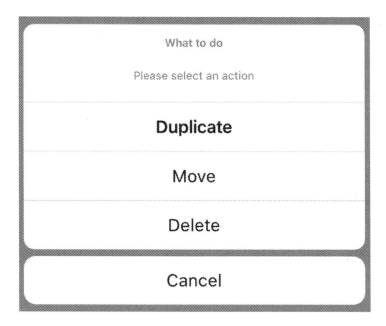

Figure 8-4. *iOS action sheet*

8-9. Showing Material Design Menus

Problem

You want to show menus in Material Design apps.

Solution

Use showMenu() function and implementations of PopupMenuEntry class.

Discussion

To use showMenu() function, you need to have a list of PopupMenuEntry objects. There are different types of PopupMenuEntry implementations:

- PopupMenuItem – Menu item for a single value

- CheckedPopupMenuItem – Menu item with a checkmark

- PopupMenuDivider – Horizontal divider between menu items

PopupMenuItem is a generic with the type of its value. Table 8-3 shows parameters of PopupMenuItem constructor. CheckedPopupMenuItem is a subclass of PopupMenuItem. CheckedPopupMenuItem has the checked property to specify whether to display a checkmark.

Table 8-3. *Parameters of PopupMenuItem constructor*

Name	Type	Description
child	Widget	Content of the menu item.
value	T	Value for the menu item.
enabled	bool	Whether this menu item can be selected.
height	double	Height of the menu item. Default to 48.

The showMenu() function returns a Future<T> object which resolves to the value of selected menu item. This function also uses Navigator. push() method to show the menu. Table 8-4 shows major parameters of showMenu() function. When initialValue is specified, the first item with a matching value is highlighted.

Table 8-4. *Parameters of showMenu()*

Name	Type	Description
items	List<PopupMenuEntry<T>>	A list of menu items.
initialValue	T	Initial value to highlight menu item.
position	RelativeRect	Position to show the menu.

The menu in Listing 8-14 contains a PopupMenuItem, a PopupMenuDivider, and a CheckedPopupMenuItem.

Listing 8-14. Show menu

```
RaisedButton(
  child: Text('Show Menu'),
  onPressed: () async {
    String result = await showMenu<String>(
      context: context,
      position: RelativeRect.fromLTRB(0, 0, 0, 0),
      items: [
        PopupMenuItem(
          value: 'red',
          child: Text('Red'),
        ),
        PopupMenuDivider(),
        CheckedPopupMenuItem(
          value: 'green',
          checked: true,
          child: Text('Green'),
        )
      ],
      initialValue: 'green',
    );
    print(result);
  },
);
```

The main difficulty of using showMenu() function is to provide proper value for the position parameter. If the menu is triggered by pressing a button, using PopupMenuButton is a better choice, because the menu position is calculated automatically based on the button's position.

Table 8-5 shows major parameters of PopupMenuButton constructor. PopupMenuItemBuilder function takes a BuildContext object as the argument and returns a List<PopupMenuEntry<T>> object.

Table 8-5. *Parameters of PopupMenuButton*

Name	Type	Description
itemBuilder	PopupMenu ItemBuilder<T>	Builder function to create menu items.
initialValue	T	Initial value.
onSelected	PopupMenu ItemSelected<T>	Callback when a menu item is selected.
onCanceled	PopupMenuCanceled	Callback when the menu is dismissed without selection.
tooltip	String	Tooltip of the button.
child	Widget	Content of the button.
icon	Icon	Icon of the button.

Listing 8-15 shows how to use PopupMenuButton to implement the same menu as in Listing 8-14.

Listing 8-15. Use PopupMenuButton

```
PopupMenuButton(
  itemBuilder: (BuildContext context) {
    return <PopupMenuEntry<String>>[
      PopupMenuItem(
        value: 'red',
        child: Text('Red'),
      ),
```

```
      PopupMenuDivider(),
      CheckedPopupMenuItem(
        value: 'green',
        checked: true,
        child: Text('Green'),
      )
    ];
  },
  initialValue: 'green',
  child: Text('Select color'),
  onSelected: (String value) {
    print(value);
  },
  onCanceled: () {
    print('no selections');
  },
);
```

Figure 8-5 shows the screenshot of the menu created in Listings 8-14 and 8-15.

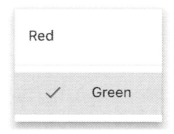

Figure 8-5. *Material Design menu*

8-10. Managing Complicated Page Flows Using Nested Navigators

Problem

You want to have complicated page flows.

Solution

Use nested Navigator instances.

Discussion

A Navigator instance manages its own stack of routes. For simple apps, one Navigator instance is generally enough, and you can simply use the Navigator instance created by WidgetsApp, MaterialApp, or CupertinoApp. If your app has complicated page flows, you may need to use nested navigators. Since Navigator itself is also a widget, Navigator instances can be created like normal widgets. The Navigator instance created by WidgetsApp, MaterialApp, or CupertinoApp becomes the root navigator. All navigators are organized in a hierarchy. To get the root navigator, you can set rootNavigator parameter to true when invoking Navigator.of() method. Table 8-6 shows parameters of Navigator constructor.

Table 8-6. *Parameters of Navigator*

Name	Type	Description
onGenerateRoute	RouteFactory	Generate a route for a given RouteSettings object.
onUnknownRoute	RouteFactory	Handle unknown routes.
initialRoute	String	Name of the first route.
observers	List<Navigator Observer>	Observers of state changes in the navigator.

Let's use a concrete example to explain how nested navigators can be used. Suppose that you are building a social news reading app, after a new user is signed up, you want to show the user an optional on-boarding page. This on-boarding page has several steps for the user to complete. The user can go back and forth to only complete interested steps. The user can also skip this page and return to app's home page. The on-boarding page has its own navigator to handle navigation of steps.

In Listing 8-16, the navigator has two named routes. The initial route is set to on_boarding/topic, so UserOnBoardingTopicPage is displayed first.

Listing 8-16. User on-boarding page

```
class UserOnBoardingPage extends StatelessWidget {
  @override
  Widget build(BuildContext context) {
    return Scaffold(
      appBar: AppBar(
        title: Text('Get Started'),
      ),
      body: Navigator(
        initialRoute: 'on_boarding/topic',
        onGenerateRoute: (RouteSettings settings) {
          WidgetBuilder builder;
          switch (settings.name) {
            case 'on_boarding/topic':
              builder = (BuildContext context) {
                return UserOnBoardingTopicPage();
              };
              break;
            case 'on_boarding/follower':
              builder = (BuildContext context) {
                return UserOnBoardingFollowPage();
              };
```

```
            break;
        }
        return MaterialPageRoute(
          builder: builder,
          settings: settings,
        );
      },
    ),
  );
  }
}
```

In Listing 8-17, pressing the "Next" button navigates to the next step with route name on_boarding/follower. Pressing the "Done" button uses the root navigator to pop off the on-boarding page.

Listing 8-17. Step to select topics

```
class UserOnBoardingTopicPage extends StatelessWidget {
  @override
  Widget build(BuildContext context) {
    return Column(
      children: <Widget>[
        Text('Select interested topics'),
        RaisedButton.icon(
          icon: Icon(Icons.arrow_forward),
          label: Text('Next'),
          onPressed: () {
            Navigator.pushNamed(context, 'on_boarding/
            follower');
          },
        ),
```

```
    RaisedButton.icon(
      icon: Icon(Icons.check),
      label: Text('Done'),
      onPressed: () {
        Navigator.of(context, rootNavigator: true).pop();
      },
    )
  ],
);
}
}
```

Figure 8-6 shows the screenshot of code in Listing 8-17.

Figure 8-6. *Step to select topics*

CupertinoTabView has its own navigator instance. When creating
CupertinoTabView, you can provide routes, onGenerateRoute,
onUnknownRoute, and navigatorObservers parameters. These
parameters are used to configure the Navigator instance. When using
CupertinoTabScaffold to create tab layout, each tab view has its own
navigation state and history.

When using nested navigators, it's important to make sure that the
correct navigator instance is used. If you want to show and close full-
screen pages or modal dialogs, you should use the root navigator obtained

by `Navigator.of(context, rootNavigator: true)`. Invoking `Navigator.of(context)` can only get the nearest enclosing `Navigator` instance. There is no way to get intermediate `Navigator` instances in the hierarchy. You need to use the `BuildContext` object at the correct location of the widgets tree. Functions like `showDialog()` and `showMenu()` always use `Navigator.of(context)` internally. You can only use the passed-in `BuildContext` object to control which `Navigator` instance is used by these functions.

8-11. Observing Navigator State Changes
Problem

You want to get notified when state of navigator is changed.

Solution

Use `NavigatorObserver`.

Discussion

Sometimes, you may want to get notified when the state of navigator is changed. For example, you want to analyze the page flows of users using the app to improve user experiences. When creating `Navigator` instances, you can provide a list of `NavigatorObserver` objects as the observers of navigator state changes. Table 8-7 shows methods of `NavigatorObserver` interface.

Table 8-7. *Methods of NavigatorObserver*

Name	Description
didPop(Route route, Route previousRoute)	The route is popped and previousRoute is the newly active route.
didPush(Route route, Route previousRoute)	The route is pushed and previousRoute is the previously active route.
didRemove(Route route, Route previousRoute)	The route is removed and previousRoute is the route immediately below the removed route.
didReplace(Route newRoute, Route oldRoute)	The oldRoute is replaced with newRoute.
didStartUserGesture(Route route, Route previousRoute)	User starts moving the route using gesture. The route immediately below route is previousRoute.
didStopUserGesture()	User stops moving route using gesture.

In Listing 8-18, LoggingNavigatorObserver class logs messages when routes are pushed and popped.

Listing 8-18. Logging navigator observer

```
class LoggingNavigatorObserver extends NavigatorObserver {
  @override
  void didPush(Route<dynamic> route, Route<dynamic>
  previousRoute) {
    print('push: ${_routeName(previousRoute)} ->
    ${_routeName(route)}');
  }
```

```
@override
void didPop(Route<dynamic> route, Route<dynamic>
previousRoute) {
  print(' pop: ${_routeName(route)} -> ${_
  routeName(previousRoute)}');
}

String _routeName(Route<dynamic> route) {
  return route != null
      ? (route.settings?.name ?? route.runtimeType.
      toString())
      : 'null';
}
}
```

NavigatorObserver interface is useful when you want to have a global handler for all state changes in a navigator. If you are only interested in state changes related to a particular route, then using RouteObserver class is a better choice. RouteObserver class is also an implementation of NavigatorObserver interface.

To get notified of state changes related to a Route object, your class needs to implement RouteAware interface. Table 8-8 shows methods of RouteAware interface.

Table 8-8. *Methods of RouteAware*

Name	Description
didPop()	Callback when the current route is popped off.
didPopNext()	Called when the current route becomes active after the top route is popped off.
didPush()	Called when the current route is pushed.
didPushNext()	Called when the current route is no longer active after a new route is pushed.

To actually get notified for a Route object, you need to use subscribe() method of RouteObserver to subscribe a RouteAware object to a Route object. When the subscription is no longer required, you should use unsubscribe() to unsubscribe the RouteAware object.

In Listing 8-19, _ObservedPageState class implements RouteAware interface and overrides didPush() and didPop() methods to print out some messages. ModalRoute.of(context) gets the nearest enclosing ModalRoute object from build context, which is the route that ObservedPage is in. By using ModalRoute.of(context), there is no need for explicitly passing Route objects. The current _ObservedPageState object subscribes to state changes in current route using the subscribe() method of the passed-in RouteObserver object. The subscription is removed when the _ObservedPageState object is disposed.

Listing 8-19. Use RouteObserver

```
class ObservedPage extends StatefulWidget {
  ObservedPage(this.routeObserver);
  final RouteObserver<PageRoute<dynamic>> routeObserver;

  @override
  _ObservedPageState createState() => _ObservedPageState(routeO
  bserver);
}

class _ObservedPageState extends State<ObservedPage> with
RouteAware {
  _ObservedPageState(this._routeObserver);
  final RouteObserver<PageRoute<dynamic>> _routeObserver;

  @override
  void didChangeDependencies() {
    super.didChangeDependencies();
```

```dart
    _routeObserver.subscribe(this, ModalRoute.of(context));
  }

  @override
  void dispose() {
    _routeObserver.unsubscribe(this);
    super.dispose();
  }

  @override
  void didPush() {
    print('pushed');
  }

  @override
  void didPop() {
    print('popped');
  }

  @override
  Widget build(BuildContext context) {
    return Scaffold(
      appBar: AppBar(
        title: Text('Observed (Stateful)'),
      ),
    );
  }
}
```

8-12. Stopping Routes from Popping

Problem

You want to stop routes from popping off the navigator.

Solution

Use `WillPopCallback` with `ModalRoute` objects.

Discussion

When a route is pushed to a navigator, the route can be popped off using the back button in the `Scaffold` or system's back button in Android. Sometimes you may want to stop the route from being popped off. For example, if there are unsaved changes in the page, you may want to show an alert dialog first to ask for confirmation. When `Navigator.maybePop()` method is used instead of `Navigator.pop()` method, you have a chance to decide whether the request to pop off a route should proceed.

ModalRoute class has `addScopedWillPopCallback()` method to add `WillPopCallback` that decides whether the route should be popped off. `WillPopCallback` is a typedef of function type `Future<bool> ()`. If the returned `Future<bool>` object resolves to `true`, then the route can be popped off. Otherwise, the route cannot be popped off. You can add multiple `WillPopCallback` functions to a ModalRoute object. If any of the `WillPopCallback` function vetoes the request, the route won't be popped off.

In Listing 8-20, a `WillPopCallback` function is added to the current route. The return value of `WillPopCallback` function is the `Future<bool>` object returned by `showDialog()`.

Listing 8-20. Veto route popping request

```
class VetoPopPage extends StatelessWidget {
  @override
  Widget build(BuildContext context) {
    ModalRoute.of(context).addScopedWillPopCallback(() {
      return showDialog<bool>(
        context: context,
        builder: (BuildContext context) {
          return AlertDialog(
            title: Text('Exit?'),
            actions: <Widget>[
              FlatButton(
                child: Text('Yes'),
                onPressed: () {
                  Navigator.pop(context, true);
                },
              ),
              FlatButton(
                child: Text('No'),
                onPressed: () {
                  Navigator.pop(context, false);
                },
              ),
            ],
          );
        },
      );
    });
    return Scaffold(
      appBar: AppBar(
```

```
        title: Text('Veto Pop'),
      ),
      body: Container(),
    );
  }
}
```

8-13. Summary

It's common to have multiple pages in Flutter apps. This chapter discusses basic concepts of implementing page navigation in Flutter. This chapter also covers dialogs, menus, and action sheets. In the next chapter, we'll discuss backend service interaction in Flutter.

CHAPTER 9

Service Interaction

Many non-trivial mobile apps require interaction with backend services. This chapter covers essential concepts related to service interactions in Flutter.

9-1. Working with Futures

Problem

You want to work with Future objects.

Solution

Use then() and catchError() methods to handle results of Future objects.

Discussion

When using code from Flutter and Dart libraries, you may encounter functions that return Future objects. Future<T> class from dart:async library is a representation of delayed computations. A Future object represents a potential value or error that will be available in the future. When given a Future object, you can register callbacks to handle the value or error once it is available. Future class is one of the basic building blocks of asynchronous programming in Dart.

© Fu Cheng 2019
F. Cheng, *Flutter Recipes*, https://doi.org/10.1007/978-1-4842-4982-6_9

Given a Future object, there are three different cases regarding its result:

- The computation never completes. No callbacks will be invoked.

- The computation completes with a value. Value callbacks are invoked with the value.

- The computation completes with an error. Error callbacks are invoked with the error.

To register callbacks to a Future object, you can use then() method to register a value callback and an optional error callback or use catchError() method to register an error callback only. It's recommended to use then() method to only register a value callback. This is because if an error callback is registered using onError parameter of then() method, this error callback cannot handle the error thrown in the value callback. Most of the time, you want the error callback to handle all possible errors. If an error of a Future object is not handled by its error callbacks, this error will be handled by the global handler.

In Listing 9-1, the Future object may complete with value 1 or an Error object. Both value and error callbacks are registered to handle the result.

Listing 9-1. Use then() and catchError() methods to handle result

```
Future.delayed(
  Duration(seconds: 1),
  () {
    if (Random().nextBool()) {
      return 1;
    } else {
      throw Error();
    }
  },
```

```
).then((value) {
  print(value);
}).catchError((error) {
  print('error: $error');
});
```

Return values of then() and catchError() methods are also Future objects. Given a Future object A, the result of invoking A.then(func) is another Future object B. If the func callback runs successfully, the Future B will complete with the return value of invoking func function. Otherwise, Future B will complete with the error thrown when invoking func function. Invoking B.catchError(errorHandler) returns a new Future object C. The error handler can handle errors thrown in Future B, which may be thrown in Future A itself or in its value handler. By using then() and catchError() methods, Future objects form a chain of handling asynchronous computations.

In Listing 9-2, multiple then() methods are chained together to process the result in sequence.

Listing 9-2. Chained then() methods

```
Future.value(1)
  .then((value) => value + 1)
  .then((value) => value * 10)
  .then((value) => value + 2)
  .then((value) => print(value));
```

If you want to call functions when a future completes, you can use whenComplete() method. Functions added using whenComplete() are called when this future completes, no matter it completes with a value or an error. The whenComplete() method is equivalent of a finally block in other programming languages. The chain of then().catchError(). whenComplete() is equivalent of "try-catch-finally".

Listing 9-3 shows an example of using whenComplete() method.

Listing 9-3. Using whenComplete()

```
Future.value(1).then((value) {
  print(value);
}).whenComplete(() {
  print('complete');
});
```

It's possible for the computation of Future object to take a long time to complete. You can use timeout() method to set the time limit on the computation. When invoking timeout() method, you need to provide a Duration object as the time limit and an optional onTimeout function to provide the value when a timeout happens. The return value of timeout() method is a new Future object. If the current Future object doesn't complete before the time limit, the result of calling onTimeout function is the result of the new Future object. If no onTimeout function is provided, the new Future object will complete with a TimeoutException when current future is timed out.

In Listing 9-4, the Future object will complete in 5 seconds with value 1, but the time limit is set to 2 seconds. The value 10 returned by onTimeout function will be used instead.

Listing 9-4. Use timeout() method

```
Future.delayed(Duration(seconds: 5), () => 1)
  .timeout(
    Duration(seconds: 2),
    onTimeout: () => 10,
  )
  .then((value) => print(value));
```

9-2. Using async and await to Work with Futures

Problem

You want to work with Future objects like they are synchronous.

Solution

Use async and await.

Discussion

Future objects represent asynchronous computations. The usual way to work with Future objects is registering callbacks to handle results. This callback-based style may create a barrier for developers that are used to synchronous operations. Using async and await is a syntax sugar in Dart to make working with Future objects like normal synchronous operations.

Given a Future object, await can wait for its completion and return its value. The code after the await can use the returned value directly, just like it is the result of a synchronous call. When await is used, its enclosing function must be marked as async. This means the function returns a Future object.

In Listing 9-5, the return value of getValue() function is a Future object. In calculate() function, await is used to get the return value of getValue() function and assign to value variable. Since await is used, calculate() function is marked as async.

Listing 9-5. Use async/await

```
Future<int> getValue() {
  return Future.value(1);
}
```

```
Future<int> calculate() async {
  int value = await getValue();
  return value * 10;
}
```

When await is used to handle Future objects, you can use try-catch-finally to handle errors thrown in Future objects. This allows Future objects to be used just like normal synchronous operations. Listing 9-6 shows an example of using try-catch-finally and await/async together.

Listing 9-6. Use try-catch-finally and await/async

```
Future<int> getErrorValue() {
  return Future.error('invalid value');
}

Future<int> calculateWithError() async {
  try {
    return await getErrorValue();
  } catch (e) {
    print(e);
    return 1;
  } finally {
    print('done');
  }
}
```

9-3. Creating Futures
Problem

You want to create Future objects.

Solution

Use Future constructors Future(), Future.delayed(), Future.sync(), Future.value(), and Future.error() to create Future objects.

Discussion

If you need to create Future objects, you can use its constructors, Future(), Future.delayed(), Future.sync(), Future.value(), and Future.error():

- Future() constructor creates a Future object that runs the computation asynchronously.

- Future.delayed() constructor creates a Future object that runs the computation after a delay specified using a Duration object.

- Future.sync() constructor creates a Future object that runs the computation immediately.

- Future.value() constructor creates a Future object that completes with the given value.

- Future.error() constructor creates a Future object that completes with the given error and optional stack trace.

Listing 9-7 shows examples of using different Future constructors.

Listing 9-7. Create Future objects

```
Future(() => 1).then(print);
Future.delayed(Duration(seconds: 3), () => 1).then(print);
Future.sync(() => 1).then(print);
Future.value(1).then(print);
Future.error(Error()).catchError(print);
```

9-4. Working with Streams

Problem

You want to work with a stream of events.

Solution

Use Stream<T> class and its subclasses.

Discussion

With Future class, we can represent a single value which may be available in the future. However, we may also need to work with a sequence of events. Stream<T> class in dart:async library represents a source of asynchronous events. To help with this, the Future class has asStream() method to create a Stream containing the result of the current Future object.

If you have experiences with Reactive Streams (www.reactive-streams.org/), you may find Stream in Dart is a similar concept. There can be three types of events in a stream:

- Data event represents actual data in the stream. These events are also called elements in the stream.

- Error event represents errors occurred.

- Done event represents that the end of stream has reached. No more events will be emitted.

To receive events from a stream, you can use the listen() method to set up listeners. The return value of listen() method is a StreamSubscription object representing the active subscription. Depending on the number of subscriptions allowed on the stream, there are two types of streams:

- A single-subscription stream allows only a single listener during the whole lifecycle of the stream. It only starts emitting events when a listener is set up, and it stops emitting events when the listener unsubscribes.

- A broadcast stream allows any number of listeners. Events are emitted when they are ready, even though there are no subscribed listener.

Given a Stream object, the property isBroadcast can be used to check whether it is a broadcast stream. You can use the asBroadcastStream() method to create a broadcast stream from a single-subscription stream.

Stream Subscription

Table 9-1 shows parameters of listen() method. You can provide any number of handlers for different events and ignore those uninterested events.

Table 9-1. *Parameters of listen() method*

Name	Type	Description
onData	void (T event)	Handler of data events.
onError	Function	Handler of error events.
onDone	void ()	Handler of done event.
cancelOnError	bool	Whether to cancel the subscription when the first error event is emitted.

In Listing 9-8, handlers for three types of events are provided.

Listing 9-8. Use listen() method

```
Stream.fromIterable([1, 2, 3]).listen(
  (value) => print(value),
  onError: (error) => print('error: $error'),
  onDone: () => print('done'),
  cancelOnError: true,
);
```

With the StreamSubscription object returned by listen() method, you can manage the subscription. Table 9-2 show methods of StreamSubscription class.

Table 9-2. *Methods of StreamSubscription*

Name	Description
cancel()	Cancels this subscription.
pause([Future resumeSignal])	Requests the stream to pause events emitting. If resumeSignal is provided, the stream will resume when the future completes.
resume()	Resumes the stream after a pause.
onData()	Replaces the data event handler.
onError()	Replaces the error event handler.
onDone()	Replaces the done event handler.
asFuture([E futureValue])	Returns a future that handles the completion of stream.

The asFuture() method is useful when you want to handle the completion of a stream. Since a stream can complete normally or with an error, using this method overwrites existing onDone and onError callbacks. In the case of an error event, the subscription is cancelled, and the returned Future object is completed with the error. In the case of a done event, the Future object completes with the given futureValue.

Stream Transformation

The power of stream is to apply various transformations on the stream to get another stream or a value. Table 9-3 shows methods in Stream class that return another Stream object.

Table 9-3. *Stream transformations*

Name	Description
asyncExpand<E>(Stream<E> convert(T event))	Transforms each element into a stream and concatenates elements in these streams as the new stream.
asyncMap<E>(FutureOr<E> convert(T event))	Transforms each element into a new event.
distinct([bool equals (T previous, T next)])	Skips duplicate elements.
expand<S>(Iterable<S> convert(T element))	Transforms each element into a sequence of elements.
handleError(Function onError, { bool test(dynamic error) })	Handles errors in the stream.
map<S>(S convert(T event))	Transforms each element into a new event.
skip(int count)	Skips elements in the stream.
skipWhile(bool test (T element))	Skips elements while they match the predicate.

(continued)

Table 9-3. (*continued*)

Name	Description
`take(int count)`	Takes only the first count elements from the stream.
`takeWhile(bool test (T element))`	Takes elements while they match the predicate.
`timeout(Duration timeLimit, { void onTimeout(EventSink<T> sink) })`	Handles error when the time between two events exceeds the time limit.
`transform<S>(StreamTransformer <T, S> streamTransformer)`	Transforms the stream.
`where(bool test(T event))`	Filters elements in the stream.

Listing 9-9 shows examples of using stream transformations. Code below each statement shows the result of the execution.

Listing 9-9. Stream transformations

```
Stream.fromIterable([1, 2, 3]).asyncExpand((int value) {
  return Stream.fromIterable([value * 5, value * 10]);
}).listen(print);
// -> 5, 10, 10, 20, 15, 30

Stream.fromIterable([1, 2, 3]).expand((int value) {
  return [value * 5, value * 10];
}).listen(print);
// -> 5, 10, 10, 20, 15, 30

Stream.fromIterable([1, 2, 3]).asyncMap((int value) {
  return Future.delayed(Duration(seconds: 1), () => value * 10);
```

```
}).listen(print);
// -> 10, 20, 30

Stream.fromIterable([1, 2, 3]).map((value) => value * 10).
listen(print);
// -> 10, 20, 30

Stream.fromIterable([1, 1, 2]).distinct().listen(print);
// -> 1, 2

Stream.fromIterable([1, 2, 3]).skip(1).listen(print);
// -> 2, 3

Stream.fromIterable([1, 2, 3])
    .skipWhile((value) => value % 2 == 1)
    .listen(print);
// -> 2, 3

Stream.fromIterable([1, 2, 3]).take(1).listen(print);
// -> 1

Stream.fromIterable([1, 2, 3])
    .takeWhile((value) => value % 2 == 1)
    .listen(print);
// -> 1

Stream.fromIterable([1, 2, 3]).where((value) => value % 2 ==
1).listen(print);
// -> 1, 3
```

There are other methods in Stream class that return a Future object; see Table 9-4. These operations return a single value instead of a stream.

Table 9-4. *Methods for single values*

Name	Description
any(bool test(T element))	Checks whether any element in the stream matches the predicate.
every(bool test(T element))	Checks whether all elements in the stream match the predicate.
contains(Object needle)	Checks whether the stream contains the given element.
drain<E>([E futureValue])	Discards all elements in the stream.
elementAt(int index)	Gets the element at the given index.
firstWhere(bool test(T element), { T orElse() })	Finds the first element matching the predicate.
lastWhere(bool test(T element), { T orElse() })	Finds the last element matching the predicate.
singleWhere(bool test(T element), { T orElse() })	Finds the single element matching the predicate.
fold<S>(S initialValue, S combine(S previous, T element))	Combines elements in the stream into a single value.
forEach(void action(T element))	Runs an action on each element of the stream.
join([String separator = ""])	Combines the elements into a single string.
pipe(StreamConsumer<T> streamConsumer)	Pipes the events into a StreamConsumer.

(continued)

Table 9-4. (*continued*)

Name	Description
reduce(T combine(T previous, T element))	Combines elements in the stream into a single value.
toList()	Collects the elements into a list.
toSet()	Collects the elements into a set.

Listing 9-10 shows examples of using methods in Table 9-4. Code below each statement shows the result of the execution.

Listing 9-10. Methods return Future objects

```
Stream.fromIterable([1, 2, 3]).forEach(print);
// -> 1, 2, 3

Stream.fromIterable([1, 2, 3]).contains(1).then(print);
// -> true

Stream.fromIterable([1, 2, 3]).any((value) => value % 2 ==
0).then(print);
// -> true

Stream.fromIterable([1, 2, 3]).every((value) => value % 2 ==
0).then(print);
// -> false

Stream.fromIterable([1, 2, 3]).fold(0, (v1, v2) => v1 + v2).
then(print);
// -> 6

Stream.fromIterable([1, 2, 3]).reduce((v1, v2) => v1 * v2).
then(print);
// -> 6
```

```
Stream.fromIterable([1, 2, 3])
    .firstWhere((value) => value % 2 == 1)
    .then(print);
// -> 1

Stream.fromIterable([1, 2, 3])
    .lastWhere((value) => value % 2 == 1)
    .then(print);
// -> 3

Stream.fromIterable([1, 2, 3])
    .singleWhere((value) => value % 2 == 1)
    .then(print);
// -> Unhandled exception: Bad state: Too many elements
```

9-5. Creating Streams

Problem

You want to create Stream objects.

Solution

Use different Stream constructors.

Discussion

There are different Stream constructors to create Stream objects:

- Stream.empty() constructor creates an empty broadcast stream.

- Stream.fromFuture() constructor creates a single-subscription stream from a Future object.

- `Stream.fromFutures()` constructor creates a stream from a list of `Future` objects.

- `Stream.fromInterable()` constructor creates a single-subscription stream from elements of an `Iterable` object.

- `Stream.periodic()` constructor creates a stream that periodically emits data events at the given intervals.

Listing 9-11 shows examples of different `Stream` constructors.

Listing 9-11. Use Stream constructors

```
Stream.fromIterable([1, 2, 3]).listen(print);
Stream.fromFuture(Future.value(1)).listen(print);
Stream.fromFutures([Future.value(1), Future.error('error'),
Future.value(2)])
    .listen(print);
Stream.periodic(Duration(seconds: 1), (int count) => count * 2)
    .take(5)
    .listen(print);
```

Another way to create streams is using `StreamController` class. A `StreamController` object can send different events to the stream it controls. The default `StreamController()` constructor creates a single-subscription stream, while `StreamController.broadcast()` constructor creates a broadcast stream. With `StreamController`, you can generate elements in stream programmatically.

In Listing 9-12, different events are sent to the stream controlled by the `StreamController` object.

Listing 9-12. Use StreamController

```
StreamController<int> controller = StreamController();
controller.add(1);
controller.add(2);
controller.stream.listen(print, onError: print, onDone: () =>
print('done'));
controller.addError('error');
controller.add(3);
controller.close();
```

9-6. Building Widgets Based on Streams and Futures

Problem

You want to build a widget that updates its content based on the data in a stream or a future.

Solution

Use StreamBuilder<T> or FutureBuilder<T> widget.

Discussion

Given a Steam or Future object, you may want to build a widget that updates its content based on the data in it. You can use StreamBuilder<T> widget to work with Stream objects and FutureBuilder<T> widget to work with Future objects. Table 9-5 shows parameters of StreamBuilder<T> constructor.

Table 9-5. *Parameters of StreamBuilder<T>*

Name	Type	Description
stream	Stream<T>	The stream for the builder.
builder	AsyncWidgetBuilder<T>	Builder function for the widget.
initialData	T	Initial data to build the widget.

AsyncWidgetBuilder is a typedef of function type Widget (BuildContext context, AsyncSnapshot<T> snapshot). AsyncSnapshot class represents the snapshot of interaction with an asynchronous computation. Table 9-6 shows properties of AsyncSnapshot<T> class.

Table 9-6. *Properties of AsyncSnapshot<T>*

Name	Type	Description
connectionState	ConnectionState	State of connection to the asynchronous computation.
data	T	The latest data received by the asynchronous computation.
error	Object	The latest error object received by the asynchronous computation.
hasData	bool	Whether data property is not null.
hasError	bool	Whether error property is not null.

You can determine the connection state using the value of connectionState. Table 9-7 shows values of ConnectionState enum.

Table 9-7. *Values of ConnectionState*

Name	Description
none	Not connected to the asynchronous computation.
waiting	Connected to the asynchronous computation and waiting for interaction.
active	Connected to an active asynchronous computation.
done	Connected to a terminated asynchronous computation.

When using `StreamBuilder` widget to build the UI, the typical way is to return different widgets according to the connection state. For example, if the connection state is waiting, then a process indicator may be returned.

In Listing 9-13, the stream has five elements that are generated every second. If the connection state is none or waiting, a `CircularProgressIndicator` widget is returned. If the state is active or done, a `Text` widget is returned according to the value of data and error properties.

Listing 9-13. Use StreamBuilder

```
class StreamBuilderPage extends StatelessWidget {
  final Stream<int> _stream =
      Stream.periodic(Duration(seconds: 1), (int value) =>
      value * 10).take(5);

  @override
  Widget build(BuildContext context) {
    return Scaffold(
      appBar: AppBar(
        title: Text('Stream Builder'),
      ),
```

```
    body: Center(
      child: StreamBuilder(
        stream: _stream,
        initialData: 0,
        builder: (BuildContext context, AsyncSnapshot<int>
        snapshot) {
          switch (snapshot.connectionState) {
            case ConnectionState.none:
            case ConnectionState.waiting:
              return CircularProgressIndicator();
            case ConnectionState.active:
            case ConnectionState.done:
              if (snapshot.hasData) {
                return Text('${snapshot.data ?? "}');
              } else if (snapshot.hasError) {
                return Text(
                  '${snapshot.error}',
                  style: TextStyle(color: Colors.red),
                );
              }
          }
          return null;
        },
      ),
    ),
  );
  }
}
```

The usage of FutureBuilder widget is similar with StreamBuilder widget. When using a FutureBuilder with a Future object, you can convert the Future object to a Stream object using asStream() method first, then use StreamBuilder with the converted Stream object.

In Listing 9-14, we use a different way to build the UI. Instead of checking the connection state, hasData and hasError properties are used to check the status.

Listing 9-14. Use FutureBuilder

```
class FutureBuilderPage extends StatelessWidget {
  final Future<int> _future = Future.delayed(Duration(seconds: 1),
  () {
    if (Random().nextBool()) {
      return 1;
    } else {
      throw 'invalid value';
    }
  });

  @override
  Widget build(BuildContext context) {
    return Scaffold(
      appBar: AppBar(
        title: Text('Future Builder'),
      ),
      body: Center(
        child: FutureBuilder(
          future: _future,
          builder: (BuildContext context, AsyncSnapshot<int>
          snapshot) {
            if (snapshot.hasData) {
              return Text('${snapshot.data}');
            } else if (snapshot.hasError) {
              return Text(
                '${snapshot.error}',
                style: TextStyle(color: Colors.red),
```

```
      );
    } else {
      return CircularProgressIndicator();
    }
  },
 ),
),
);
  }
}
```

9-7. Handle Simple JSON Data

Problem

You want to have a simple way to handle JSON data.

Solution

Use jsonEncode() and jsonDecode() functions from dart:convert library.

Discussion

JSON is a popular data format for web services. To interact with backend services, you may need to handle JSON data in two scenarios:

- JSON data serialization converts objects in Dart to JSON strings.

- JSON data deserialization converts JSON strings to objects in Dart.

For both scenarios, if you only need to handle simple JSON data occasionally, then using jsonEncode() and jsonDecode() functions from dart:convert library is a good choice. The jsonEncode() function converts Dart objects to strings, while jsonDecode() function converts strings to Dart objects. In Listing 9-15, data object is serialized to JSON string first, then the JSON string is deserialized to Dart object again.

Listing 9-15. Handle JSON data

```
var data = {
  'name': 'Test',
  'count': 100,
  'valid': true,
  'list': [
    1,
    2,
    {
      'nested': 'a',
      'value': 123,
    },
  ],
};
String str = jsonEncode(data);
print(str);
Object obj = jsonDecode(str);
print(obj);
```

The JSON encoder in dart:convert library only supports a limited number of data types, including numbers, strings, booleans, null, lists, and maps with string keys. To encode other types of objects, you need to use the toEncodable parameter to provide a function which converts the object to an encodable value first. The default toEncodable function calls

toJson() method on the object. It's a common practice to add toJson()
method to custom classes that need to be serialized as JSON strings.

In Listing 9-16, toJson() method of ToEncode class returns a list which
will be used as the input of JSON serialization.

Listing 9-16. Use toJson() function

```
class ToEncode {
  ToEncode(this.v1, this.v2);

  final String v1;
  final String v2;

  Object toJson() {
    return [v1, v2];
  }
}
print(jsonEncode(ToEncode('v1', 'v2')));
```

If you want to have indent in the serialized JSON strings, you need to
use JsonEncoder class directly. In Listing 9-17, two spaces are used as the
indent.

Listing 9-17. Add indent

```
String indentString = JsonEncoder.withIndent('  ').
convert(data);
print(indentString);
```

9-8. Handle Complex JSON Data
Problem

You want to have a type-safe way to handle JSON data.

Solution

Use json_annotation and json_serializable libraries.

Discussion

Using jsonEncode() and jsonDecode() functions from dart:convert library can easily work with simple JSON data. When the JSON data has a complicated structure, using these two functions is not quite convenient. When deserializing JSON strings, the results are usually lists or maps. If the JSON data has a nested structure, it's not easy to extract the values from lists or maps. When serializing objects, you need to add toJson() methods to these classes to build the lists or maps. These tasks can be simplified using code generation with json_annotation and json_serializable libraries.

The json_annotation library provides annotations to customize JSON serialization and deserialization behavior. The json_serializable library provides the build process to generate code that handles JSON data. To use these two libraries, you need to add them into pubspec.yaml file. In Listing 9-18, json_serializable library is added to dependencies, while json_serializable library is added to dev_dependencies.

Listing 9-18. Add json_annotation and json_serializable

```
dependencies:
  json_annotation: ^2.0.0

dev_dependencies:
  build_runner: ^1.0.0
  json_serializable: ^2.0.0
```

In Listing 9-19, Person class is in the json_serialize.dart file. The annotation @JsonSerializable() means generating code for Person

class. The generated code is in the json_serialize.g.dart file. Functions
_$PersonFromJson() and _$PersonToJson() used in Listing 9-19 come
from the generated file. The _$PersonFromJson() function is used in the
Person.fromJson() constructor, while _$PersonToJson() function is used
in the toJson() method.

Listing 9-19. Use json_serializable

```
import 'package:json_annotation/json_annotation.dart';

part 'json_serialize.g.dart';

@JsonSerializable()
class Person {
  Person({this.firstName, this.lastName, this.email});

  final String firstName;
  final String lastName;
  final String email;

  factory Person.fromJson(Map<String, dynamic> json) =>
_$PersonFromJson(json);

  Map<String, dynamic> toJson() => _$PersonToJson(this);
}
```

To generate the code, you need to run flutter packages pub run
build_runner build command. Listing 9-20 shows the generated file.

Listing 9-20. Generated code to handle JSON data

```
part of 'json_serialize.dart';

Person _$PersonFromJson(Map<String, dynamic> json) {
  return Person(
      firstName: json['firstName'] as String,
```

```
      lastName: json['lastName'] as String,
      email: json['email'] as String);
}

Map<String, dynamic> _$PersonToJson(Person instance) =>
<String, dynamic>{
      'firstName': instance.firstName,
      'lastName': instance.lastName,
      'email': instance.email
    };
```

JsonSerializable annotation has different properties to customize the behavior; see Table 9-8.

Table 9-8. *Properties of JsonSerializable*

Name	Default value	Description
anyMap	false	When true, use Map as the map type; otherwise, Map<String, dynamic> is used.
checked	false	Whether to add extra checks to validate data types.
createFactory	true	Whether to generate the function that converts maps to objects.
createToJson	true	Whether to generate the function that can be used as toJson() function.
disallow UnrecognizedKeys	false	When true, unrecognized keys are treated as an error; otherwise, they are ignored.
explicitToJson	false	When true, generated toJson() function uses toJson on nested objects.

(continued)

Table 9-8. (*continued*)

Name	Default value	Description
fieldRename	FieldRename. none	Strategy to convert names of class fields to JSON map keys.
generateTo JsonFunction	true	When true, generate top-level function; otherwise, generate a mixin class with toJson() function.
includeIfNull	true	Whether to include fields with null values.
nullable	true	Whether to handle null values gracefully.
useWrappers	false	Whether to use wrapper classes to minimize the usage of Map and List instances during serialization.

The generateToJsonFunction property determines how toJson() functions are generated. When the value is true, top-level functions like _$PersonToJson() in Listing 9-20 will be generated. In Listing 9-21, generateToJsonFunction property is set to false for User class.

Listing 9-21. User class

```
@JsonSerializable(
  generateToJsonFunction: false,
)
class User extends Object with _$UserSerializerMixin {
  User(this.name);

  final String name;
}
```

In Listing 9-22, instead of a function, the _$UserSerializerMixin class is generated with toJson() method. User class in Listing 9-21 only needs to use this mixin class.

Listing 9-22. Generated code for User class

```
User _$UserFromJson(Map<String, dynamic> json) {
  return User(json['name'] as String);
}

abstract class _$UserSerializerMixin {
  String get name;
  Map<String, dynamic> toJson() => <String, dynamic>{'name':
  name};
}
```

JsonKey annotation specifies how a field is serialized. Table 9-9 shows properties of JsonKey.

Table 9-9. *Properties of JsonKey*

Name	Description
name	JSON map key. If null, the field name is used.
nullable	Whether to handle null values gracefully.
includeIfNull	Whether to include this field if the value is null.
ignore	Whether to ignore this field.
fromJson	A function to deserialize this field.
toJson	A function to serialize this field.
defaultValue	The value to use as the default value.
required	Whether this field is required in the JSON map.
disallowNullValue	Whether to disallow null values.

Listing 9-23 shows an example of using JsonKey.

Listing 9-23. Use JsonKey

```
@JsonKey(
  name: 'first_name',
  required: true,
  includeIfNull: true,
)
final String firstName;
```

JsonValue annotation specifies the enum value used for serialization. In Listing 9-24, JsonValue annotation is added to all enum values of Color.

Listing 9-24. Use JsonValue

```
enum Color {
  @JsonValue('R')
  Red,
  @JsonValue('G')
  Green,
  @JsonValue('B')
  Blue
}
```

JsonLiteral annotation reads JSON data from a file and converts the content into an object. It allows easy access to content of static JSON data files. In Listing 9-25, JsonLiteral annotation is added to the data getter. _$dataJsonLiteral is the generated variable of the data in the JSON file.

Listing 9-25. Use JsonLiteral

```
@JsonLiteral('data.json', asConst: true)
Map get data => _$dataJsonLiteral;
```

9-9. Handling XML Data

Problem

You want to handle XML data in Flutter apps.

Solution

Use xml library.

Discussion

XML is a popular data exchange format. You can use xml library to handle XML data in Flutter apps. You need to add xml: ^3.3.1 to dependencies of pubspec.yaml file first. Similar with JSON data, there are two usage scenarios of XML data:

- Parse XML documents and query data.

- Build XML documents.

Parse XML Documents

To parse XML documents, you need to use parse() function which takes a XML string as the input and returns parsed XmlDocument object. With the XmlDocument object, you can query and traverse the XML document tree to extract data from it.

To query the document tree, you can use findElements() and findAllElements() methods. These two methods accept a tag name and an optional namespace as the parameters and return an Iterable<XmlElement> object. The difference is that findElements() method only searches direct children, while findAllElements() method searches all descendant children. To traverse the document tree, you can use properties shown in Table 9-10.

Table 9-10. *Properties of XmlParent*

Name	Type	Description
children	XmlNodeList<XmlNode>	Direct children of this node.
ancestors	Iterable<XmlNode>	Ancestors of this node in reverse document order.
descendants	Iterable<XmlNode>	Descendants of this node in document order.
attributes	List<XmlAttribute>	Attribute nodes of this node in document order.
preceding	Iterable<XmlNode>	Nodes preceding the opening tag of this node in document order.
following	Iterable<XmlNode>	Nodes following the closing tag of this node in document order.
parent	XmlNode	Parent of this node, can be null.
firstChild	XmlNode	First child of this node, can be null.
lastChild	XmlNode	Last child of this node, can be null.
nextSibling	XmlNode	Next sibling of this node, can be null.
previousSibling	XmlNode	Previous sibling of this node, can be null.
root	XmlNode	Root of the tree.

In Listing 9-26, the input XML string (excerpt from `https://msdn.`
`microsoft.com/en-us/windows/desktop/ms762271`) is parsed and queried
for the first book element. Then text of the `title` element and value of the
`id` attribute are extracted.

Listing 9-26. XML document parsing and querying

```
String xmlStr = "'
  <?xml version="1.0"?>
  <catalog>
    <book id="bk101">
      <Author>Gambardella, Matthew</author>
      <title>XML Developer's Guide</title>
      <genre>Computer</genre>
      <price>44.95</price>
      <publish_date>2000-10-01</publish_date>
      <description>An in-depth look at creating applications
        with XML.</description>
    </book>
    <book id="bk102">
      <Author>Ralls, Kim</author>
      <title>Midnight Rain</title>
      <genre>Fantasy</genre>
      <price>5.95</price>
      <publish_date>2000-12-16</publish_date>
      <description>A former architect battles corporate
        zombies, an evil sorceress, and her own childhood to
        become queen of the world.</description>
    </book>
  </catalog>
"';
```

```
XmlDocument document = parse(xmlStr);
XmlElement firstBook = document.rootElement.
findElements('book').first;
String title = firstBook.findElements('title').single.text;
String id = firstBook.attributes
    .firstWhere((XmlAttribute attr) => attr.name.local == 'id')
    .value;
print('$id => $title');
```

Build XML Documents

To build XML documents, you can use XmlBuilder class. XmlBuilder class provides methods to build different components of XML documents; see Table 9-11. With these methods, we can build XML documents in a top-down fashion, which starts from the root element and build nested content layer by layer.

Table 9-11. *Methods of XmlBuilder*

Name	Description
element()	Creates a XmlElement node with specified tag name, namespaces, attributes, and nested content.
attribute()	Creates a XmlAttribute node with specified name, value, namespace, and type.
text()	Creates a XmlText node with specified text.
namespace()	Binds namespace prefix to the uri.
cdata()	Creates a XmlCDATA node with specified text.
comment()	Creates a XmlComment node with specified text.
processing()	Creates a XmlProcessing node with specified target and text.

After finishing the building, the build() method of XmlBuilder can be used to build the XmlNode as the result. In Listing 9-27, the root element is a note element with id attribute. Value of nest parameter is a function which uses builder methods to build the content of the node element.

Listing 9-27. Use XmlBuilder

```
XmlBuilder builder = XmlBuilder();
builder.processing('xml', 'version="1.0"');
builder.element(
  'note',
  attributes: {
    'id': '001',
  },
  nest: () {
    builder.element('from', nest: () {
      builder.text('John');
    });
    builder.element('to', nest: () {
      builder.text('Jane');
    });
    builder.element('message', nest: () {
      builder
        ..text('Hello!')
        ..comment('message to send');
    });
  },
);
XmlNode xmlNode = builder.build();
print(xmlNode.toXmlString(pretty: true));
```

Listing 9-28 shows the built XML document by code in Listing 9-27.

348

Listing 9-28. Built XML document

```
<?xml version="1.0"?>
<note id="001">
  <from>John</from>
  <to>Jane</to>
  <message>Hello!
    <!--message to send-->
  </message>
</note>
```

9-10. Handling HTML Data

Problem

You want to parse HTML document in Flutter apps.

Solution

Use html library.

Discussion

Even though JSON and XML data format are popular in Flutter apps, you may still need to parse HTML document to extract data. This process is called screen scraping. You can use html library to parse HTML document. To use this library, you need to add html: ^0.13.4+1 to the dependencies of pubspec.yaml file.

The parse() function parses HTML strings into Document objects. These Document objects can be queried and manipulated using W3C DOM API. In Listing 9-29, HTML string is parsed first, then getElementsByTagName()

349

method is used to get the li elements, and finally id attribute and text are extracted from li elements.

Listing 9-29. Parse HTML document

```
import 'package:html/dom.dart';
import 'package:html/parser.dart' show parse;

void main() {
  String htmlStr = "'
  <ul>
    <li id="001">John</li>
    <li id="002">Jane</li>
    <li id="003">Mary</li>
  </ul>
  "';
  Document document = parse(htmlStr);
  var users = document.getElementsByTagName('li').map((Element
element) {
    return {
      'id': element.attributes['id'],
      'name': element.text,
    };
  });
  print(users);
}
```

9-11. Sending HTTP Requests
Problem

You want to send HTTP requests to backend services.

Solution

Use HttpClient from dart:io library.

Discussion

HTTP protocol is a popular choice to expose web services. The representation can be JSON or XML. By using HttpClient class from dart:io library, you can easily interact with backend services over HTTP.

To use HttpClient class, you need to choose a HTTP method first, then prepare the HttpClientRequest object for the request, and process the HttpClientResponse object for the response. HttpClient class has different pairs of methods corresponding to different HTTP methods. For example, get() and getUrl() methods are both used to send HTTP GET requests. The difference is that get() method accepts host, port, and path parameters, while getUrl() method accepts url parameter of type Uri. You can see other pairs like post() and postUrl(), put() and putUrl(), patch() and patchUrl(), delete() and deleteUrl(), and head() and headUrl().

These methods return Future<HttpClientRequest> objects. You need to chain the returned Future objects with then() method to prepare HttpClientRequest object. For example, you can modify HTTP request headers or write request body. The then() method needs to return the value of HttpClientRequest.close() method, which is a Future<HttpClientResponse> object. In the then() method of the Future<HttpClientResponse> object, you can use this object to get response body, headers, cookies, and other information.

In Listing 9-30, request.close() method is called directly in the first then() method, because we don't need to do anything to the HttpClientRequest object. The _handleResponse() function decodes

HTTP response as UTF-8 strings and prints them out. HttpClientResponse class implements Stream<List<int>>, so the response body can be read as streams.

Listing 9-30. Send HTTP GET request

```
void _handleResponse(HttpClientResponse response) {
  response.transform(utf8.decoder).listen(print);
}

HttpClient httpClient = HttpClient();
httpClient
    .getUrl(Uri.parse('https://httpbin.org/get'))
    .then((HttpClientRequest request) => request.close())
    .then(_handleResponse);
```

If you need to send HTTP POST, PUT, and PATCH requests with body, you can use HttpClientRequest.write() method to write the body; see Listing 9-31.

Listing 9-31. Write HTTP request body

```
httpClient
    .postUrl(Uri.parse('https://httpbin.org/post'))
    .then((HttpClientRequest request) {
  request.write('hello');
  return request.close();
}).then(_handleResponse);
```

If you need to modify HTTP request headers, you can use the HttpClientRequest.headers property to modify the HttpHeaders object; see Listing 9-32.

Listing 9-32. Modify HTTP request headers

```
httpClient
    .getUrl(Uri.parse('https://httpbin.org/headers'))
    .then((HttpClientRequest request) {
  request.headers.set(HttpHeaders.userAgentHeader, 'my-agent');
  return request.close();
}).then(_handleResponse);
```

If you need to support HTTP basic authentication, you can use `HttpClient.addCredentials()` method to add `HttpClientBasicCredentials` objects; see Listing 9-33.

Listing 9-33. Basic authentication

```
String username = 'username', password = 'password';
Uri uri = Uri.parse('https://httpbin.org/basic-
auth/$username/$password');
httpClient.addCredentials(
    uri, null, HttpClientBasicCredentials(username, password));
httpClient
    .getUrl(uri)
    .then((HttpClientRequest request) => request.close())
    .then(_handleResponse);
```

9-12. Connecting to WebSocket
Problem

You want to connect to WebSocket servers in Flutter apps.

Solution

Use WebSocket class in dart:io library.

Discussion

WebSockets are widely used in web apps to provide bidirectional communications between browser and server. They can also provide real-time updates of data in the backend. If you already have a WebSocket server that interacts with the web app running in the browser, you may also want the same feature to be available in Flutter apps. WebSocket class in dart:io library can be used to implement the WebSocket connections.

The static WebSocket.connect() method connects to a WebSocket server. You need to provide the server URL with scheme ws or wss. You can optionally provide a list of subprotocols and a map of headers. The return value of connect() method is a Future<WebSocket> object. WebSocket class implements Stream class, so you can read data sent from server as streams. To send data to the server, you can use add() and addStream() methods.

In Listing 9-34, the WebSocket connects to the demo echo server. By using listen() method to subscribe to the WebSocket object, we can process data sent from the server. The two add() method calls send two messages to the server.

Listing 9-34. Connect to WebSocket

```
WebSocket.connect('ws://demos.kaazing.com/echo').
then((WebSocket webSocket) {
  webSocket.listen(print, onError: print);
  webSocket.add('hello');
  webSocket.add('world');
  webSocket.close();
}).catchError(print);
```

9-13. Connecting to Socket

Problem

You want to connect to socket servers.

Solution

Use Socket class in dart:io library.

Discussion

If you want to connect to socket servers in Flutter apps, you can use Socket class from dart:io library. The static Socket.connect() method connects to a socket server at specified host and port and returns a Future<Socket> object. Socket class implements Stream<List<int>>, so you can read data from server by subscribing to the stream. To send data to the server, you can use add() and addStream() methods.

In Listing 9-35, a socket server is started on port 10080. This server converts the received strings into uppercase and sends back the results.

Listing 9-35. Simple socket server

```
import 'dart:io';
import 'dart:convert';

void main() {
  ServerSocket.bind('127.0.0.1', 10080).then((serverSocket) {
    serverSocket.listen((socket) {
      socket.addStream(socket
          .transform(utf8.decoder)
          .map((str) => str.toUpperCase())
          .transform(utf8.encoder));
```

```
    });
  });
}
```

In Listing 9-36, `Socket.connect()` method is used to connect to the socket server shown in Listing 9-35. Data received from the server is printed out. Two strings are sent to the server.

Listing 9-36. Connect to socket server

```
void main() {
  Socket.connect('127.0.0.1', 10080).then((socket) {
    socket.transform(utf8.decoder).listen(print);
    socket.write('hello');
    socket.write('world');
    socket.close();
  });
}
```

9-14. Interacting JSON-Based REST Services

Problem

You want to use JSON-based REST services.

Solution

Use `HttpClient`, `json_serialize` library, and `FutureBuilder` widget.

Discussion

It's a popular choice for mobile apps backend to expose services over HTTP protocol with JSON as the representation. By using HttpClient, json_serialize library, and FutureBuilder widget, you can build the UI to work with these REST services. This recipe provides a concrete example which combines content in Listings 9-6, 9-8, and 9-11.

This example uses GitHub Jobs API (https://jobs.github.com/api) to get job listings on GitHub web site. In Listing 9-37, Job class represents a job listing. In the JsonSerializable annotation, createToJson property is set to false, because we only need to parse JSON response from the API. The _parseDate function parses the string in created_at field of the JSON object. You need to add intl library to use DateFormat class.

Listing 9-37. Job class

```
part 'github_jobs.g.dart';

DateFormat _dateFormat = DateFormat('EEE MMM dd HH:mm:ss
yyyy');
DateTime _parseDate(String str) =>
    _dateFormat.parse(str.replaceFirst(' UTC', ''), true);

@JsonSerializable(
  createToJson: false,
)
class Job {
  Job();

  String id;
  String type;
  String url;
  @JsonKey(name: 'created_at', fromJson: _parseDate)
  DateTime createdAt;
```

```
String company;
@JsonKey(name: 'company_url')
String companyUrl;
@JsonKey(name: 'company_logo')
String companyLogo;
String location;
String title;
String description;
@JsonKey(name: 'how-to-apply')
String howToApply;

factory Job.fromJson(Map<String, dynamic> json) =>
_$JobFromJson(json);
}
```

In Listing 9-38, a HttpClient object is used to send a HTTP GET request to GitHub Jobs API and parse the JSON response using jsonDecode() function. The Future object of type Future<List<Job>> is used by FutureBuilder widget to build the UI. JobsList widget takes a List<Job> object and displays the list using ListView widget.

Listing 9-38. Widget to show jobs

```
class GitHubJobsPage extends StatelessWidget {
  final Future<List<Job>> _jobs = HttpClient()
      .getUrl(Uri.parse('https://jobs.github.com/positions.
      json'
        '?description=java&location=new+york'))
      .then((HttpClientRequest request) => request.close())
      .then((HttpClientResponse response) {
    return response.transform(utf8.decoder).join(").
    then((String content) {
      return (jsonDecode(content) as List<dynamic>)
```

```
        .map((json) => Job.fromJson(json))
        .toList();
  });
});

@override
Widget build(BuildContext context) {
  return Scaffold(
    appBar: AppBar(
      title: Text('GitHub Jobs'),
    ),
    body: FutureBuilder<List<Job>>(
      future: _jobs,
      builder: (BuildContext context,
      AsyncSnapshot<List<Job>> snapshot) {
        if (snapshot.hasData) {
          return JobsList(snapshot.data);
        } else if (snapshot.hasError) {
          return Center(
            child: Text(
              '${snapshot.error}',
              style: TextStyle(color: Colors.red),
            ),
          );
        } else {
          return Center(
            child: CircularProgressIndicator(),
          );
        }
      },
    ),
  );
```

```
  }
}

class JobsList extends StatelessWidget {
  JobsList(this.jobs);
  final List<Job> jobs;

  @override
  Widget build(BuildContext context) {
    return ListView.separated(
      itemBuilder: (BuildContext context, int index) {
        Job job = jobs[index];
        return ListTile(
          title: Text(job.title),
          subtitle: Text(job.company),
        );
      },
      separatorBuilder: (BuildContext context, int index) {
        return Divider();
      },
      itemCount: jobs.length,
    );
  }
}
```

9-15. Interacting with gRPC Services

Problem

You want to interact with gRPC services.

Solution

Use grpc library.

Discussion

gRPC (https://grpc.io/) is a high-performance, open-source universal RPC framework. This recipe shows how to interact with gRPC services. The gRPC service to interact is the greeter service from gRPC official examples (https://github.com/grpc/grpc/tree/master/examples/node). You need to start the gRPC server first.

To use this gRPC service in Flutter apps, you need to install Protocol Buffers compiler (https://github.com/protocolbuffers/protobuf) first. After downloading the release file for your platform and extracting its content, you need to add the extracted bin directory to the PATH environment variable. You can run protoc --version command to verify the installation. The version used in this recipe is 3.7.1.

You also need to install Dart protoc plugin (https://github.com/dart-lang/protobuf/tree/master/protoc_plugin). The easiest way to install is to run the following command.

```
$ flutter packages pub global activate protoc_plugin
```

Because we use flutter packages to run the installation, the binary file is put under the .pub-cache/bin directory of the Flutter SDK. You need to add this path to PATH environment variable. The plugin requires dart command to be available, so you also need to add bin/cache/dart-sdk/bin directory of Flutter SDK to PATH environment variable. Now we can use protoc to generate Dart files for interactions with the greeter service. In the following command, lib/grpc/generated is the output path of generated files. proto_file_path is the path of proto files. helloworld.proto file contains the definition for greeter service. Libraries protobuf and grpc also need to be added to the dependencies of pubspec.yaml file.

```
$ protoc --dart_out=grpc:lib/grpc/generated --proto_
path=<proto_file_path> <proto_file_path>/helloworld.proto
```

The generated `helloworld.pbgrpc.dart` file provides `GreeterClient` class to interact with the service. In Listing 9-39, a `ClientChannel` is created to connect to the gRPC server. The channel is required when creating a `GreeterClient` object. The `sayHello()` method sends requests to the server and receives responses.

Listing 9-39. Interact with gRPC service

```
import 'package:grpc/grpc.dart';

import 'generated/helloworld.pbgrpc.dart';

void main() async {
  final channel = new ClientChannel('localhost',
      port: 50051,
      options: const ChannelOptions(
          credentials: const ChannelCredentials.insecure()));
  final stub = new GreeterClient(channel);

  try {
    var response = await stub.sayHello(new HelloRequest()..name =
    'John');
    print('Received: ${response.message}');
  } catch (e) {
    print('Caught error: $e');
  }
  await channel.shutdown();
}
```

9-16. Summary

This chapter focuses on different ways to interact with backend services, including HTTP, WebSocket, Socket, and gRPC. Futures and Streams play an important role in asynchronous computations. This chapter also discusses how to handle JSON, XML, and HTML data. In the next chapter, we'll discuss state management in Flutter apps.

CHAPTER 10

State Management

When building Flutter apps, you need to manage the state when the apps are running. The state may change due to user interactions or background tasks. This chapter covers recipes that use different solutions for state management in Flutter.

10-1. Managing State Using Stateful Widgets

Problem

You want to have a simple way to manage state in the UI.

Solution

Create your own subclasses of StatefulWidget.

Discussion

StatefulWidget class is the fundamental way in Flutter to manage state. A stateful widget rebuilds itself when its state changes. If the state to manage is simple, using stateful widgets is generally good enough. You don't need to use third-party libraries discussed in other recipes.

© Fu Cheng 2019   365
F. Cheng, *Flutter Recipes*, https://doi.org/10.1007/978-1-4842-4982-6_10

Stateful widgets use State objects to store the state. When creating your own subclasses of StatefulWidget, you need to override createState() method to return a State object. For each subclass StatefulWidget, there will be a corresponding subclass of State class to manage the state. The createState() method returns an object of the corresponding subclass of State. The actual state is usually kept as private variables of the subclass of State.

In the subclass of State, you need to implement build() method to return a Widget object. When the state changes, the build() method will be called to get the new widget to update the UI. To trigger the rebuild of the UI, you need to call setState() method explicitly to notify the framework. The parameter of setState() method is a VoidCallback function that contains the logic to update the internal state. When rebuilding, the build() method uses the latest state to create widget configurations. Widgets are not updated but replaced when necessary.

SelectColor widget in Listing 10-1 is a typical example of stateful widget. _SelectColorState class is the State implementation for SelectColor widget. _selectedColor is the internal variable that maintains the current selected color. The value of _selectedColor is used by the DropdownButton widget to determine the selected option to render and the Text widget to determine the text to display. In the onChanged handler of DropdownButton, setState() method is called to update the value of _selectedColor variable, which notifies the framework to run _SelectColorState.build() method again to get the new widget configuration to update the UI.

Listing 10-1. Example of stateful widget

```
class SelectColor extends StatefulWidget {
  @override
  _SelectColorState createState() => _SelectColorState();
}
```

```
class _SelectColorState extends State<SelectColor> {
  final List<String> _colors = ['Red', 'Green', 'Blue'];
  String _selectedColor;

  @override
  Widget build(BuildContext context) {
    return Column(
      children: <Widget>[
        DropdownButton(
          value: _selectedColor,
          items: _colors.map((String color) {
            return DropdownMenuItem(
              value: color,
              child: Text(color),
            );
          }).toList(),
          onChanged: (value) {
            setState(() {
              _selectedColor = value;
            });
          },
        ),
        Text('Selected: ${_selectedColor ?? "}'),
      ],
    );
  }
}
```

State objects have their own lifecycle. You can override different lifecycle methods in subclasses of State to perform actions on different stages. Table 10-1 shows these lifecycle methods.

Table 10-1. *Lifecycle methods of State*

Name	Description
initState()	Called when this object is inserted into the widgets tree. Should be used to perform initialization of state.
didChangeDependencies()	Called when a dependency of this object changes.
didUpdateWidget (T oldWidget)	Called when the widget of this object changes. Old widget is passed as a parameter.
reassemble()	Called when the app is reassembled during debugging. This method is only called during development.
build(BuildContext context)	Called when the state changes.
deactivate()	Called when this object is removed from the widgets tree.
dispose()	Called when this object is removed from the widgets tree permanently. This method is called after deactivate().

Of the methods listed in Table 10-1, initState() and dispose() methods are easy to understand. These two methods will only be called once during the lifecycle. However, other methods may be invoked multiple times.

The didChangeDependencies() method is typically used when the state object uses inherited widgets. This method is called when an inherited widget changes. Most of the time, you don't need to override this method, because the framework calls build() method automatically after a dependency changes. Sometimes you may need to perform some expensive tasks after a dependency changes. In this case, you should put the logic into didChangeDependencies() method instead of performing the task in build() method.

The reassemble() method is only used during development, for example, during hot reload. This method is not called in release builds. Most of the time, you don't need to override this method.

The didUpdateWidget() method is called when the state's widget changes. You should override this method if you need to perform cleanup tasks on the old widget or reuse some state from the old widget. For example, _TextFieldState class for TextField widget overrides didUpdateWidget() method to initialize TextEditingController object based on the value of the old widget.

The deactivate() method is called when the state object is removed from the widgets tree. This state object may be inserted back to the widgets tree at a different location. You should override this method if the build logic depends on the widget's location. For example, FormFieldState class for FormField widget overrides deactivate() method to unregister the current form field from the enclosing form.

In Listing 10-1, the whole content of the widget is built in the build() method, so you can simply call setState() method in the onPressed callback of DropdownButton. If the widget has a complex structure, you can pass down a function that updates the state to the children widgets. In Listing 10-2, the onPressed callback of RaisedButton is set by the constructor parameter of CounterButton. When the CounterButton is used in Counter widget, the provided handler function uses setState() to update the state.

Listing 10-2. Pass state change function to descendant widget

```
class Counter extends StatefulWidget {
  @override
  _CounterState createState() => _CounterState();
}
```

```
class _CounterState extends State<Counter> {
  int count = 0;
  @override
  Widget build(BuildContext context) {
    return Column(
      children: <Widget>[
        CounterButton(() {
          setState(() {
            count++;
          });
        }),
        CounterText(count),
      ],
    );
  }
}

class CounterText extends StatelessWidget {
  CounterText(this.count);
  final int count;

  @override
  Widget build(BuildContext context) {
    return Text('Value: ${count ?? "}');
  }
}

class CounterButton extends StatelessWidget {
  CounterButton(this.onPressed);
  final VoidCallback onPressed;

  @override
  Widget build(BuildContext context) {
```

```
    return RaisedButton(
      child: Text('+'),
      onPressed: onPressed,
    );
  }
}
```

10-2. Managing State Using Inherited Widgets

Problem

You want to propagate state down the widgets tree.

Solution

Create your own subclasses of InheritedWidget.

Discussion

When using stateful widgets to manage state, the state is stored in State objects. If a descendant widget needs to access the state, the state needs to be passed down to it from the root of subtree, just like how count state is passed in Listing 10-2. When the widget has a relatively deep subtree structure, it's inconvenient to add constructor parameters for passing the state down. In this case, using InheritedWidget is a better choice.

When InheritedWidget is used, the method BuildContext. inheritFromWidgetOfExactType() can get the nearest instance of a particular type of inherited widget from the build context. Descendant widgets can easily access state data stored in an inherited widget. When inheritFromWidgetOfExactType() method is called, the build context registers itself to the inherited widget. When the inherited widget changes, the build context is rebuilt automatically to get the new values from the inherited widget. This means no manual updates are required for descendant widgets that use state from the inherited widget.

The Config class in Listing 10-3 represents the state. It has color and fontSize properties. Config class overrides == operator and hashCode property to implement correct equality check. The copyWith() method can be used to create new instances of Config class by updating a partial set of properties. The Config.fallback() constructor creates a Config object with default values.

Listing 10-3. Config class for inherited widget

```
class Config {
  const Config({this.color, this.fontSize});

  const Config.fallback()
      : color = Colors.red,
        fontSize = 12.0;

  final Color color;
  final double fontSize;

  Config copyWith({Color color, double fontSize}) {
    return Config(
      color: color ?? this.color,
      fontSize: fontSize ?? this.fontSize,
    );
  }

  @override
  bool operator ==(other) {
    if (other.runtimeType != runtimeType) return false;
    final Config typedOther = other;
```

```
    return color == typedOther.color && fontSize == typedOther.
    fontSize;
  }

  @override
  int get hashCode => hashValues(color, fontSize);
}
```

The ConfigWidget in Listing 10-4 is an inherited widget. It keeps a Config object as its internal state. The updateShouldNotify() method is called to check whether registered build contexts should be notified after the inherited widget changes. This is a performance optimization to avoid unnecessary updates. The static of() method is a common practice to get the inherited widget or the state associated with the inherited widget. The of() method of ConfigWidget uses inheritFromWidgetOfExactType() to get the nearest enclosing ConfigWidget instance from build context and gets config property from the widget. If no ConfigWidget object is found, the default Config instance is returned.

Listing 10-4. ConfigWidget as inherited widget

```
class ConfigWidget extends InheritedWidget {
  const ConfigWidget({
    Key key,
    @required this.config,
    @required Widget child,
  }) : super(key: key, child: child);

  final Config config;

  static Config of(BuildContext context) {
    final ConfigWidget configWidget =
        context.inheritFromWidgetOfExactType(ConfigWidget);
    return configWidget?.config ?? const Config.fallback();
  }
```

```
  @override
  bool updateShouldNotify(ConfigWidget oldWidget) {
    return config != oldWidget.config;
  }
}
```

In Listing 10-5, both ConfiguredText and ConfiguredBox widgets use
ConfigWidget.of(context) to get the Config object and use its properties
when building the UI.

Listing 10-5. Use ConfigWidget to get the Config object

```
class ConfiguredText extends StatelessWidget {
  @override
  Widget build(BuildContext context) {
    Config config = ConfigWidget.of(context);
    return Text(
      'Font size: ${config.fontSize}',
      style: TextStyle(
        color: config.color,
        fontSize: config.fontSize,
      ),
    );
  }
}

class ConfiguredBox extends StatelessWidget {
  @override
  Widget build(BuildContext context) {
    Config config = ConfigWidget.of(context);
    return Container(
      decoration: BoxDecoration(color: config.color),
      child: Text('Background color: ${config.color}'),
```

```
    );
  }
}
```

ConfigUpdater widget in Listing 10-6 is used to update the Config object. It also uses ConfigWidget.of(context) to get the Config object to update. The onColorChanged and onFontSizeIncreased callbacks are used to trigger update of Config object.

Listing 10-6. ConfigUpdater to update Config object

```
typedef SetColorCallback = void Function(Color color);

class ConfigUpdater extends StatelessWidget {
  const ConfigUpdater({this.onColorChanged, this.
onFontSizeIncreased});

  static const List<Color> _colors = [Colors.red, Colors.green,
Colors.blue];
  final SetColorCallback onColorChanged;
  final VoidCallback onFontSizeIncreased;

  @override
  Widget build(BuildContext context) {
    Config config = ConfigWidget.of(context);
    return Column(
      children: <Widget>[
        DropdownButton(
          value: config.color,
          items: _colors.map((Color color) {
            return DropdownMenuItem(
              value: color,
              child: Text(color.toString()),
            );
```

```
      }).toList(),
      onChanged: onColorChanged,
    ),
    RaisedButton(
      child: Text('Increase font size'),
      onPressed: onFontSizeIncreased,
    )
   ],
  );
 }
}
```

Now we can put these widgets together to build the whole UI. In Listing 10-7, ConfiguredPage is a stateful widget with a Config object as its state. ConfigUpdater widget is a child of ConfiguredPage to update the Config object. ConfiguredPage constructor also has child parameter to provide child widget that uses ConfigWidget.of(context) to get the correct Config object. For the onColorChanged and onFontSizeIncreased callbacks of ConfigWidget, setState() method is used to update the state of ConfiguredPage widget and triggers update of ConfigWidget. The framework notifies ConfigUpdater and other widgets to update with latest value of Config object.

Listing 10-7. ConfiguredPage to use ConfigWidget

```
class ConfiguredPage extends StatefulWidget {
  ConfiguredPage({Key key, this.child}) : super(key: key);
  final Widget child;

  @override
  _ConfiguredPageState createState() => _ConfiguredPageState();
}
```

```
class _ConfiguredPageState extends State<ConfiguredPage> {
  Config _config = Config(color: Colors.green, fontSize: 16);

  @override
  Widget build(BuildContext context) {
    return ConfigWidget(
      config: _config,
      child: Column(
        children: <Widget>[
          ConfigUpdater(
            onColorChanged: (Color color) {
              setState(() {
                _config = _config.copyWith(color: color);
              });
            },
            onFontSizeIncreased: () {
              setState(() {
                _config = _config.copyWith(fontSize: _config.
                fontSize + 1.0);
              });
            },
          ),
          Container(
            decoration: BoxDecoration(border: Border.all()),
            padding: EdgeInsets.all(8),
            child: widget.child,
          ),
        ],
      ),
    );
  }
}
```

In Listing 10-8, ConfigWidgetPage widget uses ConfiguredPage widget to wrap ConfiguredText and ConfiguredBox widgets.

Listing 10-8. ConfigWidgetPage to build the UI

```
class ConfigWidgetPage extends StatelessWidget {
  @override
  Widget build(BuildContext context) {
    return Scaffold(
      appBar: AppBar(
        title: Text('Inherited Widget'),
      ),
      body: ConfiguredPage(
        child: Column(
          children: <Widget>[
            ConfiguredText(),
            ConfiguredBox(),
          ],
        ),
      ),
    );
  }
}
```

10-3. Managing State Using Inherited Model

Problem

You want to get notified and rebuild UI based on aspects of changes.

Solution

Create your own subclasses of InheritedModel.

Discussion

If we take a closer look at the `ConfiguredText` and `ConfiguredBox` widgets in Listing 10-5 of Recipe 10-2, we can see that `ConfiguredBox` widget only depends on the `color` property of the `Config` object. If the `fontSize` property changes, there is no need for `ConfiguredBox` widget to rebuild. These unnecessary rebuilds may cause performance issues, especially if the widget is complex.

`InheritedModel` widget allows you to divide a state into multiple aspects. A build context can register to get notified only for a particular aspect. When state changes in `InheritedModel` widget, only dependent build contexts registered to matching aspects will be notified.

`InheritedModel` class extends from `InheritedWidget` class. It has a type parameter to specify the type of aspect. `ConfigModel` class in Listing 10-9 is the `InheritedModel` subclass for `Config` object. The type of aspect is `String`. When implementing `InheritedModel` class, you still need to override `updateShouldNotify()` method to determine whether dependents should be notified. The `updateShouldNotifyDependent()` method determines whether a dependent should be notified based on the set of aspects it depends on. The `updateShouldNotifyDependent()` method is only called when `updateShouldNotify()` method returns `true`. For the `ConfigModel`, only "color" and "fontSize" aspects are defined. If the dependent depends on the "color" aspect, then it's notified only when the `color` property of `Config` object changes. This is also applied to "fontSize" aspect for `fontSize` property.

The static `of()` method has an extra `aspect` parameter to specify the aspect the build context depends on. The static `InheritedModel.inheritFrom()` method is used to make the build context depend on specified aspect. When aspect is `null`, this method is the same as using `BuildContext.inheritFromWidgetOfExactType()` method.

Listing 10-9. ConfigModel as InheritedModel

```
class ConfigModel extends InheritedModel<String> {
  const ConfigModel({
    Key key,
    @required this.config,
    @required Widget child,
  }) : super(key: key, child: child);

  final Config config;

  static Config of(BuildContext context, String aspect) {
    ConfigModel configModel =
        InheritedModel.inheritFrom(context, aspect: aspect);
    return configModel?.config ?? Config.fallback();
  }

  @override
  bool updateShouldNotify(ConfigModel oldWidget) {
    return config != oldWidget.config;
  }

  @override
  bool updateShouldNotifyDependent(
      ConfigModel oldWidget, Set<String> dependencies) {
    return (config.color != oldWidget.config.color &&
            dependencies.contains('color')) ||
        (config.fontSize != oldWidget.config.fontSize &&
            dependencies.contains('fontSize'));
  }
}
```

In Listing 10-10, ConfiguredModelText widget uses null as the aspect, because it depends on both "color" and "fontSize" aspects.

ConfiguredModelBox widget uses color as the aspect. If font size is
updated, only ConfiguredModelText widget is rebuilt.

Listing 10-10. Use ConfigModel to get Config object

```
class ConfiguredModelText extends StatelessWidget {
  @override
  Widget build(BuildContext context) {
    Config config = ConfigModel.of(context, null);
    return Text(
      'Font size: ${config.fontSize}',
      style: TextStyle(
        color: config.color,
        fontSize: config.fontSize,
      ),
    );
  }
}

class ConfiguredModelBox extends StatelessWidget {
  @override
  Widget build(BuildContext context) {
    Config config = ConfigModel.of(context, 'color');
    return Container(
      decoration: BoxDecoration(color: config.color),
      child: Text('Background color: ${config.color}'),
    );
  }
}
```

10-4. Managing State Using Inherited Notifier

Problem

You want dependent widgets to rebuild based on notifications from Listenable objects.

Solution

Create your own subclasses of InheritedNotifier widget.

Discussion

Listenable class is typically used to manage listeners and notify clients for updates. You can use the same pattern to notify dependents to rebuild with InheritedNotifier. InheritedNotifier widget also extends from InheritedWidget class. When creating InheritedNotifier widgets, you need to provide Listenable objects. When the Listenable object sends notifications, dependents of this InheritedNotifier widget are notified for rebuilding.

In Listing 10-11, ConfigNotifier uses ValueNotifier<Config> as the type of Listenable. The static of() method gets the Config object from ConfigNotifier object.

Listing 10-11. ConfigNotifier as InheritedNotifier

```
class ConfigNotifier extends InheritedNotifier<ValueNotifier
<Config>> {
  ConfigNotifier({
    Key key,
    @required notifier,
```

```
    @required Widget child,
  }) : super(key: key, notifier: notifier, child: child);

  static Config of(BuildContext context) {
    final ConfigNotifier configNotifier =
        context.inheritFromWidgetOfExactType(ConfigNotifier);
    return configNotifier?.notifier?.value ?? Config.
fallback();
  }
}
```

To use ConfigNotifier widget, you need to create a new instance of
ValueNotifier<Config>. To update the Config object, you can simply
set the value property to a new value. ValueNotifier object will send
notifications, which notify dependent widgets to rebuild.

Listing 10-12. ConfiguredNotifierPage to use ConfigNotifier

```
class ConfigurcdNotifierPage extends StatelessWidget {
  ConfiguredNotifierPage({Key key, this.child}) : super(key:
key);
  final Widget child;
  final ValueNotifier<Config> _notifier =
      ValueNotifier(Config(color: Colors.green, fontSize: 16));

  @override
  Widget build(BuildContext context) {
    return ConfigNotifier(
      notifier: _notifier,
      child: Column(
        children: <Widget>[
          ConfigUpdater(
            onColorChanged: (Color color) {
```

```
              _notifier.value = _notifier.value.copyWith(color:
              color);
          },
          onFontSizeIncreased: () {
            Config oldConfig = _notifier.value;
            _notifier.value =
                oldConfig.copyWith(fontSize: oldConfig.
                fontSize + 1.0);
          },
        ),
        Container(
          decoration: BoxDecoration(border: Border.all()),
          padding: EdgeInsets.all(8),
          child: child,
        ),
      ],
    ),
  );
  }
}
```

10-5. Managing State Using Scoped Model

Problem

You want to have a simple solution to handle model changes.

Solution

Use scoped_model package.

Discussion

In Recipes 10-1, 10-2, 10-3, and 10-4, you have seen the usage of StatefulWidget, InheritedWidget, InheritedModel, and InheritedNotifier widgets to manage state. These widgets are provided by Flutter framework. These widgets are low-level APIs, so they are inconvenient to use in complex apps. The scoped_model package (https://pub.dev/packages/scoped_model) is a library to allow easily passing a data model from a parent widget down to its descendants. It's built on top of InheritedWidget, but with an easy-to-use API. To use this package, you need to add scoped_model: ^1.0.1 to the dependencies of pubspec.yaml file. We'll use the same example as in Recipe 10-2 to demonstrate the usage of scoped_model package.

Listing 10-13 shows the Config model using scoped_model package. The Config class extends from Model class. It has private fields to store the state. The setColor() and increaseFontSize() methods update _color and _fontSize fields, respectively. These two methods use notifyListeners() internally to notify descendant widgets to rebuild.

Listing 10-13. Config model as scoped model

```
import 'package:scoped_model/scoped_model.dart';

class Config extends Model {
  Color _color = Colors.red;
  double _fontSize = 16.0;

  Color get color => _color;
  double get fontSize => _fontSize;

  void setColor(Color color) {
    _color = color;
    notifyListeners();
  }
}
```

```
  void increaseFontSize() {
    _fontSize += 1;
    notifyListeners();
  }
}
```

In Listing 10-14, ScopedModelText widget shows how to use the model in descendant widgets. ScopedModelDescendant widget is used to get the nearest enclosing model object. The type parameter determines the model object to get. The builder parameter specified the build function to build the widget. The build function has three parameters. The first parameter of type BuildContext is common for build functions. The last parameter is the model object. If a portion of the widget UI doesn't rely on the model and should not be rebuilt when model changes, you can specify it as the child parameter of ScopedModelDescendant widget and access it in the second parameter of the build function.

Listing 10-14. ScopedModelText uses ScopedModelDescendant

```
class ScopedModelText extends StatelessWidget {
  @override
  Widget build(BuildContext context) {
    return ScopedModelDescendant<Config>(
      builder: (BuildContext context, Widget child, Config
      config) {
        return Text(
          'Font size: ${config.fontSize}',
          style: TextStyle(
            color: config.color,
            fontSize: config.fontSize,
          ),
        );
      },
```

```
  );
  }
}
```

In Listing 10-15, ScopedModelUpdater widget simply uses setColor() and increaseFontSize() methods to update the state.

Listing 10-15. ScopedModelUpdater to update Config object

```
class ScopedModelUpdater extends StatelessWidget {
  static const List<Color> _colors = [Colors.red, Colors.green,
Colors.blue];

  @override
  Widget build(BuildContext context) {
    return ScopedModelDescendant<Config>(
      builder: (BuildContext context, Widget child, Config
      config) {
        return Column(
          children: <Widget>[
            DropdownButton(
              value: config.color,
              items: _colors.map((Color color) {
                return DropdownMenuItem(
                  value: color,
                  child: Text(color.toString()),
                );
              }).toList(),
              onChanged: (Color color) {
                config.setColor(color);
              },
            ),
            RaisedButton(
```

```
            child: Text('Increase font size'),
            onPressed: () {
              config.increaseFontSize();
            },
          )
        ],
      );
    },
  );
}
}
```

ScopedModel widget in Listing 10-16 is the last piece to put Model and ScopedModelDescendant together. The model parameter specifies the model object managed by the ScopedModel object. All the ScopedModelDescendant widgets under the ScopedModel object get the same model object.

Listing 10-16. ScopedModelPage uses ScopedModel

```
class ScopedModelPage extends StatelessWidget {
  @override
  Widget build(BuildContext context) {
    return Scaffold(
      appBar: AppBar(
        title: Text('Scoped Model'),
      ),
      body: ScopedModel(
        model: Config(),
        child: Column(
          children: <Widget>[
            ScopedModelUpdater(),
            ScopedModelText()
```

```
      ],
    ),
  ),
);
  }
}
```

You can also use static `ScopedModel.of()` method to get the `ScopedModel` object, then use its `model` property to get the model object.

10-6. Managing State Using Bloc

Problem

You want to use Bloc pattern to manage state.

Solution

Use `bloc` and `flutter_bloc` packages.

Discussion

Bloc (Business Logic Component) is an architecture pattern to separate presentation from business logic. Bloc was designed to be simple, powerful, and testable. Let's start from core concepts in Bloc.

States represent a part of the application's state. When state changes, UI widgets are notified to rebuild based on the latest state. Each application has its own way to define states. Typically, you'll use Dart classes to describe states.

Events are sources of changes to states. Events can be generated by user interactions or background tasks. For example, pressing a button may generate an event that describes the intended action. When the response of a HTTP request is ready, an event can also be generated to include the response body. Events are typically described as Dart classes. Events may also have payload carried with them.

When events are dispatched, handling these events may cause the current state transits to a new state. UI widgets are then notified to rebuild using the new state. An event transition consists of the current state, the event, and the next state. If all state transitions are recorded, we can easily track all user interactions and state changes. We can also implement time-travelling debugging.

Now we can have a definition of Bloc. A Bloc component transforms a stream of events into a stream of states. A Bloc has an initial state as the state before any events are received. For each event, a Bloc has a `mapEventToState()` function that takes a received event and returns a stream of states to be consumed by the presentation layer. A Bloc also has the `dispatch()` method to dispatch events to it.

In this recipe, we'll use the GitHub Jobs API (`https://jobs.github.com/api`) to get job listings on GitHub. The user can input a keyword for search and see the results. To consume this, we will be using the http package (`https://pub.dev/packages/http`). Add this package to your pubspec.yaml file.

Let's start from the states. Listing 10-17 shows classes for different states. `JobsState` is the abstract base class for all state classes. `JobsState` class extends from `Equatable` class in the `equatable` package. `Equatable` class is used to provide implantations for `==` operator and `hashCode` property. `JobsEmpty` is the initial state. `JobsLoading` means the job listing data is still loading. `JobsLoaded` means job listing data is loaded. The payload type of `JobsLoaded` event is `List<Job>`. `JobsError` means an error occurred when fetching the data.

Listing 10-17. Bloc states

```
import 'package:http/http.dart' as http;

abstract class JobsState extends Equatable {
  JobsState([List props = const []]) : super(props);
}

class JobsEmpty extends JobsState {}

class GetJobsEvent extends JobsEvent {
  GetJobsEvent({@required this.keyword})
      : assert(keyword != null),
        super([keyword]);

  final String keyword;
}

class GitHubJobsClient {
  Future<List<Job>> getJobs(keyword) async {
    final response = await http.get('https://jobs.github.com/
    positions.json?description=${keyword}');
    if (response.statusCode != 200) {
      throw new Exception("Unable to fetch data");
    }else{
      var result = new List<Job>();
      final rawResult = json.decode(response.body);
      for(final jsonJob in rawResult){
        result.add(Job.fromJson(jsonJob));
      }
    }
  }
}
```

```
class JobsLoading extends JobsState {}

class JobsLoaded extends JobsState {
  JobsLoaded({@required this.jobs})
      : assert(jobs != null),
        super([jobs]);

  final List<Job> jobs;
}

class JobsError extends JobsState {}
```

Listing 10-18 shows the events. JobsEvent is the abstract base class for event classes. GetJobsEvent class represents the event to get jobs data.

Listing 10-18. Bloc events

```
abstract class JobsEvent extends Equatable {
  JobsEvent([List props = const []]) : super(props);
}

class GetJobsEvent extends JobsEvent {
  GetJobsEvent({@required this.keyword})
      : assert(keyword != null),
        super([keyword]);

  final String keyword;
}
```

Listing 10-19 shows the Bloc. JobsBloc class extends from Bloc<JobsEvent, JobsState> class. Type parameters of Bloc are event and state classes. JobsEmpty is the initial state. In the mapEventToState() method, if the event is GetJobsEvent, a JobsLoading state is emitted first to the stream. Then GitHubJobsClient object is used to fetch the data. If the data is fetched successfully, a JobsLoaded state is emitted with the loaded data. Otherwise, a JobsError state is emitted instead.

Listing 10-19. Bloc

```
class JobsBloc extends Bloc<JobsEvent, JobsState> {
  JobsBloc({@required this.jobsClient}) : assert(jobsClient !=
  null);

  final GitHubJobsClient jobsClient;

  @override
  JobsState get initialState => JobsEmpty();

  @override
  Stream<JobsState> mapEventToState(JobsEvent event) async* {
    if (event is GetJobsEvent) {
      yield JobsLoading();
      try {
        List<Job> jobs = await jobsClient.getJobs(event.
        keyword);
        yield JobsLoaded(jobs: jobs);
      } catch (e) {
        yield JobsError();
      }
    }
  }
}
```

GitHubJobs class in Listing 10-20 is the widget to use the JobsBloc class in Listing 10-19. The JobsBloc object is created in initState() method and disposed in dispose() method. In the KeywordInput widget, when user inputs the keyword in the text field and presses the search button, a GetJobsEvent is dispatched to the JobsBloc object. In the JobsView widget, BlocBuilder widget is used to build UI based on the state in the Bloc. Here we check the actual type of JobsState and return different widgets.

Listing 10-20. GitHub jobs widget using Bloc

```
class GitHubJobs extends StatefulWidget {
  GitHubJobs({Key key, @required this.jobsClient})
      : assert(jobsClient != null),
        super(key: key);

  final GitHubJobsClient jobsClient;

  @override
  _GitHubJobsState createState() => _GitHubJobsState();
}

class _GitHubJobsState extends State<GitHubJobs> {
  JobsBloc _jobsBloc;

  @override
  void initState() {
    super.initState();
    _jobsBloc = JobsBloc(jobsClient: widget.jobsClient);
  }

  @override
  Widget build(BuildContext context) {
    return Column(
      children: <Widget>[
        Padding(
          padding: const EdgeInsets.all(8.0),
          child: KeywordInput(
            jobsBloc: _jobsBloc,
          ),
        ),
        Expanded(
          child: JobsView(
```

```
            jobsBloc: _jobsBloc,
          ),
        ),
      ],
    );
  }

  @override
  void dispose() {
    _jobsBloc.dispose();
    super.dispose();
  }
}

class KeywordInput extends StatefulWidget {
  KeywordInput({this.jobsBloc});

  final JobsBloc jobsBloc;

  @override
  _KeywordInputState createState() => _KeywordInputState();
}

class _KeywordInputState extends State<KeywordInput> {
  final GlobalKey<FormFieldState<String>> _keywordFormKey =
GlobalKey();

  @override
  Widget build(BuildContext context) {
    return Row(
      children: <Widget>[
        Expanded(
          child: TextFormField(
            key: _keywordFormKey,
          ),
```

```
      ),
      IconButton(
        icon: Icon(Icons.search),
        onPressed: () {
          String keyword = _keywordFormKey.currentState?.
          value ?? ";
          if (keyword.isNotEmpty) {
            widget.jobsBloc.dispatch(GetJobsEvent(keyword:
            keyword));
          }
        },
      ),
    ],
  );
 }
}

class JobsView extends StatelessWidget {
  JobsView({this.jobsBloc});

  final JobsBloc jobsBloc;

  @override
  Widget build(BuildContext context) {
    return BlocBuilder(
      bloc: jobsBloc,
      builder: (BuildContext context, JobsState state) {
        if (state is JobsEmpty) {
          return Center(
            child: Text('Input keyword and search'),
          );
        } else if (state is JobsLoading) {
          return Center(
```

```
        child: CircularProgressIndicator(),
      );
    } else if (state is JobsError) {
      return Center(
        child: Text(
          'Failed to get jobs',
          style: TextStyle(color: Colors.red),
        ),
      );
    } else if (state is JobsLoaded) {
      return JobsList(state.jobs);
    }
  },
);
  }
}
```

10-7. Managing State Using Redux
Problem

You want to use Redux as the state management solution.

Solution

Use redux and flux_redux packages.

Discussion

Redux (https://redux.js.org/) is a popular library to manage state in apps. Originated for React, Redux has been ported to different languages. The redux package is a Dart implementation of Redux. The flux_redux

package allows using Redux store when building Flutter widgets. If you
have used Redux before, the same concepts are used in Flutter.

Redux uses a single global object as the state. This object is the single
source of truth for the app, and it's called the store. Actions are dispatched
to the store to update the state. Reducer functions accept the current state
and an action as the parameters and return the next state. The next state
becomes the input of the next run of the reducer function. UI widgets can
select partial data from the store to build the content.

To use flutter_redux package, you need to add flutter_redux:
^0.5.3 to the dependencies of pubspec.yaml file. We'll use the same
example of listing jobs on GitHub to demonstrate the usage of Redux in
Flutter.

Let's start from the state. JobsState class in Listing 10-21 represents
the global state. The state has three properties, loading represents whether
the data is still loading, error represents whether an error occurred
when loading the data, and data presents the list of data. By using the
copyWith() method, we can new JobsState objects by updating some
properties.

Listing 10-21. JobsState for Redux

```
class JobsState extends Equatable {
  JobsState({bool loading, bool error, List<Job> data})
      : _loading = loading,
        _error = error,
        _data = data,
        super([loading, error, data]);

  final bool _loading;
  final bool _error;
  final List<Job> _data;

  bool get loading => _loading ?? false;
  bool get error => _error ?? false;
```

```
List<Job> get data => _data ?? [];
bool get empty => _loading == null && _error == null && _data
== null;

JobsState copyWith({bool loading, bool error, List<Job>
data}) {
  return JobsState(
    loading: loading ?? this._loading,
    error: error ?? this._error,
    data: data ?? this._data,
  );
}
}
```

Listing 10-22 shows the actions. These actions trigger state changes.

Listing 10-22. Actions for Redux

```
abstract class JobsAction extends Equatable {
  JobsAction([List props = const []]) : super(props);
}

class LoadJobAction extends JobsAction {
  LoadJobAction({@required this.keyword})
      : assert(keyword != null),
        super([keyword]);

  final String keyword;
}

class JobLoadedAction extends JobsAction {
  JobLoadedAction({@required this.jobs})
      : assert(jobs != null),
        super([jobs]);
```

```
  final List<Job> jobs;
}
```

```
class JobLoadErrorAction extends JobsAction {}
```

Listing 10-23 shows the reducer function to update state according to the action.

Listing 10-23. Reducer function for Redux

```
JobsState jobsReducers(JobsState state, dynamic action) {
  if (action is LoadJobAction) {
    return state.copyWith(loading: true);
  } else if (action is JobLoadErrorAction) {
    return state.copyWith(loading: false, error: true);
  } else if (action is JobLoadedAction) {
    return state.copyWith(loading: false, data: action.jobs);
  }
  return state;
}
```

Actions defined in Listing 10-22 can only be used for synchronous operations. For example, if you want to dispatch the JobLoadedAction, you need to have the List<Job> object ready first. However, the operation to load jobs data is asynchronous. You'll need to use thunk functions as the middleware of Redux store. A thunk function takes the store as the only parameter. It uses the store to dispatch actions. A thunk action can be dispatched to the store, just like other normal actions.

The getJobs() function in Listing 10-24 takes a GitHubJobsClient object and a search keyword as the parameters. This function returns a thunk function of type ThunkAction<JobsState>. ThunkAction comes from redux_thunk package. In the thunk function, a LoadJobAction is dispatched first. Then GitHubJobsClient object is used to get the jobs data. Depending on the result of data loading, a JobLoadedAction or JobLoadErrorAction is dispatched.

Listing 10-24. Thunk function for Redux

```
ThunkAction<JobsState> getJobs(GitHubJobsClient jobsClient,
String keyword) {
  return (Store<JobsState> store) async {
    store.dispatch(LoadJobAction(keyword: keyword));
    try {
      List<Job> jobs = await jobsClient.getJobs(keyword);
      store.dispatch(JobLoadedAction(jobs: jobs));
    } catch (e) {
      store.dispatch(JobLoadErrorAction());
    }
  };
}
```

Now we can use the Redux store to build the widgets. You can use two helper widgets to access data in the store. In Listing 10-25, StoreBuilder widget is used to provide direct access to the store. The store is available as the second parameter of the build function. StoreBuilder widget is usually used when you need to dispatch actions. StoreConnector widget allows using a converter function to transform the state first. When the search icon is pressed, the getJobs() function in Listing 10-24 is called first to create the thunk function, then dispatches the thunk function to the store. When using StoreConnector widget, the converter function simply gets the current state from the store. The state object is then used in build function.

Listing 10-25. GitHub jobs widget using Redux store

```
class GitHubJobs extends StatefulWidget {
  GitHubJobs({
    Key key,
    @required this.store,
    @required this.jobsClient,
  })  : assert(store != null),
        assert(jobsClient != null),
        super(key: key);

  final Store<JobsState> store;
  final GitHubJobsClient jobsClient;

  @override
  _GitHubJobsState createState() => _GitHubJobsState();
}

class _GitHubJobsState extends State<GitHubJobs> {
  @override
  Widget build(BuildContext context) {
    return StoreProvider<JobsState>(
      store: widget.store,
      child: Column(
        children: <Widget>[
          Padding(
            padding: const EdgeInsets.all(8.0),
            child: KeywordInput(
              jobsClient: widget.jobsClient,
            ),
          ),
          Expanded(
            child: JobsView(),
```

```
        ),
      ],
    ),
  );
  }
}

class KeywordInput extends StatefulWidget {
  KeywordInput({this.jobsClient});

  final GitHubJobsClient jobsClient;

  @override
  _KeywordInputState createState() => _KeywordInputState();
}

class _KeywordInputState extends State<KeywordInput> {
  final GlobalKey<FormFieldState<String>> _keywordFormKey =
GlobalKey();

  @override
  Widget build(BuildContext context) {
    return Row(
      children: <Widget>[
        Expanded(
          child: TextFormField(
            key: _keywordFormKey,
          ),
        ),
        StoreBuilder<JobsState>(
          builder: (BuildContext context, Store<JobsState>
          store) {
            return IconButton(
              icon: Icon(Icons.search),
```

```
            onPressed: () {
              String keyword = _keywordFormKey.currentState?.
              value ?? ";
              if (keyword.isNotEmpty) {
                store.dispatch(getJobs(widget.jobsClient,
                keyword));
              }
            },
          );
        },
      ),
    ],
  );
}
}

class JobsView extends StatelessWidget {
  @override
  Widget build(BuildContext context) {
    return StoreConnector<JobsState, JobsState>(
      converter: (Store<JobsState> store) => store.state,
      builder: (BuildContext context, JobsState state) {
        if (state.empty) {
          return Center(
            child: Text('Input keyword and search'),
          );
        } else if (state.loading) {
          return Center(
            child: CircularProgressIndicator(),
          );
        } else if (state.error) {
          return Center(
```

```
      child: Text(
        'Failed to get jobs',
        style: TextStyle(color: Colors.red),
      ),
    );
  } else {
    return JobsList(state.data);
  }
},
    );
  }
}
```

The last step is to create the store. The store in Listing 10-26 is created with the reducer function, the initial state, and the thunk middleware from redux_thunk package.

Listing 10-26. Create the store

```
final store = new Store<JobsState>(
  jobsReducers,
  initialState: JobsState(),
  middleware: [thunkMiddleware],
);
```

10-8. Managing State Using Mobx

Problem

You want to use Mobx to manage state.

Solution

Use mobx and flutter_mobx packages.

Discussion

Mobx (https://mobx.js.org) is a state management library which connects reactive data with the UI. MobX originates from developing web apps using JavaScript. It's also ported to Dart (https://mobx.pub). In Flutter apps, we can use mobx and flutter_mobx packages to build apps with Mobx. Mobx for Flutter uses build_runner package to generate code for the store. The build_runner and mobx_codegen packages need to be added as dev_dependencies to pubspec.yaml file.

Mobx uses observables to manage the state. The whole state of an app consists of core state and derived state. Derived state is computed from core state. Actions mutate observables to update the state. Reactions are observers of the state and get notified whenever an observable they track is changed. In Flutter app, the reactions are used to update the widgets.

Comparing to Redux for Flutter, Mobx uses code generation to simplify the usage of store. You don't need to write boilerplate code to create actions. Mobx provides several annotations. You just annotate the code with these annotations. This is similar with how json_annotation and json_serialize packages work. We'll use the same example of showing job listings on GitHub to demonstrate the usage of Mobx. Add this package to your pubspec.yaml file if it is not already present.

Listing 10-27 shows the basic code of jobs_store.dart file for the Mobx store. This file uses the generated part file jobs_store.g.dart. _JobsStore is the abstract class of the store for jobs. It implements Store class from Mobx. Here we defined two observables using @observable annotation. The first observable keyword is a simple string that manages the current search keyword. The getJobsFuture observable is an ObservableFuture<List<Job>> object that manages the asynchronous operation to get the jobs using API. Those properties marked using @ computed annotation are derived observables to check the status of data loading. We also define two actions using @action annotation. The setKeyword() action sets the getJobsFuture observable to an empty state and keyword observable to the provided value. The getJobs() action uses GitHubJobsClient.getJobs() method to load the data. The getJobsFuture observable is updated to an ObservableFuture object wrapping the returned future.

Listing 10-27. Mobx store

```
import 'package:meta/meta.dart';
import 'package:mobx/mobx.dart';

part 'jobs_store.g.dart';

class JobsStore = _JobsStore with _$JobsStore;

abstract class _JobsStore implements Store {
  _JobsStore({@required this.jobsClient}) : assert(jobsClient
  != null);

  final GitHubJobsClient jobsClient;

  @observable
  String keyword = '';

  @observable
  ObservableFuture<List<Job>> getJobsFuture = emptyResponse;

  @computed
  bool get empty => getJobsFuture == emptyResponse;

  @computed
  bool get hasResults =>
      getJobsFuture != emptyResponse &&
      getJobsFuture.status == FutureStatus.fulfilled;
```

```
@computed
bool get loading =>
    getJobsFuture != emptyResponse &&
    getJobsFuture.status == FutureStatus.pending;

@computed
bool get hasError =>
    getJobsFuture != emptyResponse &&
    getJobsFuture.status == FutureStatus.rejected;

static ObservableFuture<List<Job>> emptyResponse =
ObservableFuture.value([]);

List<Job> jobs = [];

@action
Future<List<Job>> getJobs() async {
  jobs = [];
  final future = jobsClient.getJobs(keyword);
  getJobsFuture = ObservableFuture(future);

  return jobs = await future;
}

@action
void setKeyword(String keyword) {
  getJobsFuture = emptyResponse;
  this.keyword = keyword;
}
}
}
```

The flutter packages pub run build_runner build command is required to generate code. JobsStore class is the store to use. Listing 10-28 shows the widget that uses the store. In the onPressed callback of the search button, setKeyword() method is called first to update the keyword, then getJobs() method is called to trigger the data loading. The Observer widget uses a build function to build the UI using computed observables and fields in JobsStore object. Whenever these observables change, Observer widget rebuilds to update the UI.

Listing 10-28. GitHub jobs widget using Mobx store

```
class GitHubJobs extends StatefulWidget {
  GitHubJobs({Key key, @required this.jobsStore})
      : assert(jobsStore != null),
        super(key: key);

  final JobsStore jobsStore;

  @override
  _GitHubJobsState createState() => _GitHubJobsState();
}

class _GitHubJobsState extends State<GitHubJobs> {
  @override
  Widget build(BuildContext context) {
    JobsStore jobsStore = widget.jobsStore;
    return Column(
      children: <Widget>[
        Padding(
          padding: const EdgeInsets.all(8.0),
          child: KeywordInput(
            jobsStore: jobsStore,
          ),
        ),
        Expanded(
          child: JobsView(
            jobsStore: jobsStore,
```

```
        ),
      ),
    ],
  );
  }
}

class KeywordInput extends StatefulWidget {
  KeywordInput({this.jobsStore});

  final JobsStore jobsStore;

  @override
  _KeywordInputState createState() => _KeywordInputState();
}

class _KeywordInputState extends State<KeywordInput> {
  final GlobalKey<FormFieldState<String>> _keywordFormKey =
GlobalKey();

  @override
  Widget build(BuildContext context) {
    return Row(
      children: <Widget>[
        Expanded(
          child: TextFormField(
            key: _keywordFormKey,
          ),
        ),
        IconButton(
          icon: Icon(Icons.search),
          onPressed: () {
            String keyword = _keywordFormKey.currentState?.
            value ?? ";
```

```
            if (keyword.isNotEmpty) {
              widget.jobsStore.setKeyword(keyword);
              widget.jobsStore.getJobs();
            }
          },
        ),
      ],
    );
  }
}

class JobsView extends StatelessWidget {
  JobsView({this.jobsStore});

  final JobsStore jobsStore;

  @override
  Widget build(BuildContext context) {
    return Observer(
      builder: (BuildContext context) {
        if (jobsStore.empty) {
          return Center(
            child: Text('Input keyword and search'),
          );
        } else if (jobsStore.loading) {
          return Center(
            child: CircularProgressIndicator(),
          );
        } else if (jobsStore.hasError) {
          return Center(
            child: Text(
              'Failed to get jobs',
              style: TextStyle(color: Colors.red),
```

```
          ),
        );
      } else {
        return JobsList(jobsStore.jobs);
      }
    },
  );
  }
}
```

10-9. Summary

This chapter discusses different state management solutions for Flutter apps. In these solutions, StatefulWidget, InheritedWidget, InheritedModel, and InheritedNotifier widgets are provided by Flutter framework. Scoped model, Bloc, Redux, and Mobx libraries are third-party solutions. You are free to choose whatever solution that suits best for your requirement. In the next chapter, we'll discuss animations in Flutter.

CHAPTER 11

Animations

Animations play an important role in mobile apps to provide visual
feedback for end users. This chapter covers recipes related to animations
in Flutter.

11-1. Creating Simple Animations
Problem

You want to create simple animations.

Solution

Use `AnimationController` class to create simple animations.

Discussion

Animations in Flutter have a value and a status. The value of an animation
may change over time. Animations are represented using abstract
`Animation<T>` class. Animation class extends from `Listenable` class. You
can add listeners to `Animation` objects to get notified for changes of value
or status.

   `AnimationController` class is a subclass of `Animation<double>` class.
`AnimationController` class provides control over the animation it creates.
To create an `AnimationController` object, you can provide a lower bound,

© Fu Cheng 2019
F. Cheng, *Flutter Recipes*, https://doi.org/10.1007/978-1-4842-4982-6_11

an upper bound, and a duration. The value of AnimationController object changes from the lower bound to the upper bound over the duration. A TickerProvider object is also required. For stateful widget, you can use TickerProviderStateMixin or SingleTickerProviderStateMixin class as the mixin of the state class. If only one AnimationController object is used for the state, using SingleTickerProviderStateMixin is more efficient.

Listing 11-1 shows an example of using AnimationController in stateful widgets to animate the size of an image. The AnimationController object is created in the body of initState() method and disposed in dispose() method. This is a typical pattern of using AnimationController. _GrowingImageState class has the SingleTickerProviderStateMixin mixin, so the AnimationController constructor uses this object as the vsync parameter. In the listener of AnimationController object, setState() method is called to trigger the rebuild of the widget. The forward() method starts the running of the animation in forward direction. In the build() method, the current value of AnimationController object is used to control the size of the SizedBox widget. In the runtime, the size of SizedBox widget grows from 0 to 400 in 10 seconds.

Listing 11-1. Using AnimationController

```
class GrowingImage extends StatefulWidget {
  @override
  _GrowingImageState createState() => _GrowingImageState();
}

class _GrowingImageState extends State<GrowingImage>
    with SingleTickerProviderStateMixin {
  AnimationController controller;

  @override
  void initState() {
```

```
    super.initState();
    controller = AnimationController(
      lowerBound: 0,
      upperBound: 400,
      duration: const Duration(seconds: 10),
      vsync: this,
    )
      ..addListener(() {
        setState(() {});
      })
      ..forward();
  }

  @override
  Widget build(BuildContext context) {
    return SizedBox(
      width: controller.value,
      height: controller.value,
      child: Image.network('https://picsum.photos/400'),
    );
  }

  @override
  void dispose() {
    controller.dispose();
    super.dispose();
  }
}
```

Table 11-1 shows methods of AnimationController to control the progress of animation.

Table 11-1. *Methods to control animation*

Name	Description
forward()	Starts the running of animation in forward direction.
reverse()	Starts the running of animation in backward direction.
stop()	Stops the running of animation.
repeat()	Starts the running of animation and restarts when it completes.
reset()	Sets the value to the lower bound and stops the animation.

An animation may be in different status. AnimationStatus enum represents different statuses for an animation. Table 11-2 shows all values of this enum. You can use addStatusListener() method to add a listener to get notified when the status changes.

Table 11-2. *Values of AnimationStatus*

Name	Description
forward	The animation is running in forward direction.
reverse	The animation is running in backward direction.
dismissed	The animation is stopped at the beginning.
completed	The animation is stopped at the end.

In Listing 11-2, a status listener is added to the AnimationController object. When the animation is in the completed status, it starts running in backward direction.

Listing 11-2. Status listener

```
var controller = AnimationController(
  lowerBound: 0,
  upperBound: 300,
```

```
  duration: const Duration(seconds: 10),
  vsync: this,
)
  ..addListener(() {
    setState(() {});
  })
  ..addStatusListener((AnimationStatus status) {
    if (status == AnimationStatus.completed) {
      controller.reverse();
    }
  })
  ..forward();
```

Listing 11-1 shows a typical pattern to use animations with stateful widgets. AnimatedWidget widget makes the use of animations much easier. AnimatedWidget constructor requires a Listenable object. Whenever the Listenable object emits a value, the widget rebuilds itself. Listing 11-3 shows an example of using AnimatedWidget. Although AnimatedWidget class is typically used with Animation objects, you can still use it with any Listenable object.

Listing 11-3. Example of AnimatedWidget

```
class AnimatedImage extends AnimatedWidget {
  AnimatedImage({Key key, this.animation})
      : super(key: key, listenable: animation);

  final Animation<double> animation;

  @override
  Widget build(BuildContext context) {
    return SizedBox(
      width: animation.value,
      height: animation.value,
```

```
      child: Image.network('https://picsum.photos/300'),
   );
  }
}
```

11-2. Creating Animations Using Linear Interpolation

Problem

You want to create animations for other data types using linear interpolation.

Solution

Use Tween class and its subclasses.

Discussion

AnimationController class uses double as its value type. Double values are useful for animations with size or position. You may still need to animate other types of data. For example, you can animate the background color from red to green. For these scenarios, you can use Tween class and its subclasses.

Tween class represents linear interpolation between a beginning and ending value. To create a Tween object, you need to provide these two values. Tween objects can provide values for animations to use. By using the animate() method with another Animation object, you can create a new Animation object that is driven by the provided Animation object but uses values from the Tween object. Subclasses of Tween need to implement the lerp() method that takes an animation value and returns the interpolated value.

In Listing 11-4, AnimatedColor widget uses Animation<Color> object to update the background color. ColorTween object is created with beginning value Colors.red and ending value Colors.green.

Listing 11-4. Example of ColorTween

```
class AnimatedColorTween extends StatefulWidget {
  @override
  _AnimatedColorTweenState createState() => _
AnimatedColorTweenState();
}

class _AnimatedColorTweenState extends
State<AnimatedColorTween>
    with SingleTickerProviderStateMixin {
  AnimationController controller;
  Animation<Color> animation;

  @override
  void initState() {
    super.initState();
    controller = AnimationController(
      duration: const Duration(seconds: 10),
      vsync: this,
    );
    animation =
        ColorTween(begin: Colors.red, end: Colors.green).
        animate(controller);
    controller.forward();
  }
```

```
  @override
  Widget build(BuildContext context) {
    return AnimatedColor(
      animation: animation,
    );
  }

  @override
  void dispose() {
    controller.dispose();
    super.dispose();
  }
}

class AnimatedColor extends AnimatedWidget {
  AnimatedColor({Key key, this.animation})
      : super(key: key, listenable: animation);

  final Animation<Color> animation;

  @override
  Widget build(BuildContext context) {
    return Container(
      width: 300,
      height: 300,
      decoration: BoxDecoration(color: animation.value),
    );
  }
}
```

There are many other subclasses of Tween for different objects, including AlignmentTween, BorderTween, BoxConstraintsTween, DecorationTween, EdgeInsetsTween, SizeTween, TextStyleTween, and more.

11-3. Creating Curved Animations

Problem

You want to create curved animations.

Solution

Use CurvedAnimation or CurveTween class.

Discussion

Except from linear animations, you can also create curved animations that use curves to adjust the rate of changes. A curve is a mapping of unit interval to another unit interval. Curve class and its subclasses are built-in types of curves. The transform() method of Curve class returns the mapped value of the curve for a given point. A curve must map the input 0.0 to 0.0 and 1.0 to 1.0. Table 11-3 shows different types of curves.

Table 11-3. *Different types of curves*

Name	Description
Cubic	Cubic curve defined by two control points. Created with four double values as x and y coordinates of these two points.
ElasticInCurve	Oscillation curve that grows in magnitude while overshooting its bounds. Created with duration of the oscillation.
ElasticOutCurve	Oscillation curve that shrinks in magnitude while overshooting its bounds. Created with duration of the oscillation.

(*continued*)

Table 11-3. (*continued*)

Name	Description
ElasticInOutCurve	Oscillation curve that grows then shrinks in magnitude while overshooting its bounds. Created with duration of the oscillation.
Interval	Created with begin, end, and a curve. Its value is 0.0 until begin and 1.0 after end. Values between begin and end are defined by the curve.
SawTooth	A sawtooth curve that repeats the given number of times.
Threshold	A curve that is 0.0 until the threshold, then jumps to 1.0.

You can use either constructors of Curve subclasses in Table 11-3 to create new curves or use constants in Curves class. Constants in Curves class are generally good enough for most cases. For a Curve object, you can use the flipped property to get a new curve that is the inversion of this one.

With Curve objects, you can create curved animations using CurvedAnimation class. Table 11-4 shows parameters of CurvedAnimation constructor. If reverseCurve parameter is null, the specified curve is used in both directions.

Table 11-4. *Parameters of CurvedAnimation*

Name	Type	Description
parent	Animation<double>	The animation to apply the curve.
curve	Curve	The curve to use in forward direction.
reverseCurve	Curve	The curve to use in backward direction.

In Listing 11-5, AnimatedBox widget uses the animation value to determine the left position of the box. The CurvedAnimation object is created with Curves.easeInOut curve.

Listing 11-5. CurvedAnimation

```
class CurvedPosition extends StatefulWidget {
  @override
  _CurvedPositionState createState() => _CurvedPositionState();
}

class _CurvedPositionState extends State<CurvedPosition>
    with SingleTickerProviderStateMixin {
  AnimationController controller;
  Animation<double> animation;

  @override
  void initState() {
    super.initState();
    controller = AnimationController(
      duration: const Duration(seconds: 5),
      vsync: this,
    )..forward();
    animation = CurvedAnimation(parent: controller, curve:
    Curves.easeInOut);
  }

  @override
  Widget build(BuildContext context) {
    return AnimatedBox(
      animation: animation,
    );
  }

  @override
  void dispose() {
    controller.dispose();
    super.dispose();
```

```
  }
}

class AnimatedBox extends AnimatedWidget {
  AnimatedBox({Key key, this.animation})
      : super(key: key, listenable: animation);

  final Animation<double> animation;
  final double _width = 400;

  @override
  Widget build(BuildContext context) {
    return Container(
      width: _width,
      height: 20,
      child: Stack(
        children: <Widget>[
          Positioned(
            left: animation.value * _width,
            bottom: 0,
            child: Container(
              width: 10,
              height: 10,
              decoration: BoxDecoration(color: Colors.red),
            ),
          )
        ],
      ),
    );
  }
}
```

CurveTween class uses a Curve object to transform the value of the animation. You can use CurveTween objects when you need to chain a curve animation with another Tween object.

11-4. Chaining Tweens
Problem

You want to chain tweens.

Solution

Use chain() method of Animatable class or drive() method of Animation class.

Discussion

Animatable is the superclass of Tween, CurveTween, and TweenSequence classes. Given an Animatable object, you can use the chain() method with another Animatable object as the parent. For a given input value, the parent Animatable object is evaluated first, then the result is used as the input of the current Animatable object. You can use multiple chain() methods to create complex animations.

In Listing 11-6, the Tween object is chained with another CurveTween object.

Listing 11-6. Chain tweens

```
var animation = Tween(begin: 0.0, end: 300.0)
  .chain(CurveTween(curve: Curves.easeOut))
  .animate(controller);
```

You can also use the drive() method of Animation class to chain an Animatable object.

11-5. Creating Sequences of Tweens

Problem

You want to create a sequence of tweens for different stages.

Solution

Use TweenSequence class.

Discussion

By using TweenSequence class, you can use different Animatable objects
for different stages of an animation. A TweenSequence object is defined
by a list of TweenSequenceItem objects. Each TweenSequenceItem object
has an Animatable object and a weight. The weight defines the relative
percentage of this TweenSequenceItem object in the whole duration of its
parent TweenSequence object.

In Listing 11-7, the animation is created with 40% of linear tween and
60% of curved tween.

Listing 11-7. Example of TweenSequence

```
var animation = TweenSequence([
  TweenSequenceItem(
    tween: Tween(begin: 0.0, end: 100.0),
    weight: 40,
  ),
  TweenSequenceItem(
    tween: Tween(begin: 100.0, end: 300.0)
        .chain(CurveTween(curve: Curves.easeInOut)),
    weight: 60,
  )
]).animate(controller);
```

426

11-6. Running Simultaneous Animations
Problem

You want to run simultaneous animations in AnimatedWidget.

Solution

Use evaluate() method of Animatable class.

Discussion

AnimatedWidget constructor only supports a single Animation object. If you want to use multiple animations in an AnimatedWidget object, you need to create multiple Tween objects in the AnimatedWidget object and use evaluate() method to get the values for the Animation object.

In Listing 11-8, _leftTween and _bottomTween objects determine the left and bottom properties, respectively.

Listing 11-8. Simultaneous animations

```
class AnimatedBox extends AnimatedWidget {
  AnimatedBox({Key key, this.animation})
      : super(key: key, listenable: animation);

  final Animation<double> animation;
  final double _width = 400;
  final double _height = 300;
  static final _leftTween = Tween(begin: 0, end: 1.0);
  static final _bottomTween = CurveTween(curve: Curves.ease);

  @override
  Widget build(BuildContext context) {
    return Container(
```

```
      width: _width,
      height: _height,
      margin: EdgeInsets.all(10),
      decoration: BoxDecoration(border: Border.all()),
      child: Stack(
        children: <Widget>[
          Positioned(
            left: _leftTween.evaluate(animation) * _width,
            bottom: _bottomTween.evaluate(animation) * _height,
            child: Container(
              width: 10,
              height: 10,
              decoration: BoxDecoration(color: Colors.red),
            ),
          )
        ],
      ),
    );
  }
}
```

11-7. Creating Staggered Animations
Problem

You want to create sequential or overlapping animations.

Solution

Use Interval class.

Discussion

With TweenSequence class, you can create a sequence of tweens. However, tweens specified in TweenSequence objects cannot be overlapping. To create overlapping animations, you can use Interval curve to specify the begin and end time of an animation.

In Listing 11-9, three Tween objects animate in different intervals specified in Interval objects. These Tween objects are controlled by the same Animation object.

Listing 11-9. Staggered animations

```
class AnimatedContainer extends StatelessWidget {
  AnimatedContainer({Key key, this.animation})
     : width = Tween(begin: 0.0, end: 300.0).
    animate(CurvedAnimation(
         parent: animation,
         curve: Interval(0.0, 0.5, curve: Curves.
         easeInOut))),
     height = Tween(begin: 0.0, end: 200.0).
     animate(CurvedAnimation(
         parent: animation,
         curve: Interval(0.2, 0.7, curve: Curves.
         bounceInOut))),
     backgroundColor = ColorTween(begin: Colors.red, end:
     Colors.green)
         .animate(CurvedAnimation(
             parent: animation,
             curve: Interval(0.3, 1.0, curve: Curves.
             elasticInOut))),
     super(key: key);
```

```
final Animation<double> animation;
final Animation<double> width;
final Animation<double> height;
final Animation<Color> backgroundColor;

Widget _build(BuildContext context, Widget child) {
  return Container(
    width: width.value,
    height: height.value,
    decoration: BoxDecoration(color: backgroundColor.value),
    child: child,
  );
}

@override
Widget build(BuildContext context) {
  return AnimatedBuilder(
    animation: animation,
    builder: _build,
  );
}
}
```

11-8. Creating Hero Animations
Problem

You want to animate an element across two routes.

Solution

Use Hero widget.

Discussion

When switching from the current route to a new route, it's better to have some elements in the new route to indicate the navigation context. For example, the current route displays a list of items. When the user taps one item to navigate to the details route, the new route should have a widget to show brief information about the selected item.

Hero widget is shared between two routes. A Hero widget is created with a tag and a child widget. The tag is the unique identifier of a Hero widget. If the source route and target route both have a Hero widget with the same tag, then during route transition, the Hero widget in source route is animated to the location in the target route. Tags of Hero widget must be unique in the same widgets tree.

In Listing 11-10, ImageHero class wraps a Hero widget that displays an image in a SizedBox widget. The tag is set to the image's URL.

Listing 11-10. Hero widget

```
class ImageHero extends StatelessWidget {
  ImageHero({Key key, this.imageUrl, this.width, this.height})
      : super(key: key);

  final String imageUrl;
  final double width;
  final double height;

  @override
  Widget build(BuildContext context) {
    return SizedBox(
      width: width,
      height: height,
      child: Hero(
        tag: imageUrl,
```

```
        child: Image.network(imageUrl),
      ),
    );
  }
}
```

Listing 11-11 shows the current route that displays a list of images. ImageHero widget is wrapped in a GridTile widget. Tapping an image navigates to the new route with ImageView widget.

Listing 11-11. Current route with ImageHero

```
class ImagesPage extends StatelessWidget {
  @override
  Widget build(BuildContext context) {
    return Scaffold(
      appBar: AppBar(
        title: Text('Images'),
      ),
      body: GridView.count(
        crossAxisCount: 2,
        children: List.generate(8, (int index) {
          String imageUrl = 'https://picsum.
          photos/300?random&$index';
          return GridTile(
            child: InkWell(
              onTap: () {
                Navigator.push(
                  context,
                  MaterialPageRoute(builder: (BuildContext
                  context) {
                    return ImageView(imageUrl: imageUrl);
                  }),
```

```
              );
            },
            child: ImageHero(
              imageUrl: imageUrl,
              width: 300,
              height: 300,
            ),
          ),
        );
      }),
    ),
  );
}
}
```

Listing 11-12 shows the ImageView widget. It also has an ImageHero widget with the same tag as the selected image. This is required to make the animation work.

Listing 11-12. New route with ImageHero

```
class ImageView extends StatelessWidget {
  ImageView({Key key, this.imageUrl}) : super(key: key);
  final String imageUrl;

  @override
  Widget build(BuildContext context) {
    return Scaffold(
      appBar: AppBar(
        title: Text('Image'),
      ),
      body: Row(
        children: <Widget>[
```

```
        ImageHero(
          width: 50,
          height: 50,
          imageUrl: imageUrl,
        ),
        Expanded(
          child: Text('Image Detail'),
        ),
      ],
    ),
  );
  }
}
```

11-9. Using Common Transitions

Problem

You want to have a simple way to use different types of Tween objects for animations.

Solution

Use different types of transitions.

Discussion

It's common to use different types of Tween objects to animate different aspects of widgets. You can use AnimatedWidget or AnimatedBuilder class to work with Tween objects. Flutter SDK provides several transition widgets to make certain animations easy to use.

ScaleTransition widget animates the scale of a widget. To create a ScaleTransition object, you need to provide an Animation<double> object as the scale. The alignment parameter specifies the alignment of the origin of scaling coordinates relative to the box. Listing 11-13 shows an example of ScaleTransition.

Listing 11-13. Example of ScaleTransition

```
class ScaleBox extends StatelessWidget {
  ScaleBox({Key key, Animation<double> animation})
      : _animation = CurveTween(curve: Curves.ease).
      animate(animation),
        super(key: key);

  final Animation<double> _animation;

  @override
  Widget build(BuildContext context) {
    return ScaleTransition(
      scale: _animation,
      alignment: Alignment.centerLeft,
      child: Container(
        height: 100,
        decoration: BoxDecoration(color: Colors.red),
      ),
    );
  }
}
```

Another example of transition widget is FadeTransition widget that animates the opacity. Listing 11-14 shows an example of FadeTransition.

Listing 11-14. Example of FadeTransition

```
class FadeBox extends StatelessWidget {
  FadeBox({Key key, Animation<double> animation})
      : _animation = CurveTween(curve: Curves.ease).
      animate(animation),
        super(key: key);

  final Animation<double> _animation;

  @override
  Widget build(BuildContext context) {
    return FadeTransition(
      opacity: _animation,
      child: Container(
        height: 100,
        decoration: BoxDecoration(color: Colors.red),
      ),
    );
  }
}
```

11-10. Creating Physics Simulations
Problem

You want to use physics simulations.

Solution

Use simulations in physics library.

Discussion

Animations in the animation library are either linear or curved. The physics library provides physics simulations, including springs, friction, and gravity. Simulation class is the base class for all simulations. A simulation is also changing over time. For a point of time, the method x() returns the position, the method dx() returns the velocity, and isDone() method returns whether the simulation is done. Given a Simulation object, you can use animateWith() method of AnimationController class to drive the animation using this simulation.

SpringSimulation class represents the simulation for a particle attached to a spring. To create a SpringSimulation object, yon can provide the parameters listed in Table 11-5.

Table 11-5. *Parameters of SpringSimulation*

Name	Type	Description
spring	SpringDescription	The description of a spring.
start	double	The start distance.
end	double	The end distance.
velocity	double	The initial velocity.
tolerance	Tolerance	Magnitudes of differences for distances, durations, and velocity to be considered equal.

To create SpringDescription objects, you can use the SpringDescription() constructor with parameters to specify mass, stiffness, and damping coefficient. The SpringDescription.withDampingRatio() constructor uses a damping ratio instead of damping coefficient. Listing 11-15 shows an example of creating SpringSimulation object.

Listing 11-15. Spring simulation

```
SpringSimulation _springSimulation = SpringSimulation(
  SpringDescription.withDampingRatio(
    mass: 1.0,
    stiffness: 50,
    ratio: 1.0,
  ),
  0.0,
  1.0,
  1.0)
..tolerance = Tolerance(distance: 0.01, velocity: double.
infinity);
```

An easier way to use spring simulation is using the `fling()` method of `AnimationController` class. This method drives the animation with a critically damped spring.

`GravitySimulation` class represents a simulation for a particle that follows Newton's second law of motion. Table 11-6 shows parameters of `GravitySimulation` constructor.

Table 11-6. *Parameters of GravitySimulation*

Name	Type	Description
acceleration	double	Acceleration of the particle.
distance	double	Initial distance.
endDistance	double	End distance for the simulation to be done.
velocity	double	Initial velocity.

In Listing 11-16, `SimulationController` widget uses a Simulation object to drive the animation.

Listing 11-16. Use simulation with animation

```
typedef BuilderFunc = Widget Function(BuildContext,
Animation<double>);

class SimulationController extends StatefulWidget {
  SimulationController({Key key, this.simulation, this.
  builder})
      : super(key: key);
  final Simulation simulation;
  final BuilderFunc builder;

  @override
  _SimulationControllerState createState() =>
  _SimulationControllerState();
}

class _SimulationControllerState extends
State<SimulationController>
    with SingleTickerProviderStateMixin {
  AnimationController controller;

  @override
  void initState() {
    super.initState();
    controller = AnimationController(
      vsync: this,
    )..animateWith(widget.simulation);
  }

  @override
  Widget build(BuildContext context) {
    return widget.builder(context, controller.view);
  }
```

```
  @override
  void dispose() {
    controller.dispose();
    super.dispose();
  }
}
```

11-11. Summary

This chapter covers recipes related to animations in Flutter.
AnimationController class is used to control animations. Subclasses
of Tween class create linear animations for different types of data.
AnimatedWidget and AnimatedBuilder are useful widgets that use
animations. In the next chapter, we'll discuss integration with native
platform in Flutter.

CHAPTER 12

Platform Integration

In mobile apps, it's common to integrate with the native platform. You can write platform-specific code to use native platform API. There are a large number of plugins to perform different tasks.

12-1. Reading and Writing Files

Problem

You want to read and write files.

Solution

Use File API.

Discussion

In mobile apps, you may need to save files on the device. The `dart:io` library provides files API to read and write files. `File` class has methods to read content, write content, and query metadata of files. Operations with file system can be synchronous or asynchronous. Most of these operations have a pair of methods in `File` class. The asynchronous method returns a `Future` object, while the synchronous method uses `Sync` as the name suffix and returns the actual value. For example, `readAsString()` and `readAsStringSync()` methods are the pair for read operation that returns a string. Table 12-1 shows asynchronous methods of `File` class.

© Fu Cheng 2019
F. Cheng, *Flutter Recipes*, https://doi.org/10.1007/978-1-4842-4982-6_12

Table 12-1. *Asynchronous methods of File*

Name	Description
copy(String newPath)	Copy this file to a new path.
create({bool recursive: false})	Create this file. If recursive is true, all directories will be created.
open()	Open the file for random access with a RandomAccessFile object.
readAsBytes()	Read the entire file content as a list of bytes.
readAsString({Encoding encoding: utf8})	Read the entire file content as a string using specified encoding.
readAsLines(({Encoding encoding: utf8})	Read the entire file content as lines of text using specified encoding.
writeAsBytes(List<int> bytes)	Write a list of bytes to the file.
writeAsString(String contents)	Write a string to the file.
rename(String newPath)	Rename this file to a new path.
delete({bool recursive: false})	Delete this file.
exists()	Check whether this file exists.
stat()	Return a FileStat object that describes the file.
lastAccessed()	Get the last accessed time of this file.
lastModified()	Get the last modified time of this file.
length()	Get the length of this file.

`Directory` class represents directories in the file system. Given a `Directory` object, `list()` or `listSync()` methods can be used to list files and sub-directories.

To create `File` objects, you can use the default constructor with a path. For Flutter apps, the path may be platform-specific. There are two common places to store files for mobile apps:

- Temporary directory to store temporary files that may be cleared at any time

- Documents directory to store files that are private to the app and will only be cleared when the app is deleted

To get the platform-specific paths for these two locations, you can use the `path_provider` package (`https://pub.dev/packages/path_provider`). This package provides `getTemporaryDirectory()` function to get the path of the temporary directory and `getApplicationDocumentsDirectory()` function to get the application documents directory.

In Listing 12-1, `readConfig()` method reads the `config.txt` file from the application documents directory, while `writeConfig()` method writes a string to the same file.

Listing 12-1. Read and write files

```
class ConfigFile {
  Future<File> get _configFile async {
    Directory directory = await
    getApplicationDocumentsDirectory();
    return File('${directory.path}/config.txt');
  }

  Future<String> readConfig() async {
    return _configFile
        .then((file) => file.readAsString())
```

```
        .catchError((error) => 'default config');
  }

  Future<File> writeConfig(String config) async {
    File file = await _configFile;
    return file.writeAsString(config);
  }
}
```

12-2. Storing Key-Value Pairs

Problem

You want to store type-safe key-value pairs.

Solution

Use shared_preferences plugin.

Discussion

You can use files API to store any data on the device. Using generic files API means that you need to deal with data serialization and deserialization yourself. If the data you need to store is simple key-value pairs, using shared_preferences plugin (https://pub.dev/packages/shared_preferences) is a better choice. This plugin provides a map-based API to manage type-safe key-value pairs. The type of keys is always String. Only several types can be used as values, including String, bool, double, int, and List<String>.

To manage key-value pairs, you need to use the static SharedPreferences.getInstance() method to get the SharedPreferences object. Table 12-2 shows methods of SharedPreferences class. For each

444

supported data type, there is a pair of methods to get and set the value. For example, getBool() and setBool() methods are used to get and set bool values.

Table 12-2. *Methods of SharedPreference*

Name	Description
get(String key)	Read the value for the specified key.
containsKey(String key)	Check whether specified key exists.
getKeys()	Get a set of keys.
remove(String key)	Remove the pair with the specified key.
clear()	Remove all pairs.
setString(String key, String value)	Write a String value.
getString()	Read a String value.

In Listing 12-2, SharedPreferences class is used to read and write a key-value pair.

Listing 12-2. Use SharedPreferences

```
class AppConfig {
  Future<SharedPreferences> _getPrefs() async {
    return await SharedPreferences.getInstance();
  }

  Future<String> getName() async {
    SharedPreferences prefs = await _getPrefs();
    return prefs.getString('name') ?? ";
  }

  Future<bool> setName(String name) async {
    SharedPreferences prefs = await _getPrefs();
```

```
    return prefs.setString('name', name);
  }
}
```

12-3. Writing Platform-Specific Code

Problem

You want to write platform-specific code.

Solution

Use platform channels to pass messages between Flutter app and the underlying host platform.

Discussion

In Flutter apps, most of code is written in platform agnostic Dart code. Features provided by Flutter SDK are limited. Sometimes you may still need to write platform-specific code to use native platform APIs. A generated Flutter app already has platform-specific code in android and ios directories. Code in these two directories is required to build native bundles.

Flutter uses message passing to call platform-specific APIs and get the result back. Messages are passed through platform channels. Flutter code sends messages to the host over a platform channel. Host code listens on the platform channel and receives the message. It then uses platform-specific API to generate the response and sends it back over the same channel to the Flutter code. Messages passed are actually asynchronous method calls.

In Flutter code, platform channels are created using MethodChannel class. All channel names in an app must be unique. It's recommended to use a domain name as the prefix of channel names. To send method calls over a channel, these method calls must be encoded into binary format before being sent, and results received are decoded into Dart values. Encoding and decoding are done using subclasses of MethodCodec class:

- StandardMethodCodec class uses standard binary encoding.

- JSONMethodCodec class uses UTF-8 JSON encoding.

MethodChannel constructor has name parameter to specify the channel name and codec parameter to specify the MethodCodec object. The default MethodCodec object used is a StandardMethodCodec object.

Given a MethodChannel object, the invokeMethod() method invokes a method on the channel with specified arguments. The return value is a Future<T> object. This Future object may complete with different values:

- It completes with the result if the method call succeeds.

- It completes with a PlatformException if the method call fails.

- It completes with a MissingPluginException if the method has not been implemented.

The invokeListMethod() method also invokes a method but returns a Future<List<T>> object. The invokeMapMethod() method invokes a method and returns a Future<Map<K, V>> object. Both invokeListMethod() and invokeMapMethod() methods use invokeMethod() internally, but add extra type cast.

In Listing 12-3, the getNetworkOperator method is invoked over the channel and returns the network operator.

Listing 12-3. Get network operator

```
class NetworkOperator extends StatefulWidget {
  @override
  _NetworkOperatorState createState() =>
  _NetworkOperatorState();
}

class _NetworkOperatorState extends State<NetworkOperator> {
  static const channel = const MethodChannel('flutter-recipes/
  network');

  String _networkOperator = ";

  @override
  void initState() {
    super.initState();
    _getNetworkOperator();
  }

  Future<void> _getNetworkOperator() async {
    String operator;
    try {
      operator = await channel.invokeMethod('getNetworkOperator
      ') ?? 'unknown';
    } catch (e) {
      operator = 'Failed to get network operator: ${e.
      message}';
    }

    setState(() {
      _networkOperator = operator;
    });
  }
```

```
@override
Widget build(BuildContext context) {
  return Container(
    child: Center(
      child: Text(_networkOperator),
    ),
  );
}
}
```

The handler of getNetworkOperator method call needs to be implemented in both Android and iOS platforms. Listing 12-4 shows the Java implementation. The getNetworkOperator() method uses Android API to get network operator. In the method call handler of the channel, if the method name is getNetworkOperator, the result of getNetworkOperator() method is sent back as success response using Result.success() method. If you want to send back error response, you can use Result.error() method. If the method is unknown, you should use Result.notImplemented() to mark the method as unimplemented.

Listing 12-4. Android implementation of getNetworkOperator

```
public class MainActivity extends FlutterActivity {
  private static final String CHANNEL = "flutter-recipes/
  network";

  @Override
  protected void onCreate(Bundle savedInstanceState) {
    super.onCreate(savedInstanceState);
    GeneratedPluginRegistrant.registerWith(this);

    new MethodChannel(getFlutterView(), CHANNEL)
        .setMethodCallHandler((methodCall, result) -> {
          if ("getNetworkOperator".equals(methodCall.method)) {
```

```
            result.success(getNetworkOperator());
        } else {
            result.notImplemented();
        }
    });
  }
  private String getNetworkOperator() {
    TelephonyManager telephonyManager =
        ((TelephonyManager) getSystemService(Context.TELEPHONY_
        SERVICE));
    return telephonyManager.getNetworkOperatorName();
  }
}
```

Listing 12-5 shows the AppDelegate.swift file for iOS platform. The receiveNetworkOperator() function uses iOS API to get the carrier name and send back as response using FlutterResult.

Listing 12-5. Swift implementation of getNetworkOperator

```swift
import UIKit
import Flutter
import CoreTelephony

@UIApplicationMain
@objc class AppDelegate: FlutterAppDelegate {
  override func application(
    _ application: UIApplication,
    didFinishLaunchingWithOptions launchOptions:
    [UIApplicationLaunchOptionsKey: Any]?
  ) -> Bool {
    GeneratedPluginRegistrant.register(with: self)
```

```swift
guard let controller = window?.rootViewController as?
FlutterViewController else {
  fatalError("rootViewController is not type
  FlutterViewController")
}
let networkChannel = FlutterMethodChannel(name: "flutter-
recipes/network", binaryMessenger: controller)
networkChannel.setMethodCallHandler({
  [weak self] (call: FlutterMethodCall, result:
  FlutterResult) -> Void in
  guard call.method == "getNetworkOperator" else {
    result(FlutterMethodNotImplemented)
    return
  }
  self?.receiveNetworkOperator(result: result)
})

return super.application(application,
didFinishLaunchingWithOptions: launchOptions)
}

private func receiveNetworkOperator(result: FlutterResult) {
  let networkInfo = CTTelephonyNetworkInfo()
  let carrier = networkInfo.subscriberCellularProvider
  result(carrier?.carrierName)
}
}
```

12-4. Creating Plugins

Problem

You want to create sharable plugins that contain platform-specific code.

Solution

Create Flutter projects using the plugin template.

Discussion

Recipe 12-4 shows how to add platform-specific code to Flutter apps. Code added to a Flutter app cannot be shared between different apps. If you want to make the platform-specific code reusable, you can create Flutter plugins. Plugins are another type of projects supported in Flutter SDK. Plugins can be shared like other Dart packages using Dart pub tool (`https://pub.dev/`).

To create a new Flutter plugin, you can use `flutter create --template=plugin` command. The `template=plugin` parameter means using the `plugin` template to create a Flutter project. You can choose to use either Java or Kotlin for Android and Objective-C or Swift for iOS, respectively. By default, Java is used for Android and Objective-C is used for iOS. You can use `-a` parameter with values `java` and `kotlin` to specify the language for Android and `-i` parameter with values `objc` and `swift` to specify the language for iOS. The following command shows how to create a plugin using Swift for iOS.

```
$ flutter create --template=plugin -i swift network
```

You can also use Android Studio or VS Code to create new plugins.

The newly created plugin already has skeleton code that gets the platform version. We can use the code in Recipe 12-3 to implement the

452

plugin with new method to get the network operator. In the directory of generated plugin, there are several sub-directories:

- The lib directory contains plugin's public Dart API.

- The android directory contains Android implementation of the public API.

- The ios directory contains iOS implementation of the public API.

- The example directory contains an example Flutter app that uses this plugin.

- The test directory contains test code.

We first define the public Dart API in lib/network_plugin.dart file. In Listing 12-6, the value of the networkOperator property is retrieved by calling getNetworkOperator method using the method channel.

Listing 12-6. Plugin Dart API

```
class NetworkPlugin {
  static const MethodChannel _channel =
    const MethodChannel('network_plugin');

  static Future<String> get networkOperator async {
    return await _channel.invokeMethod('getNetworkOperator');
  }
}
```

The NetworkPlugin.java file in Listing 12-7 is the Android implementation of the plugin. NetworkPlugin class implements MethodCallHandler interface to handle method calls received from the platform channel.

Listing 12-7. Android implementation

```java
public class NetworkPlugin implements MethodCallHandler {

  public static void registerWith(Registrar registrar) {
    final MethodChannel channel = new MethodChannel(registrar.
messenger(), "network_plugin");
    channel.setMethodCallHandler(new NetworkPlugin(registrar));
  }

  NetworkPlugin(Registrar registrar) {
    this.registrar = registrar;
  }

  private final PluginRegistry.Registrar registrar;

  @Override
  public void onMethodCall(MethodCall call, Result result) {
    if (call.method.equals("getNetworkOperator")) {
      result.success(getNetworkOperator());
    } else {
      result.notImplemented();
    }
  }

  private String getNetworkOperator() {
    Context context = registrar.context();
    TelephonyManager telephonyManager =
        ((TelephonyManager) context.getSystemService(Context.
        TELEPHONY_SERVICE));
    return telephonyManager.getNetworkOperatorName();
  }
}
```

The SwiftNetworkPlugin.swift file in Listing 12-8 is the Swift implementation of the plugin.

Listing 12-8. Swift implementation

```swift
public class SwiftNetworkPlugin: NSObject, FlutterPlugin {
  public static func register(with registrar:
  FlutterPluginRegistrar) {
    let channel = FlutterMethodChannel(name: "network_plugin",
      binaryMessenger: registrar.messenger())
    let instance = SwiftNetworkPlugin()
    registrar.addMethodCallDelegate(instance, channel: channel)
  }

  public func handle(_ call: FlutterMethodCall,
      result: @escaping FlutterResult) {
    if (call.method == "getNetworkOperator") {
      self.receiveNetworkOperator(result: result)
    } else {
      result(FlutterMethodNotImplemented)
    }
  }

  private func receiveNetworkOperator(result: FlutterResult) {
    let networkInfo = CTTelephonyNetworkInfo()
    let carrier = networkInfo.subscriberCellularProvider
    result(carrier?.carrierName)
  }
}
```

The example project and test code also need to be updated with new API.

455

12-5. Displaying Web Pages

Problem

You want to display web pages.

Solution

Use `webview_flutter` plugin.

Discussion

If you want to display web pages inside of Flutter apps, you can use `webview_flutter` plugin (https://pub.dartlang.org/packages/ webview_flutter). After adding `webview_flutter: ^0.3.6` to the dependencies of `pubspec.yaml` file, you can use `WebView` widget to show web pages and interact with them. For iOS, you need to add the `io. flutter.embedded_views_preview` key with value `YES` to the `ios/Runner/ Info.plist` file.

Table 12-3 shows parameters of WebView constructor. To control the web view, you need to use `onWebViewCreated` callback to get the `WebViewController` object. The value of `javascriptMode` can be `JavascriptMode.disabled` or `JavascriptMode.unrestricted`. To enable JavaScript execution in the web pages, `JavascriptMode. unrestricted` should be set as the value. The `navigationDelegate` of type `NavigationDelegate` is a function that takes a `NavigationRequest` object and returns value of `NavigationDecision` enum. If the return value is `NavigationDecision.prevent`, the navigation request is blocked. If the return value is `NavigationDecision.navigate`, then navigation request can continue. You can use navigation delegate to block users from accessing restricted pages. The onPageFinished callback receives the URL of the loaded page.

Table 12-3. *Parameters of WebView constructor*

Name	Description
initialUrl	The initial URL to load.
onWebViewCreated	Callback when the WebView is created.
javascriptMode	Whether JavaScript is enabled.
javascriptChannels	Channels to receive messages sent by JavaScript code running in the web view.
navigationDelegate	Determines whether a navigation request should be handled.
onPageFinished	Callback when a page loading is finished.
gcstureRecognizers	Gestures recognized by the web view.

After getting the WebViewController object, you can use methods shown in Table 12-4 to interact with the web view. All these methods are asynchronous and return Future objects. For example, the canGoBack() method returns a Future<bool> object.

Table 12-4. *Methods of WebViewController*

Name	Description
evaluateJavascript(String javascriptString)	Evaluate JavaScript code in the context of current page.
loadUrl(String url, { Map<String, String> headers }	Load the specified URL.
reload()	Reload the current URL.
goBack()	Go back in the navigation history.
canGoBack()	Whether it's valid to go back in the history.
goForward()	Go forward in the navigation history.
canGoForward()	Whether it's valid to go forward in history.
clearCache()	Clear the cache.
currentUrl()	Get the current URL.

Listing 12-9 shows an example of using WebView widget to interact with Google Search page. Because the creation of WebView widget is asynchronous, the Completer<WebViewController> object is used to capture the WebViewController object. In the onWebViewCreated callback, the Completer<WebViewController> object is completed with the created WebViewController object. In the onPageFinished callback, the evaluateJavascript() method of WebViewController object is used to execute JavaScript code that sets value to the input and clicks the search button. This causes the WebView widget to load the search result page.

The JavascriptChannel object is created with a channel name and a JavascriptMessageHandler function to handle the messages sent from JavaScript code running in the web page. The message handler in Listing 12-9 uses a SnackBar widget to show the received message. The channel name "Messenger" becomes the global object that has a postMessage function to be used in JavaScript code to send messages back.

Listing 12-9. Use WebView

```
class GoogleSearch extends StatefulWidget {
  @override
  _GoogleSearchState createState() => _GoogleSearchState();
}

class _GoogleSearchState extends State<GoogleSearch> {
  final Completer<WebViewController> _controller =
      Completer<WebViewController>();

  @override
  Widget build(BuildContext context) {
    return WebView(
      initialUrl: 'https://google.com',
      javascriptMode: JavascriptMode.unrestricted,
      javascriptChannels:
          <JavascriptChannel>[_javascriptChannel(context)].
          toSet(),
      onWebViewCreated: (WebViewController webViewController) {
        _controller.complete(webViewController);
      },
      onPageFinished: (String url) {
        _controller.future.then((WebViewController
        webViewController) {
          webViewController.evaluateJavascript(
              'Messenger.postMessage("Loaded in " + navigator.
              userAgent);');
          webViewController.evaluateJavascript(
              'document.getElementsByName("q")[0].
              value="flutter";'
```

```
                'document.querySelector("button[aria-
                label*=Search]").click();');
        });
      },
    );
  }

  JavascriptChannel _javascriptChannel(BuildContext context) {
    return JavascriptChannel(
        name: 'Messenger',
        onMessageReceived: (JavascriptMessage message) {
          Scaffold.of(context).showSnackBar(
            SnackBar(content: Text(message.message)),
          );
        });
  }
}
```

12-6. Playing Videos
Problem

You want to play videos.

Solution

Use video_player plugin.

Discussion

If you want play videos from assets, file system, or network, you can use
`video_player` plugin (`https://pub.dev/packages?q=video_player`).
To use this plugin, you need to add `video_player: ^0.10.0+5` to the
dependencies of `pubspec.yaml` file. For iOS, you need to use a real device
instead of a simulator for development and testing. If you want to load
videos from arbitrary locations, you need to add the code in Listing 12-10
to `ios/Runner/Info.plist` file. Using NSAllowsArbitraryLoads reduces
the security of the app. It's better to check Apple's guide (`https://
developer.apple.com/documentation/security/preventing_insecure_
network_connections`) for network security.

Listing 12-10. iOS HTTP security config

```
<key>NSAppTransportSecurity</key>
<dict>
  <key>NSAllowsArbitraryLoads</key>
  <true/>
</dict>
```

If you need to load videos from network on Android, you need to add
code in Listing 12-11 to the `android/app/src/main /AndroidManifest.
xml` file.

Listing 12-11. Android

```
<uses-permission android:name="android.permission.INTERNET"/>
```

To play videos, you need to use constructors shown in Table 12-5 to
create `VideoPlayerController` objects.

Table 12-5. *Constructors of VideoPlayerController*

Name	Description
VideoPlayerController.asset(String dataSource, { String package })	Play a video from assets.
VideoPlayerController.file(File file)	Play a video from local file system.
VideoPlayerController.network(String dataSource)	Play a video loaded from network.

After creating a VideoPlayerController object, you can use methods shown in Table 12-6 to control the video playing. All these methods return Future objects. The initialize() method must be called first to initialize the controller. You can only call other methods after the Future object returned by initialize() method completes successfully.

Table 12-6. *Methods of VideoPlayerController*

Name	Description
play()	Play the video.
pause()	Pause the video.
seekTo(Duration moment)	Seek to the specified position.
setLooping(bool looping)	Whether to loop the video.
setVolume(double volume)	Set the volume of audio.
initialize()	Initialize the controller.
dispose()	Dispose the controller and clean up resources.

VideoPlayerController class extends from ValueNotifier<VideoPl ayerValue> class. You can get notified when the state changes by adding listeners to it. VideoPlayerValue class contains different properties to access the state of the video. VideoPlayer class is the actual widget that displays the video. It requires a VideoPlayerController object.

VideoPlayerView class in Listing 12-12 is a widget to play video loaded from specified URL. In the initState() method, VideoPlayerController.network() constructor is used to create the VideoPlayerController object. FutureBuilder widget uses the Future object returned by initialize() method to build the UI. Since VideoPlayerController object is also a Listenable object, we can use AnimatedBuilder with the VideoPlayerController object. AspectRatio widget uses the aspectRatio property to make sure the proper aspect ratio is used when playing the video. VideoProgressIndicator widget shows a progress bar to indicate video playback progress.

Listing 12-12. Playing video

```
class VideoPlayerView extends StatefulWidget {
  VideoPlayerView({Key key, this.videoUrl}) : super(key: key);

  final String videoUrl;

  @override
  _VideoPlayerViewState createState() => _
VideoPlayerViewState();
}

class _VideoPlayerViewState extends State<VideoPlayerView> {
  VideoPlayerController _controller;
  Future<void> _initializedFuture;

  @override
  void initState() {
```

463

```
    super.initState();
    _controller = VideoPlayerController.network(widget.
videoUrl);
    _initializedFuture = _controller.initialize();
  }

  @override
  Widget build(BuildContext context) {
    return FutureBuilder(
      future: _initializedFuture,
      builder: (context, snapshot) {
        if (snapshot.connectionState == ConnectionState.done) {
          return AnimatedBuilder(
            animation: _controller,
            child: VideoProgressIndicator(_controller,
            allowScrubbing: true),
            builder: (context, child) {
              return Column(
                children: <Widget>[
                  AspectRatio(
                    aspectRatio: _controller.value.aspectRatio,
                    child: VideoPlayer(_controller),
                  ),
                  Row(
                    children: <Widget>[
                      IconButton(
                        icon: Icon(_controller.value.isPlaying
                          ? Icons.pause
                          : Icons.play_arrow),
                        onPressed: () {
                          if (_controller.value.isPlaying) {
                            _controller.pause();
```

```
                } else {
                  _controller.play();
                }
              },
            ),
            Expanded(child: child),
          ],
        ),
      ],
    );
  },
);
    } else {
      return Center(child: CircularProgressIndicator());
    }
  },
);
}

@override
void dispose() {
  _controller.dispose();
  super.dispose();
}
}
```

12-7. Using Cameras

Problem

You want to use cameras to take pictures or record videos.

Solution

Use camera plugin.

Discussion

If you want to access the cameras on the device, you can use camera plugin (https://pub.dev/packages/camera). To install this plugin, you need to add camera: ^0.5.0 to the dependencies of pubspec.yaml file. For iOS, you need to add code in Listing 12-13 to the ios/Runner/Info.plist file. These two key-value pairs describe the purpose of accessing camera and microphone. This is required to protect user privacy.

Listing 12-13. Privacy requirements for iOS

```
<key>NSCameraUsageDescription</key>
<string>APPNAME requires access to your phone's camera.
</string>
<key>NSMicrophoneUsageDescription</key>
<string>APPNAME requires access to your phone's microphone.
</string>
```

For Android, the minimum Android SDK version needs to set to 21 in the android/app/build.gradle file.

To access cameras, you need to create CameraController objects. CameraController constructor requires parameters of types CameraDescription and ResolutionPreset. CameraDescription class describes a camera. ResolutionPreset enum describes the quality of screen resolution. ResolutionPreset is an enum with values low, medium, and high. To get CameraDescription objects, you can use availableCameras() function to get a list of available cameras with type List<CameraDescription>.

Table 12-7 shows methods of CameraController class. All these methods return Future objects. A CameraController object needs to be initialized first. Other methods should only be called after the Future object returned by initialize() completes successfully. CameraController class extends from ValueNotifier<CameraValue> class, so you can add listeners to it to get notified of state changes.

Table 12-7. *Methods of CameraController*

Name	Description
takePicture(String path)	Take a picture and save to a file.
prepareForVideoRecording()	Prepare for video recording.
startVideoRecording(String filePath)	Start a video recording and save to a file.
stopVideoRecording()	Stop the current video recording.
startImageStream()	Start streaming of images.
stopImageStream()	Stop the current streaming of images.
initialize()	Initialize the controller.
dispose()	Dispose the controller and clean up resources.

In Listing 12-14, the CameraController object is created with passed-in CameraDescription object. FutureBuilder widget builds the actual UI after the CameraController object is initialized. CameraPreview widget shows live preview of the camera. When the icon is pressed, a picture is taken and saved to the temporary directory.

Listing 12-14. Use camera

```
class CameraView extends StatefulWidget {
  CameraView({Key key, this.camera}) : super(key: key);
  final CameraDescription camera;
```

467

```
  @override
  _CameraViewState createState() => _CameraViewState();
}

class _CameraViewState extends State<CameraView> {
  CameraController _controller;
  Future<void> _initializedFuture;

  @override
  void initState() {
    super.initState();
    _controller = CameraController(widget.camera,
    ResolutionPreset.high);
    _initializedFuture = _controller.initialize();
  }

  @override
  Widget build(BuildContext context) {
    return FutureBuilder<void>(
      future: _initializedFuture,
      builder: (context, snapshot) {
        if (snapshot.connectionState == ConnectionState.done) {
          return Column(
            children: <Widget>[
              Expanded(child: CameraPreview(_controller)),
              IconButton(
                icon: Icon(Icons.photo_camera),
                onPressed: () async {
                  String path = join((await
                  getTemporaryDirectory()).path,
                      '${DateTime.now()}.png');
                  await _controller.takePicture(path);
                  Scaffold.of(context).showSnackBar(
```

```
                            SnackBar(content: Text('Picture saved to
                            $path')));
                    },
                  ),
                ],
              );
            } else {
              return Center(child: CircularProgressIndicator());
            }
          },
        );
      }

      @override
      void dispose() {
        _controller.dispose();
        super.dispose();
      }
    }
}
```

In Listing 12-15, availableCameras() function gets a list of CameraDescription objects and only the first one is used to create the CameraView widget.

Listing 12-15. Select camera

```
class CameraSelector extends StatelessWidget {
  final Future<CameraDescription> _cameraFuture =
      availableCameras().then((list) => list.first);

  @override
  Widget build(BuildContext context) {
    return FutureBuilder<CameraDescription>(
      future: _cameraFuture,
```

```
    builder: (context, snapshot) {
      if (snapshot.connectionState == ConnectionState.done) {
        if (snapshot.hasData) {
          return CameraView(camera: snapshot.data);
        } else {
          return Center(child: Text('No camera available!'));
        }
      } else {
        return Center(child: CircularProgressIndicator());
      }
    },
  );
 }
}
```

12-8. Using System Share Sheet
Problem

You want to allow user sharing items using system share sheet.

Solution

Use share plugin.

Discussion

If you want to allow user sharing items in the app, you can use the share plugin (https://pub.dev/packages/share) to show the system share sheet. To use this plugin, you need to add share: ^0.6.1 to the dependencies of pubspec.yaml file.

The API provided by share plugin is very simple. It only has a static `share()` method to share some text. You can share plain text or a URL. Listing 12-16 shows how to use `share()` method to share a URL.

Listing 12-16. Share a URL

```
Share.share('https://flutter.dev');
```

12-9. Summary

Flutter apps can use platform-specific code to call native platform APIs. There are a large number of community plugins to use different futures on the native platform, including cameras, microphones, sensors, and more. In the next chapter, we'll discuss miscellaneous topics in Flutter.

CHAPTER 13

Miscellaneous

This chapter covers recipes of miscellaneous topics in Flutter.

13-1. Using Assets
Problem

You want to bundle static assets in the app.

Solution

Use assets.

Discussion

Flutter apps can include both code and static assets. There are two types of assets:

* Data files including JSON, XML, and plain text files
* Binary files including images and videos

Assets are declared in the `flutter/assets` section of the `pubspec.yaml` file. During the build process, these assets files are bundled into the app's binary files. These assets can be accessed in the runtime. It's common to put assets under the `assets` directory. In Listing 13-1, two files are declared as assets in `pubspec.yaml` file.

Listing 13-1. Assets in pubspec.yaml file

```
flutter:
  assets:
    - assets/dog.jpg
    - assets/data.json
```

In the runtime, subclasses of `AssetBundle` class are used to load content from the assets. The `load()` method retrieves the binary content, while `loadString()` method retrieves the string content. You need to provide the assets key when using these two methods. The key is the same as asset path declared in `pubspec.yaml` file. The static application-level `rootBundle` property refers to the `AssetBundle` object that contains assets packaged with the app. You can use this property directly to load assets. It's recommended to use static `DefaultAssetBundle.of()` method to get the `AssetBundle` object from build context.

In Listing 13-2, the JSON file `assets/data.json` is loaded as string using `loadString()` method.

Listing 13-2. Load string assets

```
class TextAssets extends StatelessWidget {
  @override
  Widget build(BuildContext context) {
    return FutureBuilder<String>(
      future: DefaultAssetBundle.of(context)
          .loadString('assets/data.json')
          .then((json) {
        return jsonDecode(json)['name'];
      }),
      builder: (context, snapshot) {
        if (snapshot.connectionState == ConnectionState.done) {
          return Center(child: Text(snapshot.data));
```

```
      } else {
        return Center(child: CircularProgressIndicator());
      }
    },
  );
  }
}
```

If the assets file is an image, you can use AssetImage class with Image widget to display it. In Listing 13-3, AssetImage class is used to display the assets/dog.jpg image.

Listing 13-3. Use AssetImage

```
Image(
  image: AssetImage('assets/dog.jpg'),
)
```

For an image asset, it's common to have multiple variants with different resolutions for the same file. When using AssetImage class to load an asset image, the variant that most closely matches the current device pixel ratio will be used.

In Listing 13-4, the assets/2.0x/dog.jpg file is the variant of assets/dog.jpg with resolution ratio 2.0. If the device pixel ratio is 1.6, the assets/2.0x/dog.jpg file is used.

Listing 13-4. Image assets variants

```
flutter:
  assets:
    - assets/dog.jpg
    - assets/2.0x/dog.jpg
    - assets/3.0x/dog.jpg
```

13-2. Using Gestures

Problem

You want to allow user using gestures to perform actions.

Solution

Use GestureDetector widget to detect gestures.

Discussion

Users of mobiles app are used to gestures when performing actions. For example, when viewing pictures gallery, using swiping gesture can easily navigate between different pictures. In Flutter, we can use GestureDetector widget to detect gestures and invoke specified callbacks for gestures. GestureDetector constructor has a large number of parameters to provide callbacks for different events. A gesture may dispatch multiple events during its lifecycle. For example, the gesture of horizontal drag can dispatch three events. The following are the handler parameters for these three events:

- onHorizontalDragStart callback means the pointer may begin to move horizontally.

- onHorizontalDragUpdate callback means the pointer is moving in the horizontal direction.

- onHorizontalDragEnd callback means the pointer is longer in contact with the screen.

Callbacks of different events can receive details about the events. In Listing 13-5, the GestureDetector widget wraps a Container widget. In the onHorizontalDragEnd callback handler, the velocity property of DragEndDetails object is the moving velocity of the pointer. We use this property to determine the drag direction.

Listing 13-5. Use GestureDetector

```
class SwipingCounter extends StatefulWidget {
  @override
  _SwipingCounterState createState() => _SwipingCounterState();
}

class _SwipingCounterState extends State<SwipingCounter> {
  int _count = 0;

  @override
  Widget build(BuildContext context) {
    return Column(
      children: <Widget>[
        Text('$_count'),
        Expanded(
          child: GestureDetector(
            child: Container(
              decoration: BoxDecoration(color: Colors.grey.
              shade200),
            ),
            onHorizontalDragEnd: (DragEndDetails details) {
              setState(() {
                double dx = details.velocity.
                pixelsPerSecond.dx;
                _count += (dx > 0 ? 1 : (dx < 0 ? -1 : 0));
              });
            },
          ),
        ),
      ],
    );
  }
}
```

13-3. Supporting Multiple Locales

Problem

You want the app to support multiple locales.

Solution

Use `Localizations` widget and `LocalizationsDelegate` class.

Discussion

Flutter has built-in support for internalization. If you want to support multiple locales, you need to use `Localizations` widget. `Localizations` class uses a list of `LocalizationsDelegate` objects to load localized resources. `LocalizationsDelegate<T>` class is a factory of a set of localized resources of type T. The set of localized resources is usually a class with properties and methods to provide localized values.

To create a `Localizations` object, you need to provide the `Locale` object and a list of `LocalizationsDelegate` objects. Most of the time, you don't need to explicitly create a `Localizations` object. `WidgetsApp` widget already creates a `Localizations` object. `WidgetsApp` constructor has parameters that are used by the `Localizations` object. When you need to use localized values, you can use static `Localizations.of<T>(BuildContext context, Type type)` method to get the nearest enclosing localized resources object of the given type.

By default, Flutter only provides US English localizations. To support other locales, you need to add Flutter's own localizations for those locales first. This is done by adding `flutter_localizations` package to the dependencies of `pubspec.yaml` file; see Listing 13-6. With this package, you can use localized values defined in `MaterialLocalizations` class.

Listing 13-6. flutter_localizations

```
dependencies:
  flutter:
    sdk: flutter
  flutter_localizations:
    sdk: flutter
```

After adding the flutter_localizations package, we need to enable those localized values. In Listing 13-7, this is done by adding GlobalMaterialLocalizations.delegate and GlobalWidgetsLocalizations.delegate to the localizationsDelegates list of MaterialApp constructor. The value of localizationsDelegates parameter is passed to the Localizations constructor. The supportedLocales parameter specifies the supported locales.

Listing 13-7. Enable Flutter localized values

```
MaterialApp(
  localizationsDelegates: [
    GlobalMaterialLocalizations.delegate,
    GlobalWidgetsLocalizations.delegate,
  ],
  supportedLocales: [
    const Locale('en'),
    const Locale('zh', 'CN'),
  ],
);
```

In Listing 13-8, MaterialLocalizations.of() method gets the MaterialLocalizations object from the build context. The copyButtonLabel property is a localized value defined in MaterialLocalizations class. In the runtime, the label of the button depends on the device's locale. MaterialLocalizations.of()

method uses `Localizations.of()` internally to look up the
`MaterialLocalizations` object.

Listing 13-8. Use localized values

```
RaisedButton(
  child: Text(MaterialLocalizations.of(context).
copyButtonLabel),
  onPressed: () {},
);
```

   `MaterialLocalizations` class only provides a limit set of localized
values. For your own apps, you need to create custom localized
resources classes. `AppLocalizations` class in Listing 13-9 is a custom
localized resources class. `AppLocalizations` class has the `appName`
property as an example of simple localizable strings. The `greeting()`
method is an example of localizable strings that require parameters.
`AppLocalizationsEn` and `AppLocalizationsZhCn` classes are
implementations of `AppLocalizations` class for en and zh_CN locales,
respectively.

Listing 13-9. AppLocalizations and localized subclasses

```
abstract class AppLocalizations {
  String get appName;
  String greeting(String name);

  static AppLocalizations of(BuildContext context) {
    return Localizations.of<AppLocalizations>(context,
    AppLocalizations);
  }
}
```

```
class AppLocalizationsEn extends AppLocalizations {
  @override
  String get appName => 'Demo App';

  @override
  String greeting(String name) {
    return 'Hello, $name';
  }
}

class AppLocalizationsZhCn extends AppLocalizations {
  @override
  String get appName => '示例应用';

  @override
  String greeting(String name) {
    return '你好, $name';
  }
}
```

We also need to create a custom `LocalizationsDelegate` class to load `AppLocalizations` objects. There are three methods need to be implemented:

- `isSupported()` method checks whether a locale is supported.

- `load()` method loads the localized resources object for a given locale.

- `shouldReload()` method checks whether the `load()` method should be called to load the resource again.

In the `load()` method of Listing 13-10, `AppLocalizationsEn` or `AppLocalizationsZhCn` object is returned based on the given locale.

Listing 13-10. Custom LocalizationsDelegate

```
class _AppLocalizationsDelegate
    extends LocalizationsDelegate<AppLocalizations> {
  const _AppLocalizationsDelegate();

  static const List<Locale> _supportedLocales = [
    const Locale('en'),
    const Locale('zh', 'CN')
  ];

  @override
  bool isSupported(Locale locale) {
    return _supportedLocales.contains(locale);
  }

  @override
  Future<AppLocalizations> load(Locale locale) {
    return Future.value(locale == Locale('zh', 'CN')
        ? AppLocalizationsZhCn()
        : AppLocalizationsEn());
  }

  @override
  bool shouldReload(LocalizationsDelegate<AppLocalizations>
  old) {
    return false;
  }
}
```

_AppLocalizationsDelegate object needs to be added to the list of localizationsDelegates in Listing 13-7. Listing 13-11 shows an example of using AppLocalizations class.

Listing 13-11. Use AppLocalizations

```
Text(AppLocalizations.of(context).greeting('John'))
```

13-4. Generating Translation Files
Problem

You want to extract localizable strings from code and integrate translated strings.

Solution

Use tools in `intl_translation` package.

Discussion

Recipe 13-3 describes how to support multiple locales using `Localizations` widget and `LocalizationsDelegate` class. The major drawback of solution in Recipe 13-3 is that you need to manually create localized resources classes for all supported locales. Because localized strings are directly embedded in source code, it's hard to get translators involved. A better choice is to use tools provided by `intl_translation` package to automate the process. You need to add `intl_translation: ^0.17.3` to the `dev_dependencies` of the `pubspec.yaml` file.

Listing 13-12 shows the new `AppLocalizations` class which has the same `appName` property and `greeting()` method as Listing 13-9. `Intl.message()` method describes a localized string. Only the message string is required. Parameters like `name`, `desc`, `args`, and `examples` are used to help translators to understand the message string.

Listing 13-12. AppLocalizations using Intl.message()

```
class AppLocalizations {
  static AppLocalizations of(BuildContext context) {
    return Localizations.of<AppLocalizations>(context,
    AppLocalizations);
  }

  String get appName {
    return Intl.message(
      'Demo App',
      name: 'appName',
      desc: 'Name of the app',
    );
  }

  String greeting(String name) {
    return Intl.message(
      'Hello, $name',
      name: 'greeting',
      args: [name],
      desc: 'Greeting message',
      examples: const {'name': 'John'},
    );
  }
}
```

Now we can use the tool provided by `intl_translation` package to extract localized messages from source code. The following command extracts messages declared with `Intl.message()` from `lib/app_intl.dart` file and saves to `lib/l10n` directory. After running this command, you should see the generated `intl_messages.arb` file in `lib/l10n` directory. Generated files are in ARB (Application Resource Bundle) format (https://github.com/googlei18n/app-resource-bundle) which can be used as input of translation tools like Google Translator Toolkit. ARB files are actually JSON files; you can simply use text editors to modify them.

```
$ flutter packages pub run intl_translation:extract_to_arb
--locale=en --output-dir=lib/l10n lib/app_intl.dart
```

Now you can duplicate the intl_messages.arb file for each supported locale and get them translated. For example, the intl_messages_zh.arb file is the translated version for zh locale. After translated files are ready, you can use the following command to generate Dart files. After running this command, you should see a messages_all.dart file and messages_*.dart files for each locale.

```
$ flutter packages pub run intl_translation:generate_from_arb
--output-dir=lib/l10n --no-use-deferred-loading lib/app_intl.
dart lib/l10n/intl_*.arb
```

The initializeMessages() function in messages_all.dart file can be used to initialize messages for a given locale. The static load() method in Listing 13-13 uses initializeMessages() function to initialize messages first, then sets the default locale.

Listing 13-13. Load messages

```
class AppLocalizations {
  static Future<AppLocalizations> load(Locale locale) {
    final String name =
        locale.countryCode.isEmpty ? locale.languageCode :
        locale.toString();
    final String localeName = Intl.canonicalizedLocale(name);
    return initializeMessages(localeName).then((_) {
      Intl.defaultLocale = localeName;
      return AppLocalizations();
```

```
    });
  }
}
```

This static `AppLocalizations.load()` method can be used by the `load()` method of `LocalizationsDelegate` class to load `AppLocalizations` object.

13-5. Painting Custom Elements

Problem

You want to paint custom elements.

Solution

Use `CustomPaint` widget with `CustomPainter` and `Canvas` classes.

Discussion

If you want to completely customize the painting of a widget, you can use `CustomPaint` widget. `CustomPaint` widget provides a canvas on which to draw custom elements. Table 13-1 shows the parameters of `CustomPaint` constructor. During the painting process, the `painter` paints on the canvas first, then the child widget is painted, and finally the `foregroundPainter` paints on the canvas.

Table 13-1. *Parameters of CustomPaint*

Name	Type	Description
painter	CustomPainter	The painter that paints before the child.
foregroundPainter	CustomPainter	The painter that paints after the child.
size	Size	The size to paint.
child	Widget	The child widget.

To create CustomPainter objects, you need to create subclasses of CustomPainter and override paint() and shouldRepaint() methods. In paint() method, the canvas parameter can be used to draw custom elements. Canvas class has a set of methods to draw different elements; see Table 13-2.

Table 13-2. *Methods of Canvas*

Name	Description
drawArc()	Draw an arc.
drawCircle()	Draw a circle with specified center and radius.
drawImage()	Draw an Image object.
drawLine()	Draw a line between two points.
drawOval()	Draw an oval.
drawParagraph()	Draw text.
drawRect()	Draw a rectangle with specified Rect object.
drawRRect()	Draw a rounded rectangle.

Most of the methods in Canvas class have a parameter of type Paint to describe the style to use when drawing on the canvas. In Listing 13-14, Shapes class draws a rectangle and a circle on the canvas. In the CustomShapes widget, the Text widget is painted above the Shapes painter.

Listing 13-14. Use CustomPaint

```
class CustomShapes extends StatelessWidget {
  @override
  Widget build(BuildContext context) {
    return Container(
      width: 300,
      height: 300,
      child: CustomPaint(
        painter: Shapes(),
        child: Center(child: Text('Hello World')),
      ),
    );
  }
}

class Shapes extends CustomPainter {
  @override
  void paint(Canvas canvas, Size size) {
    Rect rect = Offset(5, 5) & (size - Offset(5, 5));
    canvas.drawRect(
      rect,
      Paint()
        ..color = Colors.red
        ..strokeWidth = 2
        ..style = PaintingStyle.stroke,
    );
```

```
  canvas.drawCircle(
    rect.center,
    (rect.shortestSide / 2) - 10,
    Paint()..color = Colors.blue,
  );
}

@override
bool shouldRepaint(CustomPainter oldDelegate) {
  return false;
}
}
```

13-6. Customizing Themes

Problem

You want to customize themes in Flutter apps.

Solution

Use ThemeData class for Material Design and CupertinoThemeData class for iOS.

Discussion

It's a common requirement to customize look and feel of an app. For Flutter apps, if Material Design is used, you can use ThemeData class to customize the theme. ThemeData class has a large number of parameters to configure different aspects of the theme. MaterialApp class has the theme parameter to provide the ThemeData object. For iOS style, CupertinoThemeData class has the same purpose to specify the theme. `CupertinoApp` class also has the `theme` parameter of type `CupertinoThemeData` to customize the theme.

If you need to access the current theme object, you can use static `Theme.of()` method to get nearest enclosing `ThemeData` object for a build context in Material Design. The similar `CupertinoTheme.of()` method can be used for iOS style.

In Listing 13-15, the first `Text` widget uses the `textTheme.headline` property of current `Theme` object as the style. The second `Text` widget uses the `colorScheme.error` property as the color to display error text.

Listing 13-15. Use Theme

```
class TextTheme extends StatelessWidget {
  @override
  Widget build(BuildContext context) {
    return Column(
      children: <Widget>[
        Text('Headline', style: Theme.of(context).textTheme.
        headline),
        Text('Error',
            style: TextStyle(color: Theme.of(context).
            colorScheme.error)),
      ],
    );
  }
}
```

13-7. Summary

This chapter discusses miscellaneous topics in Flutter that are useful in different scenarios. In the next chapter, we'll discuss testing and debugging in Flutter.

CHAPTER 14

Testing and Debugging

This chapter covers recipes related to testing and debugging Flutter apps.

14-1. Writing Unit Tests
Problem

You want to write unit tests.

Solution

Use API in test package.

Discussion

Unit tests are very important in app development. To write tests in Flutter apps, you need to add test: ^1.5.3 to the dev_dependencies section of pubspec.yaml file. Test files are usually put in the test directory. The MovingBox class in Listing 14-1 is the class to test. The move() method updates the internal _offset variable.

© Fu Cheng 2019
F. Cheng, *Flutter Recipes*, https://doi.org/10.1007/978-1-4842-4982-6_14

Listing 14-1. Dart class to test

```
class MovingBox {
  MovingBox({Offset initPos = Offset.zero}) : _offset =
  initPos;
  Offset _offset;

  get offset => _offset;

  void move(double dx, double dy) {
    _offset += Offset(dx, dy);
  }
}
```

Listing 14-2 shows the tests of MovingBox class. The group() function creates a group to describe a set of tests. The test() function creates a test case with the given description and body. The body is a function that uses expect() function to declare expectations to verify. To call the expect() function, you need to provide the actual value and a matcher to check the value. The matcher can be simple values or functions from the matcher package. Common matcher functions include contains(), startsWith(), endsWith(), lessThan(), greaterThan(), and inInclusiveRange().

Listing 14-2. Test of MovingBox

```
void main() {
  group('MovingBox', () {
    test('position should be (0.0) by default', () {
      expect(MovingBox().offset, Offset.zero);
    });

    test('postion should be initial value', () {
      expect(MovingBox(initPos: Offset(10, 10)).offset,
      Offset(10, 10));
    });
```

```
  test('postion should be moved', () {
    final box = MovingBox();
    box.move(5, 5);
    expect(box.offset, Offset(5, 5));
    box.move(-1, -1);
    expect(box.offset, Offset(4, 4));
  });
});
}
```

You can use async functions as body of expect() function to write
asynchronous tests. In Listing 14-3, the first test case uses an async
function with await to get the value of a Future object. In the second
test case, completion() function waits for completion of a Future object
and verify the value. The throwsA() function verifies that a Future object
throws the given error. In the third test case, expectAsync1() function
wraps another function to verify the result and checks its invocation times.

Listing 14-3. Asynchronous tests

```
void main() {
  test('future with async', () async {
    var value = await Future.value(1);
    expect(value, equals(1));
  });

  test('future', () {
    expect(Future.value(1), completion(equals(1)));
    expect(Future.error('error'), throwsA(equals('error')));
  });

  test('future callback', () {
    Future.error('error').catchError(expectAsync1((error) {
      expect(error, equals('error'));
```

```
    }, count: 1));
  });
}
```

You can use `setUp()` function to add a function to run before tests. Similarly, the `tearDown()` function is used to add a function to run after tests. The `setUp()` function should be used to prepare the context for test cases to run. The `tearDown()` function should be used to run cleanup tasks. The `setUp()` and `tearDown()` functions usually come in pairs. In Listing 14-4, setUp() and tearDown() functions will be called twice.

Listing 14-4. setUp() and tearDown() functions

```
void main() {
  setUp(() {
    print('setUp');
  });

  test('action1', () {
    print('action1');
  });

  test('action2', () {
    print('action2');
  });

  tearDown(() {
    print('tearDown');
  });
}
```

After running the test case in Listing 14-4, the output should look like what's shown in Listing 14-5.

Listing 14-5. Output with setUp() and tearDown() functions

```
setUp
action1
tearDown
setUp
action2
tearDown
```

14-2. Using Mock Objects in Tests
Problem

You want to mock dependencies in test cases.

Solution

Use mockito package.

Discussion

When writing test cases, the classes to test may have dependencies that require external resources. For example, a service class needs to access backend API to get data. When testing these classes, you don't want to use the real dependencies. Depending on external resources, introduce uncertainty to execution of test cases and make them unstable. Using live services also makes it difficult to test all possible scenarios.

A better approach is to create mock objects to replace these dependencies. With mock objects, you can easily emulate different scenarios. Mock objects are alternative implementations of classes. You can create mock objects manually or use mockito package. To use mockito package, you need to add mockito: ^4.0.0 to the dev_dependencies section of pubspec.yaml file.

GitHubJobsClient class in Listing 14-6 uses Client class from http package to access GitHub Jobs API.

Listing 14-6. GitHubJobsClient class to test

```
class GitHubJobsClient {
  GitHubJobsClient({@required this.httpClient}) :
  assert(httpClient != null);

  final http.Client httpClient;

  Future<List<Job>> getJobs(String keyword) async {
    Uri url = Uri.https(
        'jobs.github.com', '/positions.json', {'description':
        keyword});
    http.Response response = await httpClient.get(url);
    if (response.statusCode != 200) {
      throw Exception('Failed to get job listings');
    }
    return (jsonDecode(response.body) as List<dynamic>)
        .map((json) => Job.fromJson(json))
        .toList();
  }
}
```

To test GitHubJobsClient class, we can create a mock object for http.Client object. In Listing 14-7, MockHttpClient class is the mock class for http.Client class. In the first test case, when the get() method of MockHttpClient is called with the specified Uri object, a Future<Response> object with JSON string is used as the result. We can verify that getJobs() method of GitHubJobsClient can parse the response and return a List object with one element. In the second test case, the return result of get() method of MockHttpClient is set to a

Future<Response> with HTTP 500 error. We then verify an exception is thrown by calling getJobs() method.

Listing 14-7. GitHubJobsClient test with mock

```
import 'package:mockito/mockito.dart';
class MockHttpClient extends Mock implements http.Client {}

void main() {
  group('getJobs', () {
    Uri url = Uri.https(
        'jobs.github.com', '/positions.json', {'description':
        'flutter'});

    test('should return list of jobs', () {
      final httpClient = MockHttpClient();
      when(httpClient.get(url))
          .thenAnswer((_) async => http.Response('[{"id":
          "123"}]', 200));
      final jobsClient = GitHubJobsClient(httpClient:
      httpClient);
      expect(jobsClient.getJobs('flutter'),
      completion(hasLength(1)));
    });

    test('should throws an exception', () {
      final httpClient = MockHttpClient();
      when(httpClient.get(url))
          .thenAnswer((_) async => http.Response('error', 500));
      final jobsClient = GitHubJobsClient(httpClient:
      httpClient);
      expect(jobsClient.getJobs('flutter'), throwsException);
    });
  });
}
```

14-3. Writing Widget Tests

Problem

You want to write test cases to test widgets.

Solution

Use flutter_test package.

Discussion

Using test and mockito packages is enough to write tests for Dart classes. However, you need to use flutter_test package to write tests for widgets. The flutter_test package is already included in the pubspec.yaml file for new projects created by flutter create command. Test cases for widgets are declared using testWidgets() function. When calling testWidgets(), you need to provide a description and a callback to run inside the Flutter test environment. The callback receives a WidgetTester object to interact with widgets and the test environment. After the widget under test is created, you can use Finder objects and matchers to verify state of the widget.

Table 14-1 shows methods of WidgetTester class. The pumpWidget() method is usually the entry point of a test by creating the widget to test. When testing stateful widgets, after changing the state, you need to call pump() method to trigger the rebuild. If the widget uses animations, you should use pumpAndSettle() method to wait for animations to finish. Methods like enterText() and ensureVisible() use Finder objects to find the widgets to interact with.

Table 14-1. *Methods of WidgetTester*

Name	Description
pumpWidget()	Render the specified widget.
pump()	Trigger a frame that causes the widget to rebuild.
pumpAndSettle()	Repeatedly call pump() method until there are no frames scheduled.
enterText()	Enter text to a text input widget.
pageBack()	Dismiss the current page.
runAsync()	Run a callback asynchronously.
dispatchEvent()	Dispatch an event.
ensureVisible()	Make a widget visible by scrolling its ancestor Scrollable widget.
drag()	Drag the widget by given offset.
press()	Press the widget.
longPress()	Long press the widget.
tap()	Tap the widget.

ToUppercase widget in Listing 14-8 is a stateful widget to test. It has a TextField widget to input text. When the button is pressed, the uppercase of input text is displayed using a Text widget.

Listing 14-8. Widget to test

```
class ToUppercase extends StatefulWidget {
  @override
  _ToUppercaseState createState() => _ToUppercaseState();
}
```

```
class _ToUppercaseState extends State<ToUppercase> {
  final _controller = TextEditingController();

  @override
  Widget build(BuildContext context) {
    return Column(
      children: <Widget>[
        Row(
          children: <Widget>[
            Expanded(child: TextField(controller:
            _controller)),
            RaisedButton(
              child: Text('Uppercase'),
              onPressed: () {
                setState(() {});
              },
            ),
          ],
        ),
        Text((_controller.text ?? ").toUpperCase())),
      ],
    );
  }
}
```

Listing 14-9 shows the test case of ToUppercase widget. The _wrapInMaterial() function wraps the ToUppercase widget in a MaterialApp before testing. This is because TextField widget requires an ancestor Material widget. In the test case, the widget is rendered using pumpWidget() first. The find object is a top-level constant of

CommonFinders class. It has convenient methods to create different kinds of Finder objects. Here we find the widget of type TextField and uses enterText() to input the text "abc". Then the RaisedButton widget is tapped and the state is changed. The pump() method is required to trigger the rebuild. Finally, we verify that a Text widget exists with the text "ABC".

Listing 14-9. Test ToUppercase widget

```
Widget _wrapInMaterial(Widget widget) {
  return MaterialApp(
    home: Scaffold(
      body: widget,
    ),
  );
}

void main() {
  testWidgets('ToUppercase', (WidgetTester tester) async {
    await tester.pumpWidget(_wrapInMaterial(ToUppercase()));
    await tester.enterText(find.byType(TextField), 'abc');
    await tester.tap(find.byType(RaisedButton));
    await tester.pump();
    expect(find.text('ABC'), findsOneWidget);
  });
}
```

Table 14-2. *Methods of CommonFinders*

Name	Description
byType()	Find widgets by type.
byIcon()	Find Icon widgets by icon data.
byKey()	Find widgets by a particular Key object.
byTooltip()	Find Tooltip widgets with the given message.
byWidget()	Find widgets by the given widget instance.
text()	Find Text and EditableText widgets with the given text.
widgetWithIcon()	Find widgets that contain a descendant widget with the icon.
widgetWithText()	Find widgets that contain a Text descendant with the given text.

Finder objects are used with matchers to verify the state. There are four matchers to work with Finder objects:

- findsOneWidget expects exactly one widget is found.

- findsNothing expects no widgets are found.

- findsNWidgets expects specified number of widgets are found.

- findsWidgets expects at least one widget is found.

14-4. Writing Integration Tests
Problem

You want to write integration tests running on emulators or real devices.

Solution

Use `flutter_driver` package.

Discussion

Unit tests and widget tests can only test individual classes, functions, or widgets. These tests are running on development or testing machines. These tests cannot test integration between different components of an app. Integration tests should be used for this scenario.

Integration testing comes in two parts. The first part is the instrumented app deployed to an emulator or real device. The second part is the test code to drive the app and verify state of the app. The app under test is isolated from the test code to avoid interference.

The `flutter_driver` package is required to write integration tests. You need to add `flutter_driver` package to the `dev_dependencies` section of the `pubspec.yaml` file; see Listing 14-10.

Listing 14-10. Add flutter_driver package

```
dev_dependencies:
  flutter_driver:
    sdk: flutter
```

Integration test files are usually put in the `test_driver` directory. The target to test is the page to search job listings on GitHub. It's important to provide `ValueKey` objects as the key parameter of the widgets that need to be used by integration tests. This makes it easier to find those widgets in the test case. In Listing 14-11, `Key('keyword')` creates a `ValueKey` object with name "keyword".

503

Listing 14-11. Add key to widget

```
TextField(
  key: Key('keyword'),
  controller: _controller,
)
```

The github_jobs.dart file in test_driver directory contains an instrumented version of the page to test. Listing 14-12 shows the content of github_jobs.dart file. The enableFlutterDriverExtension() function from the flutter_driver package enables Flutter Driver to connect to the app.

Listing 14-12. App to test using Flutter Driver

```
void main() {
  enableFlutterDriverExtension();
  runApp(SampleApp());
}
```

Listing 14-13 shows the content of github_jobs_test.dart file. The file name is selected by appending _test suffix to the name of the app file. This is the convention used by Flutter Driver to find the Dart file to run the app under test. In the setUpAll() function, FlutterDriver. connect() is used to connect to the app. In the test case, find is the top-level constant of CommonFinders object that has convenient methods to create SerializableFinder objects. The byValueKey() method finds the TextField widget in Listing 14-11 by the specified key. The tap() method of FlutterDriver taps at the TextField widget to make it gain focus. Then enterText() method is used to input search keyword to the focused TextField widget. The search button is then tapped to trigger the loading of data. If the data is loaded successfully, the ListView widget with jobsList key is available. The waitFor() method waits for the ListView widget to appear.

Listing 14-13. Test using Flutter Driver

```
void main() {
  group('GitHub Jobs', () {
    FlutterDriver driver;

    setUpAll(() async {
      driver = await FlutterDriver.connect();
    });

    test('searches by keyword', () async {
      await driver.tap(find.byValueKey('keyword'));
      await driver.enterText('android');
      await driver.tap(find.byValueKey('search'));
      await driver.waitFor(find.byValueKey('jobsList'),
          timeout: Duration(seconds: 5));
    });

    tearDownAll(() {
      if (driver != null) {
        driver.close();
      }
    });
  });
}
```

Now we can use the following command to run the integration test. Flutter Driver deploys the app to the emulator or real device and runs the test code to verify the result.

```
$ flutter driver --target=test_driver/github_jobs.dart
```

Table 14-3 shows methods of `FlutterDriver` class that can be used to interact with the app during tests. If you want to perform custom actions, you can provide a `DataHandler` function when calling enableFlutterDriverExtension() function. Messages sent using requestData() method will be handled by the DataHandler.

Table 14-3. *Methods of FlutterDriver*

Name	Description
enterText()	Enter text into the currently focused text input.
getText()	Get text in the Text widget.
tap()	Taps at the widget.
waitFor()	Wait until the finder locates a widget.
waitForAbsent()	Wait until the finder can no longer locate a widget.
scroll()	Scroll in a widget by the given offset.
scrollIntoView()	Scroll the Scrollable ancestor of the widget until it's visible.
scrollUntilVisible(Serial izableFinder scrollable, SerializableFinder item)	Repeatedly call scroll() in the scrollable widget until the item is visible, then call scrollIntoView() on the item.
traceAction()	Run the action and return its performance trace.
startTracing()	Start recording performance traces.
stopTracingAndDownload Timeline()	Stop recording performance traces and download the result.
forceGC()	For a garbage collection to run.
getRenderTree()	Returns a dump of the current render tree.
requestData()	Sends a message to the app and receives a response.
screenshot()	Take a screenshot.

Methods in FlutterDriver class use SerializableFinder objects to locate widgets. Table 14-4 shows methods of CommonFinders class to create SerializableFinder objects. These methods only support using String or int values as parameters. This is because values need to be serialized when sending to the app.

Table 14-4. *Methods of CommonFinders in flutter_driver*

Name	Description
byType()	Find widgets by class name.
byValueKey()	Find widgets by key.
byTooltip()	Find widgets with a tooltip with the given message.
text()	Find Text and EditableText widgets with the given text.
pageBack()	Find the back button.

14-5. Debugging Apps
Problem

You want to debug issues found in the apps.

Solution

Use IDE and utilities provided by Flutter SDK.

Discussion

When the code doesn't work as you expected in the runtime, you need to debug the code to find out the cause. With the help of IDEs, it's quite straightforward to debug Flutter apps. You can add breakpoints in the code and start the app in debug mode.

Another common approach to debug code is to write outputs to the system console using print() function. These logs can be viewed using flutter logs command. Android Studio also displays these logs in the Console view. You can also use debugPrint() function to throttle the output to avoid the logs being dropped by Android.

When creating your own widgets, you should override debugFillProperties() method to add custom diagnostic properties. These properties can be viewed in Flutter Inspector. In Listing 14-14, the DebugWidget has name and price properties. In the debugFillProperties() method, two DiagnosticsProperty objects are added using DiagnosticPropertiesBuilder object.

Listing 14-14. *debugFillProperties()*

```
class DebugWidget extends StatelessWidget {
  DebugWidget({Key key, this.name, this.price}) : super(key:
  key);

  final String name;
  final double price;

  @override
  Widget build(BuildContext context) {
    return Text('$name - $price');
  }

  @override
  void debugFillProperties(DiagnosticPropertiesBuilder
properties) {
    super.debugFillProperties(properties);

    properties.add(StringProperty('name', name));
    properties.add(DoubleProperty('price', price));
  }
}
```

There are different types of DiagnosticsProperty subclasses to use based on the property type. Table 14-5 shows common DiagnosticsProperty subclasses.

Table 14-5. *Methods of CommonFinders*

Name	Description
StringProperty	For String property.
DoubleProperty	For double property.
PercentProperty	Format double property as percentage.
IntProperty	For int property.
FlagProperty	Format bool property as flags.
EnumProperty	For enum property.
IterableProperty	For Iterable property.

14-6. Summary

This chapter covers topics related to testing and debugging Flutter apps.

Index

A

Align widget, 140, 143, 152, 162
  heightFactor, 141
  widthFactor, 141
Alignment class, 141, 142
Alignment constants, 141
AlignmentDirectional class, 142
AlignmentDirectional instance, 143
AlignmentDirectional
      constants, 142
AlignmentGeometry class, 141
ancestorWidgetOfExactType()
      method, 110
android directory, 453
Animations
  creation, 413
    AnimatedWidget, 417, 418
    AnimationController class,
      413–415
    AnimationStatus,
      values, 416
    build() method, 414
    forward() method, 414
    initState() method, 414
    methods, 416
    status listener, 416, 417
  curve, 421

Curves.easeInOut curve,
    423, 424
  parameters, 422
  types, 421, 422
linear interpolation, 418
  animate() method, 418
  ColorTween, 419, 420
transitions, 434
  FadeTransition, 436
  ScaleTransition, 435
AppLocalizations.load()
      method, 486
apply() method, 125
asBroadcastStream() method, 321
AspectRatio constructor, 158
AspectRatio widget, 158, 159, 453
AssetImage class, 475
asStream() method, 320, 333
async function, 493

B

BoxConstraints class, 137
BoxConstraints instance, 138
BoxFit values, 152, 153, 155
build() method, 109–111, 116, 348,
    366, 368, 369, 414

U

V

W

Printed in the United States
By Bookmasters